THE BAD CORSET

THE BAD CORSET

A Feminist Reimagining

REBECCA GIBSON

BLOOMSBURY VISUAL ARTS
LONDON · NEW YORK · OXFORD · NEW DELHI · SYDNEY

BLOOMSBURY VISUAL ARTS
Bloomsbury Publishing Plc
50 Bedford Square, London, WC1B 3DP, UK
1385 Broadway, New York, NY 10018, USA
29 Earlsfort Terrace, Dublin 2, Ireland

BLOOMSBURY, BLOOMSBURY VISUAL ARTS and the Diana logo are trademarks of
Bloomsbury Publishing Plc

First published in Great Britain 2024

Rebecca Gibson has asserted her right under the Copyright, Designs and Patents Act,
1988, to be identified as Author of this work.

For legal purposes the Acknowledgments on p. viii constitute an extension of this
copyright page.

Cover design by Adriana Brioso
Cover image: *Arlequine* by Maurice Sand, 1855, from the private collection of
Rebecca Gibson, © Rebecca Gibson 2023.

A catalogue record for this book is available from the British Library.

A catalog record for this book is available from the Library of Congress.

ISBN: HB: 978-1-3502-9519-3
       PB: 978-1-3502-9518-6
       ePDF: 978-1-3502-9520-9
       eBook: 978-1-3502-9521-6

Typeset by RefineCatch Limited, Bungay, Suffolk
Printed and bound in India

To find out more about our authors and books, visit www.bloomsbury.com
and sign up for our newsletters.

This book is dedicated to the mistakes I've made, from which I have recovered, learned, and grown stronger. May we all pick ourselves up, dust ourselves off, and get better at the craft of living.

"If you think about it, since older corsets use whalebone, aren't all old corsets corseted skeletons?"
Schi-Lee A. Smith

CONTENTS

ACKNOWLEDGMENTS

This book would not have been possible without the kindness, generosity, and patience of many, many people, several of whom donated their time and talents to making it a better piece of scholarship. I would like to thank my parents, John and Judy Horwitz, for their love and support and for being my biggest cheerleaders; my occasional writing and editing partner Dr. Jay VanderVeen of Indiana University South Bend, who has listened to me rant about corsets and misogyny for more than a decade now, for making my arguments better, my logic more sound, and things in general brighter and nicer; Dr. Agustín Fuentes, whose constant support and kindness knows no bounds, for his beautiful words about this pet project of mine; Michael Feijoo for lending his expert opinion on various medical technicalities—it has been a true delight to see his development since his years as my student; Anne Geurts, translator and linguist, who lent her eyes to my translation; Schi-Lee A. Smith for her accidentally perfect epigraph; Dr. Rory Langton of Indiana University South Bend for his assist on the radiographs; Dr. Sarah Bendall, Hanna Polasky, and Dr. Alanna McKnight, my fellow corset scholars, who gas me up, make me smile, extend comfort and support, and whose work I am always glad to champion; and my editors at Bloomsbury, Frances Arnold and Rebecca Hamilton, as well as the entire editorial and formatting team that brought this complicated and strange book to completion. Finally, despite the text and images within this book having originally been published in 1908 and without proper notice, leading to them all being out of copyright entirely and in the public domain, the author and publisher have made every effort to trace any residual copyright holders; none have been located or come forward. However, if any have been inadvertently overlooked, the publishers will be pleased, if notified of any omissions, to make the necessary arrangement at the first opportunity.

NOTES ON THE TRANSLATION AND HOW TO READ THIS BOOK

While I have tried to stay true to O'Followell's intent throughout this translation, that has been difficult on occasion due to his sometimes quite idiomatic usage of certain terms or phrases. An example of this is in Chapter 2, where he uses the word "mamelles." This word translates in four different ways: breasts, nipples, teats, and udders. Only two—the latter, more vulgar two—are listed in my French–English dictionary, which I relied upon to teach myself the more obscure or unknown-to-me words contained herein. While I did not believe that O'Followell, a doctor, would be calling women's breasts "udders," it did take a bit of additional searching to find the non-vulgar usage of "mamelles." There are a few instances scattered through the book in which I have noted times when I could not find an appropriate translation, or where the translation did not make sense, or where the idiomatic or antiquated phrasing interfered with interpretation. All translations are imperfect interpretations of their subject matter, and this is no different, particularly as I am at a slight disadvantage in producing the first official published translation; there are no previous ones for me to refer to for help. This is a selected translation—there was far too much extraneous matter in O'Followell's text to include every word he wrote, so I have excerpted the book to highlight his intent and impact without being needlessly redundant. In typing out the French text, I have preserved O'Followell's phrasing, punctuation, inconsistencies of spelling, and occasional imprecision. In the translation, I have retained as much of the feel of the original text as possible, while still producing a readable and comprehensible manuscript. This book is organized with the French text or an illustration first, and the translation and commentary annotations afterward–the annotations are referred to by footnote number, notated in the English translation text. Because this is an excerpted translation, there may be more text in the images than there is in translation. I hope you enjoy it, and use it well.

INTRODUCTION

There is a contemporary trend that modern interpretations of historical documents and events should be apolitical. This book does not follow it.

Indeed, this book, *The Bad Corset*, is a translation and annotation of curated selections of Dr. Ludovic O'Followell's 1908 treatise on corsets *Le Corset: Médicine, Histoire, et Hygiène,* and is staunchly feminist, as am I, and so before we move to the meat of the topic at hand, we must discuss a few expectations and definitions.

CAN CORSETS BE FEMINIST? THE ARGUMENT FOR A UNIQUE MOMENT IN FASHION HISTORY

Fashion theory (Barthes 1967; Entwistle 2000), as well as discussions of semiotics and intertextual meaning (Fairclough 2003), tell us that what we wear has multiple aspects—personal choice, habitus, sexual signaling, socio-economic status, and the availability of materials all play roles in the fashion we produce and use. With something so fundamental as undergarments, it would be easy to reduce women's choices to one of the above, and with the corset in particular, much of popular discourse reduces them to sexual signaling, which is often seen as anti-feminist. This is, of course, both reductive and incorrect—the desire for sex is universal, and indicating one's own sexual desire and availability can be very feminist, as feminism's core tenets include being able to choose (when, how, and with whom) to have sex.

Before we continue, a short digression onto my use of the terms "women" and "girls" regarding the corseted people O'Followell discusses. As a modern-day researcher trained not only in human biology but also in gender studies, I embrace the use of inclusive language, and where *The Bad Corset* discusses today's corseting practices or medical knowledge, I will often use modern language conventions—women, trans men, and nonbinary and intersex people, or people with uteruses/people who ovulate/people who ejaculate. This is in respect of the fact that not all people with uteruses are women; not all women ovulate; not all physical sexes map on to the respective genders. Despite the conservative kerfuffle in the US and UK over these concepts, scientifically this much is not in dispute. However, during O'Followell's time, binary sex was accepted as the norm, and there is no indication within *Le Corset* that he treated any trans or non-binary people, nor that the women who saw him for their problems saw themselves as anything but women. Therefore, when discussing his text, his observations, and his analysis, I use women, woman, girl, girls, as he did. Let us resume.

Far from presenting a concrete condemnation of the practice of corseting, *Le Corset* condemns women. From pre-pubescent girls, to teenagers, to young women, to women over thirty, O'Followell's 306 pages of text and scores of illustrations are used to emphasize one point: women abuse the corset, harming their body, impacting their fertility, and making themselves ugly. Rather than repudiating the seemingly patriarchical practice of corseting, O'Followell enforces the *actually* patriarchical practice of disputing and negating a woman's right to control her own body; he would hand that control over to men, with himself first among them. If only women would listen to him, he pleads! The quibble over how they clothed themselves was only ever window-dressing for his wish to control them.

He draws in the expertise of doctors, philosophers, women of renown, everyone from the father of surgery, Ambroise Paré, to the father of modern philosophy, Jean-Jacques Rousseau. He quotes them, paraphrases them, argues with them, disagrees or agrees with them depending on the moment, and all of this nuance and contradiction is missed if one relies only on the illustrations.

Where possible, I have contextualized O'Followell's text with medical information from his contemporaries and twenty-first-century scholarship. Regrettably, many of the books, articles, and theses he quotes or paraphrases are out of print or otherwise unavailable, yet wherever I could find them, I have included their information. However, a remarkable number of them have been digitized, and I have done my best to track those down in order to add context to this translation. That said, O'Followell was not at all careful about the spelling of people's names (or even the inclusion of people's full names), the years in which they published, the titles of the works, maintaining both open and close quotation marks, or indicating when he was paraphrasing, so I have corrected or amended the sources where applicable and where I have been able to find them.

Lack of specificity of the sources is a strong argument in favor of a unique subtitle (something I favor in my own writing), as what stymied me in this search was the sheer volume of works that bore names such as "The Corset," "On The Corset," or "The Question of the Corset." I have supplemented this effort by making quite liberal use of modern medical scholarship, indicating where necessary information that O'Followell would have known at the time vs. things he would have not known due to their discovery or publication after the publication of *Le Corset*. For example, while he would have known that corseting did not cause wearers to cough up blood, a symptom mentioned in the preface to *Le* Corset, because that is caused by tuberculosis (the pathogen responsible for which was isolated in 1882),[1] he would not have known that Simonetta Cattaneo, supposed model for Botticelli's Venus, may have died of a pituitary tumor not phthisis, as that information was not published until 2019.

I began this project skeptical, but assuming O'Followell had good intentions. However, as I continued to work on it, I discovered ever more lies, obfuscations, falsifications, and, for lack of a better way of stating it, things he should have known as a physician, but which he got wrong. As it turns out, my skepticism was justified: the book as a whole is much more complex than the images within it would indicate. Close reading and analysis of the text lays out not only how we must not completely rely on O'Followell's images, but also how O'Followell himself manipulated the images, plagiarized his own sources, and outright lied about certain effects of the corset. Many of the radiographs were altered to support his agenda.

I acknowledge that it is not merely enough to point out his faults, to "accuse" him from our basis of contemporary knowledge, but it is imperative to point out where his work fell short of rigorousness and accuracy. Where he was as accurate as possible for 1908, even if the information was incorrect, I do note that. Where I can contextualize his inaccuracies with either contemporary or modern sources, I do that as well. Because of the limitations of the available material, this contextualization is incomplete. If a source is mentioned in the text, but not available, I have recorded that in the annotations. In this way, *The Bad Corset* is not merely a translation, but rather a work that can interrogate and correct O'Followell's occasionally deliberate wrongdoings rather than allow them to continue to poison scholarship for another century. Before we get to that, however, who was he?

CONTEXTUALIZING O'FOLLOWELL

Ludovic Marie O'Followell was born on the December 8, 1872, in Portslade-by-Sea, Sussex, England, to parents "feu" (the late) Henri Louis, and Follain Marie [sic] who resided in Bois-Colombes, a commune just northwest of

---

[1] Fascinatingly, O'Followell does not mention tuberculosis once in the entire book.

Paris. He served in the French army from 1905 to 1922, becoming a naturalized citizen by decree on May 18, 1912. In 1913, he lived at 10 rue d'Alger in the 1st arrondissement, department de la Seine, and was still there five years later. He died on January 20, 1965, at the age of ninety-three.[2] This is, regrettably, the current extent of what is known about him as a person. Also regrettable is the fact that we have no information about the creation and publication of *Le Corset*: we do not know how many copies were printed, how many and to whom they were sold, whether there were more editions, or anything that would assist in contextualizing the book itself. However, writing in Belle Époque France, O'Followell's disparaging views of female fashion may have stemmed from an ideological backlash against the excesses and fripperies of the age. He lambasts both the antique corset and the fashions of the late nineteenth century with equal fervor, clamoring for modernization, simplification, and corsets that promote and protect the health of the woman.

Ah! You see, O'Followell was not *anti*-corset. His book is bracketed front and back with advertisements for corsets, mostly created or sold by other doctors whom O'Followell quotes in his text. There is a literature of deformity and its connection to morality that begins during the Romantic Period, yet he makes strikingly little reference to this source material. Or, perhaps, one should say that he *adds* to this source material, becoming yet one more source that equates the (corset) deformed body with (female) immorality. Here we see the development of a conceptualization of medical knowledge that emphasizes the ways in which "foundational texts," or the creation of a medical canon, cause damage throughout history—and whether or not he was foundational in 1908, he certainly is considered to be so now, for twenty-first-century scholarship. Much in the way that O'Followell relied on Paré, who relied on Vesalius, we have come to rely on O'Followell—he is the most studied and referenced corseting "expert" to be passed down through the twentieth century, and yet so much of what he wrote was already inaccurate in his own time.

By this, I do not mean he is used extensively or exclusively by corset historians, and this is not to in any way criticize such esteemed fashion historians as Kunzle and Steele, who absolutely question O'Followell's results and conclusions —in fact, they use him quite sparingly. Instead, I am referencing the unchecked modern internet viral-ness of O'Followell's radiographs. First seen in Steele (2001), two of the radiographs which will be discussed in detail in Chapter 2 of this book were picked up from the *Le Corset* Wikipedia page by biological anthropologist Pamela Stone in her 2012 article "Binding Femininity," and again in her 2020 book chapter "Bound to Please," and these have been repurposed for multiple corset blogs—often without analysis or context.[3] It is these, sadly misleading, vestiges of O'Followell which are now the most well-known "facts" about corset related skeletal changes.

It is furthermore a criticism of the under-sourced nature of the corset-biological anthropology and -history discipline as a whole, until very recently. This stems from two issues which directly affect the preparation of this book and on the basis of which this book was formed: archival preservation, and misogyny. I shall address the latter first. Corseting has, historically, been seen as a "woman's" topic, and systemically devalued in academia. If you search "corset," "medicine," and "culture" in a university library, you will get only a handful of academic sources before the late 1900s, and after that point, the majority of the sources were written by women. While the primary

[2] All biographical information courtesy of archives.paris.fr
[3] A very short list that highlights this:

https://www.realclearscience.com/blog/2019/04/11/did_19th_century_corsets_really_kill_women.html
https://gizmodo.com/x-ray-images-of-women-in-corsets-show-skeletons-in-a-bi-545378783
https://dearauthor.com/features/industry-news/monday-news-x-rays-of-corsets-scientists-study-the-justification-for-oral-sex/
https://publicdomainreview.org/collection/the-corset-x-rays-of-dr-ludovic-o-followell-1908
https://www.cnet.com/culture/vintage-x-rays-reveal-the-hidden-effects-of-corsets/
https://www.thelingerieaddict.com/2013/07/corsets-and-health-should-you-be-worried-by-corseted-x-rays.html
https://www.vintag.es/2022/04/corset-x-rays.html

source material such as O'Followell, Paré, and Gaches-Sarrute abounded until the inter-war years, we, as scholars were not making use of it, and were often discouraged from doing so.

That is, if we could even access it. Before the mid-2010s, much of the corset-related primary source material was held in individual libraries or archives, and although such material was generally available for use by scholars, you had to know where to look. Once you knew where to look, you had to be able to afford the time and money to travel to the libraries and archives to do the research. Writing from my vantage point in the early 2020s, it is painfully easy to forget how recently digitization of even the *records* of these items happened, let alone digitization of the items themselves—which, it must be added, is not complete. This book, *The Bad Corset*, has mostly been composed while sitting in my apartment, surrounded by ready access to the comforts of home. Had I needed to travel to France, the UK, Germany, and Italy to access much of my supporting primary source material instead of simply using my home-based internet access, the process would have been much longer and more expensive, perhaps prohibitively so.

As for *Le Corset* itself—there may be more than three copies in the world, but perhaps not many more. I own a physical copy—the illustrations in *The Bad Corset* are scanned images from that copy. The Bibliothèque Nationale de France (BNF) holds another. And someone out in the world owns a third, as *Le Corset* has been digitized and placed, in its entirety, on French Wikipedia. Pursuant to creating *The Bad Corset*, I have made all possible attempts to ascertain who, if anyone, has a copyright-based interest in *Le Corset*—contacting the publisher, the BNF, and learning as much about O'Followell as possible to seek out any heirs—and those attempts have been futile; the book, and the images and text within it, are in public domain.

The impetus for writing *The Bad Corset* came from several times and places in my life as a biological anthropologist. My fascination with corsetry began in my twenties, and my love of bones and skeletons far earlier, but the combination of the two culminated from my graduate work on the bioarchaeology of corseting, recently published as my second monograph, *The Corseted Skeleton: A Bioarchaeology of Binding* (Palgrave 2020). I used O'Followell's book as a source in that work, and yet. . .I was never satisfied with how reliant the fashion history and biological anthropologists are on his illustrations, and how we have under-studied the text. We have used them for decades to demonstrate corseting "damage" and to discuss the patriarchy, but they seemed. . .off to me in a way I could not put into words. I acquired my physical copy of *Le Corset* in 2012—crumbling, yellowed, without binding or cover—and because I owned the book, I decided to read it, rather than merely use the photos. As mentioned above, the pages reproduced in this book are scans from my physical copy; I do hope you will forgive anomalies in printing, page integrity, and preservation.

Before moving on to the structure of *The Bad Corset*, let us lay out some key terminology.

GLOSSARY

I have already discussed why I use woman/women, girl/girls, so now I will turn to some things that require further definition. This section borrows heavily from the glossary in Chapter 1 of my previous book, *The Corseted Skeleton* (2020), with some alteration as to the wording, as many of the same concepts apply here.

Anatomical normal   Anatomical normal refers to the standard presentation of a human being, or part of the human body. The anatomically normal body or organ has no anomalies, deformations, or pathologies—no disease, damage, or congenital malformations. It is your average body or body part, looking like a typical or standard representation of a human being or body part.

Boning   The material used to stiffen a corset. Various materials were used, depending on origin, plentitude, availability, cost, and fashion. Historically, wood, leather, whalebone, and steel were prevalent, with plastic not appearing until after our time period, and whalebone eventually falling out of popularity as steel became cheaper and easier to produce.

Busk The stiff material that created the front line of the corset. Depending on the shape of the garment, busks were either single (if the garment did not lace or hook in the front), or double (if it did). Busks were initially removable and changeable, but then became fully integrated into the garment, to the point that one was no longer able to purchase them for personal use, instead being available only for dressmakers, corset-makers for the repairing done by both types of workers.

Corset An undergarment or overgarment worn usually, although not exclusively, by women. The purpose of the corset was to provide shape to the wearer's garments, creating a distinct bust, waist, and hips. Eventually the corset was replaced by the brassiere and girdle, as fashions and textile manufacture changed. The terms "corset" and "stays" are often used interchangeably in texts from the time period, including in *Le Corset*. O'Followell goes on to make a distinction between "le corset ligne" or the straight corset, and other types of corsets such as "le corset courbure" or the curved corset, both referring to the shape of the busk.

Damage/deformation Damage or deformation refers to deviation away from the anatomical normal, particularly changes in the shape and structure of body due to the long-term pressure of the corset. While O'Followell uses these terms to imply harm to the wearer, harm is incredibly subjective, and the presence of deformation from corset wearing may not indicate a lower quality of life than had the woman not corseted.

Stays The word "stay" or "stays" is occasionally used interchangeably with "corset," and refers to a bound undergarment that contains boning, but which may or may not contain a busk.

THE STRUCTURE OF THIS BOOK AND WHAT TO EXPECT

Often in popular discourse both from the early 1900s and more recently, being feminine and being feminist are set as contrasting opposites, with femininity aligned with nature and feminism aligned to culture (Ortner 1974; Teasley 1904). This intersects with O'Followell's main premise: that women wearing the corset were anti-female, and that their choice to corset during their child-bearing years rendered them unattractive, unhealthy, unlikeable, and infertile. He states in no uncertain terms, chapter after chapter, that women who are closer to their natural shape are more feminine, more desirable, healthier, and have fewer fertility issues. This is the bias that the annotations in the following chapters will address: what medical inaccuracies can be shown in O'Followell's work? Why did O'Followell hate and blame women so much, and can we reconcile these ideas—the feminine and the feminist—without being reductive and cliched? Can we rehabilitate the corset from its position as the scourge of women by women, allowing modern-day corset wearers that nuance of the multiple aspects of fashion? Can corsets be feminist? Here is what you can expect from each chapter, comprised of excerpts from *Le Corset*, and my own annotations:

Chapter 1: What Does the Corset Do For, and To, Women: Covering the Preface and Chapter 1 of *Le Corset*

The front matter and preface of O'Followell's book contain two things on which I focus: advertisements for corsets, and a justification for the book that follows it, written by Dr. Gaston Lion, a doctor from the Paris hospital. Lion was born in 1861 in Saint-Cloud (Hauts-de-Seine), and died in 1942 in Monaco. He wrote mostly on the topic of stomach ailments, but branched out to tuberculosis, syphilis, and blood disorders.

The ten advertisements, most of them for fashionable corsetry, and one for a medical-brace type corset are stunning in their contradiction—they are (all but one) focused on unnatural and unreasonable waist sizes. I will discuss waist to bust-to-hip ratios, comparing what an uncorseted waist looks like, to what an historically accurate corseted waist looks like (Gibson 2015; Gibson 2020), to what is shown in the advertisements. Corset advertising is a subgenre of advertising, and the ads follow the rules of the subgenre, showing beauty, gracefulness, slenderness, and popularity. Genres, however, rarely align with reality—the tropes are unrealistic and unable to be matched by actual people. To wear the advertised corset is to aspire to be like the ad, an aspiration that can never be attained.

The second part of Chapter 1 will discuss the history of French medicine and the sources upon which the doctors were drawing for their tutelage and anatomical knowledge. Well before modern medical licensing boards and standardized procedures, this period in time was categorized by a lack of cleanliness, a lack of anesthesia, and a lack of living subjects that would be reasonably expected to survive surgery. In many parts of Europe, including some of France, by the time they had graduated from a medical program, many students may never have worked on a living patient, having instead gained their knowledge from theoretical lectures, or from dissection laboratories that worked on cadavers. This type of knowledge production created a feedback loop of flawed information: a cadaver cannot tell you where something hurts, what is wrong, or whether or not a surgical procedure was effective. A lecture based on knowledge gained from cadavers, and on anatomical drawings, cannot give accurate medical knowledge.

While the common practice after program graduation was to have prolonged follow-up periods and remain knowledgeable about one's patient until death, this was not possible for all patients, and records kept from such cases still privileged the viewpoint of the physician (Broomhall 2004; Hildreth 1987; McHugh 2007; Wilso 1993). Until the perfection of anesthetic and the widespread acceptance of sanitization (for how long that took, see Fitzharris 2017), there was a component missing from medical and surgical procedures: the point of view of the patient. This is to be expected, of course, but gave women little recourse in terms of advocating for themselves during their medical care. When medicine is based on treating the symptoms, a cause must be assigned to the symptoms—in this case, the corset was seen to be the cause, and so women must remove the corset. While O'Followell looks at the whole body, he does not look at the patient, apart from blaming them heavily for their own fate.

Chapter 2: The Upper Torso: Covering Chapters 2–4 of *Le Corset*, on the Topics of the Lungs, Thoracic Cage, Circulation, and Lactation

This chapter will look at the upper torso, specifically concentrating on the lungs, thoracic cage (ribs, vertebrae, scapulae, and clavicles), the lymphatic system, and the breasts. O'Followell addresses the following symptoms:

- Pulmonary: repression of the diaphragm; compression of the lungs; more or less difficulty with breathing and speech; aggravation of the lungs; disposed to coughing up blood.
- Circulatory: difficulty with the venous circulation of the upper limbs; compression of the heart; palpitations of the heart; syncope; circulatory difficulty returning the blood to the veins of the heart; obstruction in the circulation of the head and the neck; difficulty in abdominal circulation.
- Lymphatic: diverse maladies of the lymph nodes or the mammary glands.

Lachmund (1999) points out that the stethoscope's invention in the early 1800s revolutionized medical diagnostics—for the first time, doctors could hear the internal workings of the body, both the breath sounds and the sounds of various liquids moving about the body. Specifically focusing on lung sounds, Lachmund discusses the codification of these sounds into symptoms, and thus into conditions. Thus, the abnormal breath sounds associated with tuberculosis (Klebs 1909) could be identified, categorized, and codified. Moving beyond the lungs, the stethoscope also allowed for examination of the heart and circulatory system, leading to identificatory categories for veinous blockages, blood clots, embolisms, and stroke.

Certainly some of the above symptoms can be attributed to corsets—the issues with the compression of lungs and lack of expansion of the diaphragm—however, the prevalence of such are not proven. Not accounted for in O'Followell's analysis are respiratory diseases, COPD, damage from coal dust and smoke, compression and movement of the organs during pregnancy, and pneumonia, all of which would also compromise lung, diaphragm, and vocal capacities.

The symptoms of the heart, if put into non-medical terms, can be read (in no particular order) as low blood pressure, high blood pressure, various arrhythmias, blockages in the arteries leading to heart attacks, and fainting. However, even if we grant that constriction of the body can lead to constriction of the veins, this problem would most often manifest acutely, rather than with long-term constriction. Long-term constriction relates a completely non-clinical observation: bodies are squishy, and they are also springy—anything related to soft tissue will spring back to shape if not scarred or obstructed by a hard object. Take, for example, the modern use of compression garments to treat edema. Edema, or the swelling of body tissues due to excess fluid build-up, is a chronic problem for people with various illnesses—diabetes and kidney or liver disease, to name a few. The treatment is very low-tech: constantly compress the area where the fluid has built up, usually with socks, arm warmers, or similar garments, supporting the veins (which are leaking the fluid) and ensuring that the fluid has less area in which to find purchase. The operative word here, however, is "constant." Constant compression is needed to ensure that the veins are supported and compressed enough to do their jobs. Anything less than that, and they continue to leak. One can, of course, produce blockages and obstructions with sudden constriction, but it seems unlikely that these would be the result of long-term pressure from the corset. Women during O'Followell's time could be wearing anything from a one-paneled corset built into a garment, to a four-paneled version that might lace in three or more places. Apart from the former, most corseting had the ability to be laced tighter or looser, depending on preference, and thus adjusted so that it was not constricting, pinching, or mashing the breasts.

Chapter 3: The Lower Torso: Covering Chapters 5–9 of *Le Corset*, on the Topics of the Liver, Spleen, Kidneys, Stomach, and Intestines

This chapter will look at the lower torso, specifically the liver, spleen, kidneys, stomach, and intestines. O'Followell addresses the following symptoms from the list in Chapter 1: [Compression of] the liver, and the other abdominal viscera, above all after a meal; deformation, displacement of the liver and swelling in the vertical dimension abutting the iliac fossa. Restriction of the lower part of the thorax; reduction of the cavities of the chest and the abdomen. Compression of the stomach, digestive lesions (ulcers); indigestion; nausea; vomiting. Slowness and easy interruption of the matter in the shrunken intestine.

The bisection and compression of the liver is one of the most pervasive myths about the wearing of the corset, and O'Followell's text, and others like it, are very much the sources responsible for this. There are two museums (the Gordon Museum of Pathology in London and the Mütter Museum in Philadelphia) which either have or discuss what they consider to be corset-damaged livers. Yet both these discussions are of either single-specimens, or tales of the "heard it from a friend who" type.

Dr. Ambroise Paré, a physician who was a contemporary of Paracelsus, tells about an autopsy where he saw a liver that was cut in half (something that has been recounted in most modern corset discourse, see Kunzle 1982; Steele 2001). However, if you look at the anatomical position of the liver, it is encompassed by the lower rib cage, protruding slightly below the bottom ribs, but not extensively. Pressure on the lower rib cage from the corset would definitely move the liver upward, compressing it slightly or making it smaller in proportion to a standard liver, but the idea of bisection is unsupported.

The spleen's main duties are to produce white blood cells and antibodies; keep a store of red blood cells; filter old red blood cells out of the circulatory system, process them into bilirubin, and send them to the liver; and to act like a very large lymph node. Damage to the spleen causes rapid and massive bleeding, leading to a very quick death if it is not stopped almost immediately. In archival research I conducted on St. Bride's Parish in London for an eighty-year period (between 1770 and 1849 CE), there were no reported deaths from damage to the spleen (Gibson 2020).

While this is not conclusive, it certainly is suggestive of the overall lack of spleen damage from corsets. The prevalence of what O'Followell calls "hypertrophy" and what is currently called splenomegaly, or enlarged spleen, is about 2 percent in adults (Chapman et al. 2020), and is almost universally attributable to disease, not injury or compression.

The kidneys filter the blood, removing toxins and water and directing them to the bladder. Kidneys are situated in the back portion of your mid-abdominal region, and in women are quite vulnerable to secondary infections from mis-handled urinary tract infections. They are also vulnerable to kidney stones, concretions of ureic acid which form spiky stones that can become lodged in various parts of the kidney and urinary tract. I know from regrettable experience that it is also possible to dislocate a rib so that it pokes directly into the kidney, but, absent a tendency to dislocation, which most people do not have, compression of the ribs—particularly long-term compression over time—would not be enough to cause kidney damage. The articulated skeletons that I examined, and which exhibited corseting damage, did not show long-term rib dislocations (Gibson 2020). The ribs remained perfectly articulated with their vertebrae, and the overall ribcage changed in shape from ovoid to circular.

In regard to the stomach/digestive tract, we can see that several of these symptoms have alternate explanations or extremely diverse causes. Specifically, ulcers are now known to be caused by the bacteria Helicobacter pylori. H. pylori is a common bacterium that occasionally infects your upper digestive tract; with overgrowth, it begins to erode the lining of the stomach and/or small intestine, causing painful lesions. Wearing a corset—putting external pressure on the abdomen—does not have a physical mechanism for influencing H. pylori growth. While this knowledge was decades away from O'Followell's time, it remains indicative to the treatment of female patients, and to the extreme reaching being done when he attributes it to corseting.

In discussing the symptoms of the intestines, we are again seeing something that O'Followell could only have viewed in a cadaver. Many things might influence intestinal atrophy, from malnutrition, to celiac disease, to gastroenteritis. During O'Followell's time, constipation was also believed to have a non-physical cause: fixation on the anal stage of psycho-sexual development. Anal-retentiveness was thought to have manifested both literally and figuratively, producing constipation and fussiness, as well as a need for order in the person's surroundings. It was contrasted with its natural digestive counterpart—diarrhea—which constituted anal-explusiveness.

Chapter 4: Population Control, Miscarriages, and Abortions: Covering Chapter 10 of *Le Corset*, on the Topic of the Genitals and Reproductive System

Being such an important subject, and central to the female medical experience both then and now, this chapter will cover the reproductive organs and genitals. I will focus on both the symptoms from Chapter 1, and on the historic and modern contextualizations of the fight for birth control and abortion rights. The symptoms are: frequent congestion in the upper genitals; prolapse of the uterus; troubles menstruating; in the enlarged state (pregnancy), disposition towards abortion (miscarriage), with uterine hemorrhage.

Gynecology, separate from obstetrics, was a very young field at the time O'Followell wrote *Le Corset*, and obstetrics itself had only recently become the purview of doctors rather than midwives or of women themselves. Women's reproductive issues were generally treated as problems only if they stopped a woman from working, or from having (more) children. In addition to a general medical disinterest in treating the whole woman, this time period suffered from a related lack of knowledge about what constituted "normal" menstruation, what influenced spontaneous abortion—though there was no lack of speculation—and a complete disregard for the two most impactful disorders that cause pain and abnormal bleeding among menstruating women: endometriosis (first described in 1870) and poly-cystic ovarian syndrome (PCOS—first described in 1935). Uterine prolapse is most often a symptom of having several children in quick succession. Menstruation can be slowed, altered, or stopped, or can increase drastically as a result of factors such as: malnourishment; prolonged periods of breastfeeding; low body fat ratio; bearing multiple children in a row; early menopause due to hormonal imbalances; and cancer.

Among conditions that can cause spontaneous abortion, also called miscarriage, we can count: malnourishment; injury to the abdomen; uterine scarring from STIs; genetic abnormalities of the fetus; ectopic pregnancy; drug use; ingestion of certain common herbs and spices including nutmeg; and just plain bad luck. Did women self-abort using their corset? Yes. It is mentioned in the text of the pamphlet on population control called "The Fruits of Philosophy" written by Charles Knowlton and reprinted and sold by famous theosophists Annie Besant and Charles Bradlaugh, who were arrested and tried for distributing the information counter to England's laws on contraception (1832/1870 in Chandrasekhar 1981). However, unlike with other abortive practices of the time, keeping one's corset laced tight before the quickening (before a woman felt movement from the child in utero) was a relatively harm-free way to control one's own reproduction, and was not seen as going against nature or God's will.

Additionally, as mentioned, pregnancy corsets existed which allowed women to remain supported during parturition. Usually without boning, but not always, the expanding corsets held and shaped a woman's body while she gestated her child, assisting with such things as making up for slack muscle tone, counteracting the effects the hormone relaxin has on connective tissue, and treating bloating and water retention. Were a woman to choose not to wear a corset, when pregnant or otherwise, this was also among the options for women during pregnancy depending on the above-mentioned factors.

Chapter 5: The Woman Wants to Look Beautiful to Please Her Man: Covering Chapters 11-15 of *Le Corset*, on the Topics of Which Corsets Women Should Wear, If They Should Wear Them at All, and Why Women Choose to Wear the Corset

This chapter will cover the social aspects of O'Followell's take on corseting and how, when, why, and which corsets women should wear (or not wear). The questions of when, how, and in what manner a child would have corseted return some of the most interesting and varied answers in fashion history. While it is evident, and uncontested, that most adult women corseted for the majority of their post-adolescent years, the practice of child corseting was unique from family to family, and no concrete practice is evident in the literature.

How young were girls beginning to corset? This, too, is unknown, though the consensus on what constituted child-corseting seems to be sometime before puberty, but after the age of six (Müller 2006). This again emphasizes how O'Followell blames women for perpetuating corset use, and in this he is correct—women were the designers, patent-holders, and ones who created the corsets, and the ones who passed on the tradition to their children. Additionally, he is also correct about the corset's effect on the musculature. Yet, what this does not take into account is, again, agency and the ability to choose for themselves—even after wearing it during childhood.

Chapter 12's title asks the question: "Should the Woman Wear the Corset?" and answers it: "No." The issue with asking (and answering) the question in this particular manner is that it treats both women and corsets as monoliths. Should the (singular and immutable) woman wear the (uniform and undifferentiated) corset? Not unless she wants pain, disease, and death! But women are not singular or immutable, and corsets are not uniform or undifferentiated. The ways a woman chose to wear her corset(s) were as numerable as possible, due to personal preference and the ability to loosen, tighten, or re-make a corset into the best tool for the woman's body.

About the garments themselves: corsets are very adaptable in terms of patterns, styles, and closure types, and the majority of women when O'Followell was writing were still either fully responsible for the creation of their own garments, or having those garments made to size, particularly if they were middle-class or above. Socioeconomic class does effect this, of course, with women on the lower end more likely to be sewing their own clothing or owning hand-me-downs or visiting second-hand stalls, and women on the higher end more likely to either have personal tailoring or, for those who did not find it déclassé, wearing off-the-rack. However, regardless of the mode of tailoring, all garments could be adjusted by lengthening or shortening the laces (by O'Followell's time, the standard style hooked in the front and laced in the back). This might have affected the beauty of the garment, but it would allow the woman to control how tight she wore her corset. Women also retained older styles due to personal preference or economic need, and many older styles had more than two panels, increasing the overall customizability of the garment.

Next, O'Followell compares various Greek statues of Venus figures to corseted women, holding the natural, unaltered form of the statues up as the paragon of female beauty. This is a common trope among detractors of the corset—that the woman's vanity has taken her too far from nature. However, further detractors of women in general agree that to be considered adult and civilized, a woman must be contained and trained up away from her natural childhood (and child-like) self, by wearing the corset. A discussion of the "ideal form" of Greek sculpture, which is then reflected in various periods of art afterward, is a common trope in news stories and magazine articles attacking the corset (Angel et al. 1985; Anonymous 1883b).

His final section on women wanting to be attractive represents one of the largest and most pervasive tropes in the modern perception of women: that whatever women do is done for men. And not even just to please men, but to attract men, to dupe men, to spite men, to keep men, to tempt men, to befuddle or ensnare men, to in any way, shape, or form, effect men. Women's existence is often seen only in relation to men, and they are granted no nuance or subtlety, no inner life or desires, goals, or aspirations, that do not somehow involve fathers, husbands, sons, or (male) bosses. Here I will also examine modern-day corset wearers, and what they have said about their reasons for corseting, looking at the ways in which the discourse is still being shaped in relation to the male gaze.

Threaded throughout this are references to the Dress Reform movement, which situate O'Followell's publication as a salvo in the interlocking temperance-based movements of the day. Dress Reform began as a movement in the 1870s to address the "unhealthiness" of women's clothing, which was seen as too heavy, too hot in some areas while too cold in others, and too restrictive. This was not a bid to completely rid women of corseting, but to adjust all areas of the female costume for maximum health benefits (Cunningham 2003). This movement was heavily led by women, and intersected with both the teetotaller and abolitionist movements, due to the latter movements' similar emphasis on health and safety. However, would this adjustment in clothing have occurred without these movements as a driving force? I posit that it would not have been nearly as successful in turning popular fashion away from the corset and toward a more flexible alternative (bra and girdle), however, the various movements were not the only force acting on fashion at the time. Another force, which is often overlooked, is that of availability.

1908, the publication year of O'Followell's book, fell during the build-up of conflicts that would lead to World War I. During this time, certain materials were being developed (synthetic rubber and cold-formed steel, to name two) that would revolutionize both corsets and war efforts. However, as certain products gained popularity, others were subject to scarcities, most notably silk, cotton, and the aforementioned steel—all of which were needed for military applications. These materials, which make up the bulk of the typical corset, were required for the production of parachutes, canvas, explosives, tanks, and ships. The massive demand on the world's resources would have killed the corset even if the reform movement did not. Within a few short decades—by the end of the 1920s—the corset had been mostly replaced in the common female wardrobe. However, its impact on the psyche lasted far beyond its physical presence.

AFTERWORD: O'FOLLOWELL'S IMPACT: WOMEN AND MEDICINE IN THE TWENTY-FIRST CENTURY AND BEYOND

Earlier, I asked if the act of corseting can be feminist. The core of feminism is belief in the equality of the sexes, and the fight for equal access to rights and responsibilities, and those rights and responsibilities include the right to wear whatever clothing suits us, unhindered by the views, desires, or expectations of any other sex. However, the feminist issues under siege by O'Followell's 306-page treatise on corsets and medicine go far beyond clothing, and to the creation of women as medical subjects. As demonstrated in *The Bad Corset*, O'Followell and doctors with similar views were instrumental in creating the female medical body. Through a lack of direct observation of internal organs in living subjects, through a violent contempt for women and their own bodily knowledge, through infantilizing women and treating them as adjuncts of their male relatives, and through a lack of holistic care for the woman inside the body, O'Followell has had a profound negative impact on the ways in which women are seen by the modern medical community.

Modern doctors and other people with professional medical training are held up as paragons of knowledge, as authorities, as people who know our bodies better than we do. There is good reason for this—their training is intensive, and few laypeople, myself included, are going to have as many answers to questions about the body as the doctor will. Yet one area where doctors often fail is their approach to the non-standard patient. There are many ways to be non-standard, but only one standard, which comes directly from O'Followell's time period: white, male, European-derived, and in relatively decent overall health. We return here to the fact that doctors are trained to treat the symptoms, rather than the whole patient, and those symptoms were defined before women became medically interesting and important. Modern medical exploration has confirmed that women experience certain things differently, from the intensity of pain to the symptoms of heart attacks, yet most medical trials are still performed with techniques and dosages calibrated to male symptoms, body weights, body fat percentages, and expected outcomes.

Women's fight to be recognized as entire medical subjects, not just defective males, is a feminist fight. The fight to be heard by doctors without the subtle historical whisper of "hysterical" coloring our symptoms is a feminist fight. The fight to have women's pain treated as valid and important is a feminist fight, and it stems from the fight against the contempt and condemnation found in O'Followell's text. This text is the go-to in terms of illustrating the effects of corseting on the bodily systems and, as shown by *The Bad Corset*, it does not make its case nearly as convincingly as the photos, drawings, and X-rays contained inside it would indicate. This translation exposes not only this lack of evidence, but also O'Followell's prejudices, and answers the question: can corseting be feminist? Yes, it can.

REFERENCES

Angel, J., et al. (1985). Bony Response to 18th Century Stays Versus Later Corsets (abstract only, unpublished).

Anonymous. (1883b). "Stays and Statues," in *Knowledge*, 3: 23–4.

Broomhall, S. (2004). *Women's Medical Work in Early Modern France*, Manchester, UK: Manchester University Press.

Barthes, R. (1967). *The Fashion System*, trans. Ward and Howard, Berkeley, CA: The University of California Press.

Chandrasekhar, S. (1981). *"A Dirty, Filthy Book": The Writings of Charles Knowlton and Annie Besant on Reproductive Physiology and Birth Control and an Account of the Bradlaugh-Besant Trial,* Berkeley, CA: University of California Press.

Chapman, J., et al. (2020). "Splenomegaly," from *NCBI bookshelf,* https://www.ncbi.nlm.nih.gov/books/NBK430907/?report=printable

Cunningham, P. (2003). *Reforming Women's Fashion, 1850–1920: Politics, Health, and Art,* Kent, Ohio: Kent State University Press.

Davis, L. (2013). X-ray Images of Women in Corsets Show Skeletons in a Bind, on Gizmodo https://gizmodo.com/x-ray-images-of-women-in-corsets-show-skeletons-in-a-bi-545378783

Entwistle, J. (2000). *The Fashioned Body*, Malden, MA: Blackwell Publishers.

Fairclough, N. (2003). *Analyzing Discourse: Textual Analysis for Social Research*, New York, NY: Routledge Publishers.

Fitzharris, L. (2017). *The Butchering Art: Joseph Lister's Quest to Transform the Grisly World of Victorian Medicine*, New York, NY: Macmillan Publishers.

Gibson, R. (2015). "Effects of Long Term Corseting on the Female Skeleton: A Preliminary Morphological Examination," in *NEXUS: The Canadian Student Journal of Anthropology*, 23 (2): 45–60.

Gibson, R. (2020). *The Corseted Skeleton: A Bioarchaeology of Binding*, Cham, Switzerland: Palgrave Macmillan.

Harrington, C. (2013). Corsets and Health: Should You Be Worried by Corseted X-Rays? on The Lingerie Addict https://www.thelingerieaddict.com/2013/07/corsets-and-health-should-you-be-worried-by-corseted-x-rays.html

Hildreth, M. (1987). *Doctors, Bureaucrats, and Public Health in France, 1888–1902*, New York, NY: Routledge.

Klebs, A. (1909). *Tuberculosis: A Treatise by American Authors on its Etiology, Pathology, Frequency, Semeiology, Diagnosis, Prognosis, Prevention, and Treatment*, New York, NY: D. Appleton and Company.

Lachmund, J. (1999). "Making Sense of Sound: Auscultation and Lung Sound Codification in Nineteenth-Century French and German Medicine," in *Science, Technology, & Human Values,* 24 (4): 419–50.

Litte, J. (2013). Monday News: X-rays of Corsets; Scientists Study the Justification for Oral Sex; Price Fixing Trial is Over, on Dear Author https://dearauthor.com/features/industry-news/monday-news-x-rays-of-corsets-scientists-study-the-justification-for-oral-sex/

McHugh, T. (2007) *Hospital Politics in Seventeenth-Century France: The Crown, Urban Elites, and the Poor,* New York, NY: Ashgate Publishing.

Müller, A. (2006). *Fashioning Childhood in the Eighteenth Century: Age and Identity*, New York, NY: Routledge.

No author. (2013). The Corset X-Rays of Dr. Ludovic O'Followell (1908), on Public Domain Review https://publicdomainreview.org/collection/the-corset-x-rays-of-dr-ludovic-o-followell-1908

No author. (2022). In 1908, a Doctor Used X-Rays to Highlight the Damaging Effects of Tight Corsets on a Woman's Body, on Vintage.es https://www.vintag.es/2022/04/corset-x-rays.html

Ortner, S. (1974). "Is Female to Male as Nature is to Culture?" from *Women, Culture and Society,* ed. Michelle Ronaldo, pp. 67–87, Stanford, CA: Stanford University Press.

Pomeroy, R. (2019). "Did 19th Century Corsets Really Kill Women?" on *Real Clear Science* https://www.realclearscience.com/blog/2019/04/11/did_19th_century_corsets_really_kill_women.html

Starr, M. (2015). Vintage X-rays Reveal the Hidden Effects of Corsets, on cnet https://www.cnet.com/culture/vintage-x-rays-reveal-the-hidden-effects-of-corsets/

Teasley, D. (1904). *Private Lectures to Mothers and Daughters On Sexual Purity: Including Love, Courtship, Marriage, Sexual Physiology, and the Evil Effects of Tight Lacing,* Moundsville, WV: Gospel Trumpet Company.

Williams, L. (2018). X-rays from *Le Corset* (1908) Explained, on Lucy's Corsetry https://lucycorsetry.com/2013/06/27/x-rays-from-le-corset-1908-explained/

Wilson, L. (1993). *Women and Medicine in the French Enlightenment: The Debate over* Maladies des Femmes, Baltimore, MD: Johns Hopkins University Press.

1

WHAT DOES THE CORSET DO FOR, AND TO, WOMEN?
Covering the Front Matter, Preface, and Chapter 1 of *Le Corset*

THE FRONT MATTER

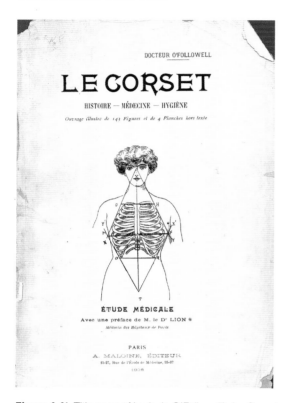

Figure 1.1[1] Title page of Ludovic O'Followell's *Le Corset*.

1 Title page: this is the first page of my copy of the book. The cover of this copy, which I purchased from a resaler as-is/sight unseen, is not extant, but there is a copy in the BNF in Paris which has the cover, if my readers would like to view it.

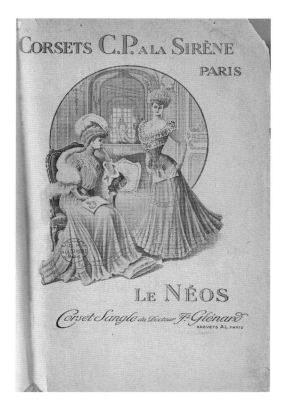

Figure 1.2[2] First advertisement, no page number.

2 First advertisement: an ad for a corset seller, "Corsets C.P. a La Sirène, Paris, Le Néox Corset Sangle du Docteur Fz Glénard, Brevets AL Paris," depicting two women, one fully dressed, one with a corset on top of an underdress. The ad is for the "Corset Sangle" or "strapped corset" of Dr. Frantz Glénard. O'Followell quotes heavily from Glénard throughout *Le Corset*, and he is the most-cited author in *Le Corset*'s bibliography.

This illustrates (literally and metaphorically) how many of the authors in *Le Corset* are saying one thing and selling another. Both O'Followell and Glénard attribute multitudinous ailments to the use, abuse, and overtightening of the corset, yet observe the bust-to-waist-to-hips ratio of the woman on the right: 1:.41:1 (Gibson 2020: 137). Only one corset out of the hundreds I examined during my research, Bath Fashion Museum's I.27.60 & 60A, had a similarly small waist (see Figures 1.16 and 1.17 below). The illustration here, and in the remaining advertisements, is not comparable to the waist size or body ratio that most women maintained, and it could certainly be considered "abuse" of the corset, yet it is the ideal image of femininity being sold by O'Followell and Glénard as the "new" and healthy corset.

Figure 1.3[3] Second and third advertisements, no page number.

3 Second and third advertisements, for general stores owned by Eugene Pemjean (top) and M. Gueudré (bottom). The top advertisement mentions corsets directly, whereas the bottom one offers a "baleine-corne" or whalebone horn. The illustration in the top advertisement shows a slender corseted woman admiring herself in a hand mirror. As discussed above, her waist size is not comparable to the "normal" or "average" woman of her time period, and conforms to the unrealistic ideals of femininity that were both expected and condemned at the time (see an 1887 unsigned letter in the Lancet titled "Corsets and Tight-Lacing"). This came directly under an argument for injections of mercury as a treatment for syphilis, and a few pages above a very serious discussion of dysacusis, or "the influence of mastication on the acuity of hearing," basically indicating that if you talk to someone who is chewing, they might not hear you (pps. 1296–7 and 1299, respectively) as well as a counter-argument from 1910, "An Anatomical Vindication of the Straight Front Corset" published anonymously in the magazine *Current Literature*, p. 172.

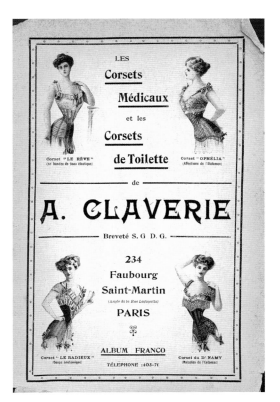

Figure 1.4[4] Fourth advertisement, no page number.

4   Fourth advertisement for "Les Corsets Médicaux et les Corsets de Toilette de A. Claverie," medical and fashion corsets sold by A. Claverie. Claverie's premises at 234 rue Faubourg Saint-Martin now holds a café and a bakery, beneath a block of apartments. As mentioned above, each of the corsets demonstrates the inaccurate, overly slender waist. The four corsets in this ad are named "Le Rêve" (the dream), "Ophélia," "Le Radieux" (the radiant), and "Corset du Dr. Namy" (Dr. Namy's corset). They are all highly decorative, with frills and stocking clips, ribbons and bows, but they also each serve a particular purpose according to the ad: Le Rêve has bands of elastic tissue, making it flexible; Ophelia is for afflictions of the abdomen; Le Radieux is "anatomically cut," indicating that it would fit the shape of the woman; and the Corset du Dr. Namy is for those suffering from stomach upsets.

That these can be advertised as so very fashionable and unrealistically small, and sold as objects meant to be beneficial to the health, highlights how the "good" corset is the one sold by O'Followell or the people chosen to advertise or be quoted in his books, and the "bad" corset is the one the woman actually wears. One may argue, as I previously have (Gibson 2020), that authors have variable (occasionally no) control over the supplemental information that is included in their publications: marketing, advertising, cover design, formatting, and size/shape of the book are often either pre-determined by the publisher, or subject to limited negotiation with the possibility of publisher override. Yet in two of the ads examined so far, a doctor has put his name to the corset being sold, and the corsets are marketed as health aides, which seems unlikely to be a coincidence given the medical focus of *Le Corset*.

This requires us to ask the following questions: 1) How can such a small corset be healthy? 2) How can O'Followell and the doctors he quotes continue to advocate for the use of corsets of this type? 3) Why are supposedly medical corsets marketed toward a woman's vanity? 4) As they are marketed to women's vanity, is this not just setting women up to be damned if they do, and damned if they don't?

Let us tackle at least the first question, although all of these questions will be revisited at various points in this book, particularly Chapter 5, where I will discuss O'Followell's chapters concerning why women wear the corset.

My own research suggests that such a small corset can indeed be, if not healthy, then not concerning. The reasons for this are two-fold: first, people began corseting at a relatively young age, which accustomed their bodies to the corset, and in the process modified their skeletons (Gibson 2020); and second, a small corset does not necessarily imply tight-lacing. A larger corset can just as easily be laced completely closed (or not) as a small one. Think of this like shoes: you want the right shoe size for your foot, after which the question of fit becomes a result of what you do with that shoe, not of the overall size of the shoe itself. For example, I wear a US size 8 ½, about the middle of the range of women's shoe sizes. If I laced it too tightly, it would hurt, despite being the correct size. If I laced it too loosely, it would chafe, despite being the correct size. Once the garment, shoe, or corset is sized for the body inside it, what the wearer does with it matters more. O'Followell will go on to suggest, however, that a bad corset can never be comfortable or healthy, and a good corset can never be uncomfortable or unhealthy, as well as implying that women damage themselves not only inadvertently, but purposefully. As though, when a shoe (or corset) is laced too tightly, there is no recourse but to continue to do so.

On the other hand, in an 1979 article entitled "Society, Physicians, and the Corset," Schwarz states that "One must not suggest that these physicians were merely bribed by the corset industry to endorse a product which had acquired the reputation of being 'unhealthy,'" which quite obviously *does* suggest this. I do not actually think they were bribed, merely that they were in on the ads being placed there, and that they knew the corset-recommending doctors in question.

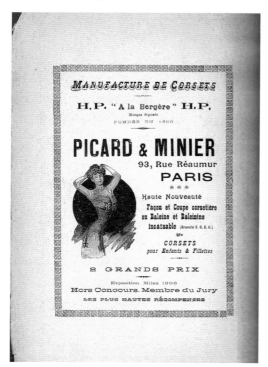

Figure 1.5[5] Fifth advertisement, no page number.

5 Fifth advertisement for Picar and Minier corsetmakers at 93 Rue Réaumur, which is now a natural foods store. The corsets are said to be "haute nouveauté" or high novelty, and this corsetier sells "corsets pour enfants &

fillettes" or corsets for children and young girls. We once again see the extremely small waist size, which the woman shows off in silhouette.

The fact that this maker is selling to children specifically (see also Balch 1904 on civilizing dress) will be discussed in Chapter 5, when I talk about O'Followell's chapters on who wears the corset and why. However, it is important to highlight the mode and importance of cultural transmission in corseting practices. Here, again, we have an ad that is aimed at women (though to be completely fair, none of these ads are aimed at men), by way of their daughters. During the centuries when corseting was prevalent, there was an informal but marked divide between domestic and public actions, where corset selling and advertising were on the public side of things, and corset purchasing and wearing were on the private side of things. Often, though not always, women would determine the clothing purchases for themselves and their children. Women, therefore, were living corseted lives, and corseting their daughters. O'Followell frames this in his later chapters as perpetuating a cycle of ignorance, but why must we assume that the women were ignorant of the potential "harms" of corseting? Is one truly ignorant of what one is currently going through? There is an analogy of a fish not recognizing water because it is born immersed in it, but a corset is not a de facto environment. We see through the vast literature (Berlanstein 1984; Cunningham 2003; Edwards 2017/18; Flood and Grant 2014; among others) that women corseted at various times in their lives, delayed the practice in certain cases, got "caught up" with it if they were delayed, removed, or altered the corset for childbearing, weight gain, and old age . . . and none of this indicates ignorance.

Figure 1.6[6] Sixth advertisement, no page number.

6 The sixth advertisement, and the only one with drawings of women where they are not shown with an exaggerated wasp-waist. Instead, on this ad for A. Delmotte, fabric-maker, located at 73 Rue de Richelieu (now a

vacant storefront), shows a woman in Grecian drapery. No woman of fashion in 1908 would be seen in society in this style of dress, so this imagery invokes something far dearer to the French woman than the wasp-waist of the other ads: "Marianne," the symbol of mother-France, the personification of the French national motto "liberté, égalité, fraternité." While Marianne can occasionally be seen in more form-fitting clothing, often with one breast exposed, she is also often pictured in loose, draped fabric, a visual throwback to antiquity, signifying a (metaphorical—as she came into prevalence post-Revolution) continuity of French nationhood (Gullickson 1996; Hunt 2004; Riberio 2003).

The ad also mentions that A. Delmotte can "fabrique de buscs sur commande" or make busks to order, and is an "atelier de baleines veritables" or a seller of true whalebones for corsets. In the latter part of the time of the corset, whalebone was falling out of favor for the now more affordable steel, but adding steel bones to an existing corset might take more modification than the wearer was willing to do.

Figure 1.7[7] Seventh and eighth advertisements, no page number.

7 Seventh and eighth advertisements; only the seventh mentions corsets. The ad is for G. Avi & Cie (G. Avi & Company), located at 89 Rue Réaumur, just down the block from Picar and Minier corsetmakers at 93 Rue Réaumur. 89 Rue Réaumur is now a McDonald's. This ad has no images of corseted women, but is outlined and decorated in the Art Nouveau style, with feminine swirls and flowers.

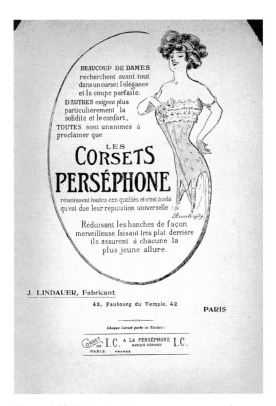

Figure 1.8[8] Ninth advertisement, no page number.

8   Ninth advertisement. This one does show the slender-waisted woman, but she is also slender hipped, indicating a shift in the way corseting was used that continued for the following two decades (Bruna 2015; Edwards 2017/18). The corset maker is J. Lindauer, located at 42 Faubourg du Temple, which is now a nondescript set of doors between a salon and a bakery. The text here is particularly relevant: "Many women search first of all for an elegant corset and a perfect fit. The others demand more particularly solidity and comfort. All are unanimous in proclaiming that the Corsets Perséphone unites all the qualities and that is what their universal reputation is about. Reducing the hips in a marvelous way and creating a very flat behind, it assures for each a very youthful allure."

This passage echoes a point made by O'Followell in a later chapter—that women do not use the corset to seek beauty, but rather to recreate the forms of youth. He considers it a deception used by women to stave off the weight of their later years and the changes wrought by childbearing in order to encourage their husbands into fidelity. What he does not mention, however, is that the advertisements in his book are selling that youth to the women. It is no secret that products exist to be sold, and selling products requires creating a need—genuine or fabricated—within the target audience. Yet, again, the emphasis on women as the ones who are using the corset to dupe, ensnare, and deceive men, rather than on the corset-makers and advertisers who play on the idea of that manufactured need, demonstrates O'Followell's bias toward misogyny.

Figure 1.9[9] Tenth advertisement, no page number.

9 In the tenth and final advertisement, we see the only true "medical" corset in *Le Corset:* one used as a treatment of scoliosis (for an archaeological discussion of similar treatments, see Moore and Buckberry 2016). The woman, pictured here from the back has three notable features: 1. Her head is grayed out—this seems unnecessary due to the fact that she is pictured from the back (those are the backs of her elbows, not the fronts), but this photographic device allows for her own anonymity, and for the viewer to identify with her only if they want or need to. There is no hair color (there is no color at all, but certainly even a black-and-white photo would allow people to distinguish between blondes and brunettes) for the viewer to compare themselves to, no facial features to recognize as one's own. The image creates a blank slate that deemphasizes identification with the subject, because who would care to associate themselves with disease and deformity if they did not have to? 2. Despite the shading out of the face/hair, the person is undeniably female, due to the hairstyle. While both women and men are susceptible to scoliosis and other spinal disorders, the choice was made here to aim the advertising at women. 3. The bust-to-waist-to-hips ratio is much more normal 1:.7:1 (Gibson 2020: 137). Presumably while wearing an orthopedic corset, one could not wear a standard or decorative corset, thus avoiding the "damage" done by the non-medical garment.

As for the corset itself, it is clearly a medical device. No effort has been made to make it pretty, or to have anything about it appeal to the eye, the vanity, or the ego. Other corsets advertised in the previous ads may have been marketed for medical purposes (see footnotes 2 and 4), but with comparison to this ad, we can see those clearly as part of a ruse to sell "healthy" corsets to women who have been blamed for "ruining" their bodies after wearing unhealthy or bad ones. Despite *Le Corset* purportedly being about the way the corset harms and deforms the body, and about what women should wear if they want to avoid those harms and deformations, there is absolutely no discussion of this actual medical corset contained within.

THE PREFACE

II

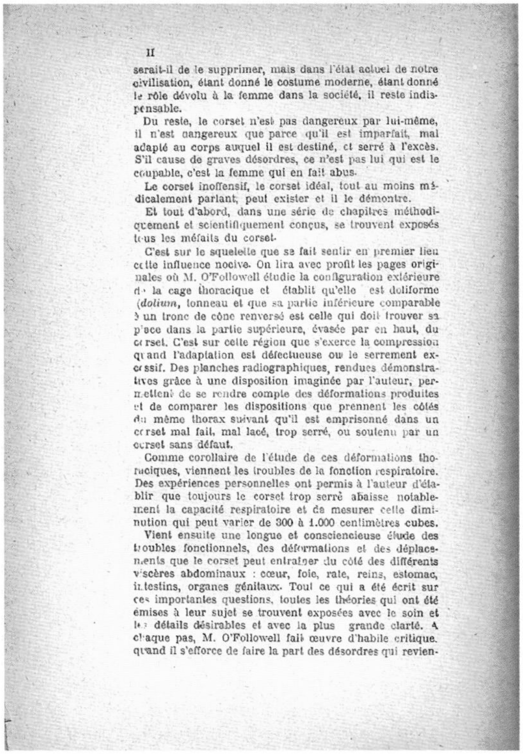

II

serait-il de le supprimer, mais dans l'état actuel de notre civilisation, étant donné le costume moderne, étant donné le rôle dévolu à la femme dans la société, il reste indispensable.

Du reste, le corset n'est pas dangereux par lui-même, il n'est dangereux que parce qu'il est imparfait, mal adapté au corps auquel il est destiné, et serré à l'excès. S'il cause de graves désordres, ce n'est pas lui qui est le coupable, c'est la femme qui en fait abus.

Le corset inoffensif, le corset idéal, tout au moins médicalement parlant, peut exister et il le démontre.

Et tout d'abord, dans une série de chapitres méthodiquement et scientifiquement conçus, se trouvent exposés tous les méfaits du corset.

C'est sur le squelette que se fait sentir en premier lieu cette influence nocive. On lira avec profit les pages originales où M. O'Followell étudie la configuration extérieure de la cage thoracique et établit qu'elle est doliforme (dolium, tonneau et que sa partie inférieure comparable à un tronc de cône renversé est celle qui doit trouver sa place dans la partie supérieure, évasée par en haut, du corset. C'est sur cette région que s'exerce la compression quand l'adaptation est défectueuse ou le serrement excessif. Des planches radiographiques, rendues démonstratives grâce à une disposition imaginée par l'auteur, permettent de se rendre compte des déformations produites et de comparer les dispositions que prennent les côtés du même thorax suivant qu'il est emprisonné dans un corset mal fait, mal lacé, trop serré, ou soutenu par un corset sans défaut.

Comme corollaire de l'étude de ces déformations thoraciques, viennent les troubles de la fonction respiratoire. Des expériences personnelles ont permis à l'auteur d'établir que toujours le corset trop serré abaisse notablement la capacité respiratoire et de mesurer cette diminution qui peut varier de 300 à 1.000 centimètres cubes.

Vient ensuite une longue et consciencieuse étude des troubles fonctionnels, des déformations et des déplacements que le corset peut entraîner du côté des différents viscères abdominaux : cœur, foie, rate, reins, estomac, intestins, organes génitaux. Tout ce qui a été écrit sur ces importantes questions, toutes les théories qui ont été émises à leur sujet se trouvent exposées avec le soin et les détails désirables et avec la plus grande clarté. A chaque pas, M. O'Followell fait œuvre d'habile critique, quand il s'efforce de faire la part des désordres qui revien-

Figure 1.10 Page II of the Preface of *Le Corset*.

Translation

. . . .the corset is not dangerous for itself, it is only dangerous because it is imperfect, maladapted to the body for which it is destined, and excessively tight. It causes many grave disorders, but it is not culpable, it is the woman who abuses it.[10]

The inoffensive corset, the ideal corset, exists—at least medically speaking—and it is demonstrated.

And first of all, in a series of method chapters and scientific conceptions, all the harms of the corset are exposed.

It is on the skeleton that this harmful influence is first felt. We will benefit from reading these original pages where Mr. O'Followell examines the external configuration of the rib cage and establishes that it is doliform (dolium,[11] barrel,[12] and the lower part of the trunk is comparable to an inverted cone which must find its place in the upper part, flared at the top, of the corset. It is on this region that compression is exerted when the person has a defective adaptation, or the tightening of the corset is excessive. Radiographic plates, made intelligible thanks to a layout thought up by the author, make it possible to realize the deformations produced and compare the arrangements made by the sides of the same chest depending on whether it is trapped in a poorly made corset, one that is too tight, or if it is supported by a flawless corset.

10   Here we have O'Followell's main premise, as stated by Dr. Lion: corsets are neutral, some that claim a medical intervention can be beneficial, but women are abusing them. Throughout *Le Corset*, the words "abuse," "excessively tight," and other pejoratives are used to describe women's use of the corset, but they are never defined clearly. How long does a woman have to wear the corset per day to abuse it? Unclear. How much does she have to reduce her waist for it to be "excessively tight"? Unclear. This is the crux of my argument: the accusations of abuse of the corset by women are not founded in medical or scientific accuracy, but rather in misogyny.

11   A dolium is a rounded ceramic pot or barrel that is almost spherical; it has a slight elongation at the bottom, which comes to a point.

12   The closing parenthesis is missing, but I assume it goes here.

CHAPTER 1

9

Par l'étude historique très détaillée qui précède et que j'ai accompagnée de si nombreux documents (1) le lecteur a pu juger combien est ancienne et universelle la mode du corset.

Cependant, cette partie du vêtement féminin a eu de tous temps et dans tous les pays des adversaires nombreux, des détracteurs acharnés.

Au chapitre VII de son livre *Des causes des maladies,* Galien, en traitant des changements de figure des parties, s'exprime ainsi: Les parties constituantes du thorax sont souvent aussi déformées par les nourrices qui les bandent mal dans la première enfance; mais c'est surtout chez les jeunes filles qu'il nous est donné de voir sans cesse se produire cet effet. Dans le but d'augmenter le volume des parties voisines des hanches et des flancs par rapport au thorax, les nourrices leur mettent des bandes, qu'elles serrent fortement sur les omoplates et tout autour de la poitrine, et comme la pression qui en résulte est souvent inégale, le thorax devient proéminent en avant, ou la région opposée, celle du rachis, devient gibbeuse. Il arrive quelquefois que le dos est pour ainsi dire brisé et entraîné de côté, de sorte qu'une épaule est soulevée saillante et en tout plus volumineuse, tandis que l'autre est affaissée et aplatie. Tous ces vices de conformation du thorax sont dus à la négligence et à l'ignorance des nour-

(1) *Le Corset*, tome I, étude historique, 1 vol., chez Maloine, rue de l'Ecole-de-Médecine.

Translation

By the very detailed historical study that precedes and that was accompanied by so many documents (1),[13] the reader has been able to judge how old and universal the fashion of the corset is.

However, this part of women's clothing has always had numerous opponents, fierce detractors.

In chapter VII of his book "The Causes of Diseases," Galen,[14] in dealing with changes to the shape of the parts of the body, states: The constituent parts of the thorax are often also deformed by the nurses who wrap them badly in early childhood; but it is especially in young girls that we see this effect happening again and again. In order to increase the volume of the neighboring parts of the hips and flanks in relation to the chest, the nurses put bands on them, which they tighten strongly on the shoulder blades and all around the chest, and since the resulting pressure is often uneven, the thorax becomes prominently pushed forward, or the opposite region, that of the spine, becomes gibbous. Sometimes the back is broken and dragged sideways, so that one shoulder is raised protruding and overall more voluminous, while the other sags and is flattened. All these defects in the conformation of the chest are due to the negligence and ignorance of the nurses

(1) *Le Corset*, book 1, historic studies, 1 vol., published by Maloine, rue de l'Ecole-de-Médecine. [Previous footnote text is sic to *Le Corset*; ed.]

13   The refers to the first volume of *Le Corset*, which covers the artwork of corseting through history. Published in 1905, it is available in the BnF. I have retained the format in which O'Followell footnoted his own writing. See footnote 63 below for a discussion of the contents of the 1905 volume.

14   Writing in the second century CE. The references in *Le Corset* are often sporadic in terms of details, but Galen's death is known to have occurred in 216 CE, meaning that at the time of writing, O'Followell's justification for this particular medical knowledge was sixteen centuries out of date. It is unclear as to whether there were more contemporary studies specifically on nursemaids' swaddling practices, many sources being unavailable in current collections, but whatever the case, O'Followell did not use them. However, there was at the time an established "bureaux de nourrices" or department of wet nurses, where the citizens of Paris could go to hire one, so therefore O'Followell could certainly have sought out more contemporaneous information.

10

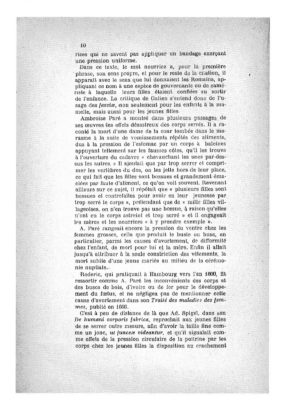

Figure 1.11 Page 10 in Chapter 1 of *Le Corset*.

Translation

who do not know how to apply a bandage that exerts uniform pressure. In this text, the word "nurse" has, for the first use, its proper meaning, and for the rest of the quotation, it appears with the meaning given to it by the Romans who apply this term to a kind of governess or maid to whom their daughters were entrusted at the end of childhood. Galen's criticism is therefore understood to be of the use of constricting fabric for both female babies and young girls.

Ambroise Paré[15] showed in several passages of his works the disastrous effects of tight corsets. He recounted the death of a courtesan who fell into a marasmus as a result of repeated vomiting of food, due to the pressure on the stomach by a whalebone corset pressing so on the false ribs that he found upon the opening of cadaver "they were overlapping one another."[16] He added that by tightening too much and compressing the vertebrae of the back, they are thrown out of place, which makes the girls hunchbacked and greatly emaciated for lack of food, which is often seen. Returning elsewhere to this subject, he repeated that "several girls are hunchbacked and forged this way from having in their youth too tight a corset," claiming that "in a thousand village girls we do not find a hunchback, because they did not have the corset forging them, and too tight" and he urged mothers and nurses "to take an example."[17]

A. Paré still classed the pressure of the belly in pregnant women, produced by the bust or busk, in particular, among the causes of abortion, deformity in the child, and the death of it and the mother.[18] Finally, he went so far as to attribute solely to the constriction of the clothes, the sudden death of a young bride in the middle of her wedding ceremony.[1920]

Roderic,[21] who practiced in Hamburg around the year 1600, pointed out like A. Paré the disadvantages of corsets and busks of wood, ivory, or iron for the development of the fetus, and did not neglect to mention this cause of abortion in his "Traité des maladies des femmes," published in 1603.

It is a short distance from there to where Ad. Spigel[22] in his *De humani corporis fabrica*, reproached young girls for tightening their corsets excessively, in order to have waists as slim as a reed, *ut junceae videantur*, and where he pointed out as effects of the circular pressure of the chest by the corset in young girls the disposition to spitting

15 Writing in the 1590s CE (the ninth edition, from which I am working, was published in 1632), Paré recounts these happenings, one of which is from 1481 CE, anecdotally. There are no drawings, no autopsy reports (or whatever would have constituted an autopsy report in the fifteenth or sixteenth centuries), and no reason to believe that he did not make the stories up entirely or that he is not playing a multi-century game of "telephone." Paré often included woodcut illustrations, including one of the later referenced iron corset, so it seems significant here that there are no illustrations, no clinical descriptions, or anything that would raise this to the level of "fact" from "anecdote with which to scare and control women." See footnote 20 for further discussion of this passage and its use in fashion history. For the subsequent quotes, I have provided the middle French text and a translation of it to clarify O'Followell's interpretation.

In this passage, "marasmus" refers to a wasting disease/failure to thrive.

16 A. Paré, *Des Oeuvres* (1632), 389. "Par trop serrer & comprimer les vertebres du dos, on les iette hors de leur place: qui fait que les filles sont boussuës, & grandement emaciées par faute d'aliment, ce qu'on void souuent. Car l'ay souuenance auoir ouuert les corps mort d'vne Dame de (Histoire.) nostre Cour, qui pour vouloir monstrer auoir le corps beau & gresle, se faisoit serrer, de sorte que ie trouuay les fausse costes cheuauchans les vnes par dessus les autres: qui faisoit que son stomach estant pressé, ne pouuoit s'estendre pour continir la viande, & apres auoir mange & beu, estoit contrainte de la reietter, & les corps n'estant nourry deuint maigre, n'ayant Presque que le cuir sur ses os, qui fut cause de la mort."

Trans.: "By squeezing and compressing the vertebrae, they are thrown out of place: this is what causes the girls to be swollen, and greatly emaciated for lack of food, which is often seen. I remember having opened the corpse of a Lady of our Court, who, in order to show off her beautiful and slender body, had squeezed herself tightly, so that I found the false ribs lying over the others: this is what caused this stomach, being squeezed, to be unable to expand to contain the meat, and after having eaten and drunk, was forced to rest & the girl's bodies [plural is sic], not being fed, became lean, having almost only leather on her bones, which was the cause of death.

17 Paré, *Des Oeuvres*, 674. "Qvelqves-vns & principalement les filles, parce qu'elles sont plus mollasse, deuuinnent bossuës, pource que leur espine n'est pas droicte, mais en arc, ou en figure de S. & tel accidentleur audient parce que quelquefois par cheute ou coups, ou quelque vice de se situer, comme nous auons amplement monstré au liure des Luxations. Ou pareillement parce que les folles meres, subit qu'ellesvoyent leurs filles se pouuoir tant soit peu tenir debout, leur apprennent à faire la reuerence, les faisant basser l'espine du dos, de la quelle estant encore les ligamens laxes, mols & glaireux, en se releuant pour la pesanteur de tout le corps, don't l'espine est le fondement comme la carine d'vne nauire, se contourne de costé & d'autre, & se ploye en figure de la lettre S. qui fait q'elles demeurent tortuës & bossuës, & quelquefois boiteuses. Aussi plusieurs filles sont bossuës & contrefaictes pour leur auoir en leur ieunesse par trop serré le corps. Qu'il soit vray, on void que de mille filles villageoises, on n'en trouue pas vne bossue : à raison qu'ils n'ont eu le corps astraint & trop serré. Parquoy les meres & nourrices y doiuent prendre exemple. Pour reparer & cacher tel vice, on leur fera porter les corcelets de fer delié, lesquels feront troüz afin qu'ils ne poisent pas tant, & seront si bien appropriez & embourrez qu'ils ne blesseront aucunement, & seront lesdits corcelets changez souuentesfois si le malade n'a accomply ses trois dimensions, & à ceux qui croissant, les faudra changer de trois mois en trois mois, plus ou moins, ainsi que l'on verra estre necessaire : car autrement en lieu de faire vn bien, on feroit vn mal. La figure du corcelet est telle."

Trans.: These are principally girls, because they are softer, more hunchbacked, because their spine is not straight, but arched or S-shaped. & one accidentally hears that sometimes by falls or blows, or some abnormal situation, as we have amply demonstrated in the book of Dislocations. Or similarly because mad mothers, suddenly seeing their daughters able to stand a little bit straighter, teach them to make a small bow, causing them to lower their spines, from which there are still the lax, soft, and mucousy ligaments, and by lifting itself up with the weight of the whole body, of which the spine is the foundation like the carene of a ship, bends to one side and the other, and bends in the shape of the letter S. which causes them to remain crooked & hunchbacked, & sometimes lame. Also several girls are hunchbacked & deformed for their asses in their youth by a too tight corps. That it be true, we see that of a thousand village girls, we do not find a hunchbacked one: because they did not have a strained and too much tightened corps. Why should mothers and nurses follow this example. To repair and hide such a defect, they will be made to wear loose iron corselets, which will be pierced so that they do not weigh so much, & will be so well fitted and stuffed that they will not hurt, & the said corselets will be changed often if the patient has not accomplished their three dimensions, & for those who grow, they will have to be changed every three months, more or less, as will be seen to be necessary: otherwise, instead of doing good, we would be doing bad. The image of the corselet is here.

18 Paré, *Des Oeuvres*, 389. "Par trop serrer le ventre aux femmes grosses, on fait que les enfans sont bossus & contrafaiçts, & la mere auortant souuent meurt auec l'enfant."

In this quote, abortion is equivalent to miscarriage, as the terms were used interchangeably and miscarriage is considered medically to be a spontaneous/involuntary abortion.

Trans.: If you tighten the stomach of the pregnant women too much, the children are hunchbacked and deformed, and the mother often dies with the child.

This is accurate—if you constrict the abdomen of a heavily pregnant person, they are at increased chance of miscarriage.

19 Paré, *Des Oeuvres*, 389. "Par trop serrer le'estomach, & les parties dediées à la respiration, on est cause d'vne suffocation & mort subite : ce que de recente memoire on a vue aduenir l'an 1481. en l'Eglise sainct Nicolas (Histoire) des Champs, où vne ieune espouse de Iean de la Forest, maistre Barbier Chirurgien à Paris, fille de defunct Jacques Ocheded Marchand Passementier, & de Claude Boufaut; laquelle pour estre trop serrée & pressée en ses habits nuptiaux, sortant de l'Autel, apres auoir pris du pain & du vin à la façon accousstumée, pensant retourner en sa place, tomba roide morte, faute de respiration, & le iour mesme fut enterrée en ladite Eglise. Et quelques iours apres, ledit de la Forest espousa à sainct Germain en Laye ladite Boufaut mere de ladicte fille defuncte: parce que son Curé auoit refuse faire ledit marriage, disant qu'aucun ne pouuoit espouser la fille & la mere."

Trans.: By tightening the stomach too much, & the parts dedicated to breathing, it is the cause of suffocation and sudden death: what in recent memory we have seen happen in the year 1481. in the church of Saint Nicholas des Champs, where a young wife of Iean de la Forest, Master Barber-Surgeon in Paris, daughter of the deceased Jacques Ocheded Marchand Passementire, & of Claude Boufaut; who, to be too tight and pressed into her nuptial garments, leaving the Altar, after having taken the bread and the wine in the accustomed way, thought to return to her place, fell stiff and dead, for lack of breath, and was that vary day buried in said church. And a few days later, the said de la Forest married in Saint Germain en Laye the said Boufaut, mother of the said deceased daughter: because their priest had refused to make the said marriage, saying that no one could marry the daughter and the mother.

20 While the passage quoted in footnotes 15 and 19 does indeed attribute the demise of the young lady to her nuptial garment, it also mentions that the erstwhile husband subsequently marries the young lady's mother within days, having to find an entirely new officiant as the first refused to marry someone to both child and parent. Without other evidence in regard to the young lady's clothing, it seems far more likely that—given that death occurred immediately after taking communion, which might indicate a poisoned Eucharist—her mother or (momentary) husband found a way to kill her so that they could marry in her stead. This illustrates the problematic nature of taking Paré's accounts as re-presented in other works at face value—Paré definitely attributed the death to constriction of the waist, but the entirety of the quote indicates that he blatantly ignored all evidence to the contrary in order to fit his thesis. This passage by Paré is used by almost all major corset historians, though they are critical of it and do not necessarily take it at face value, particularly Lord (1868/1870), Steele (2001, pp. 5, 13, 15), and Kunzle (1982, pp. 72, 79, 80), among others. And yet it is not generally reproduced in its entirety—for which I cannot blame them, as one generally operates under the assumption that the author one cites is accurate and truthful.

21 Roderic *Traité des maladies des femmes en 1603*. I am unable to find this specific text—there are many that have the title "traité des maladies des femmes," but most are not written by anyone with the name Roderic, and of those that are, there exists only citations. However, the author is most likely Estêvão Rodrigues de Castro (Roderic being a transliteration of Rodrigues), born approximately 1559 and died 1638, noted in the BnF database as a poet, a doctor, and a scientist.

22 Adriaan van de Spiegel (1552–1625). *De humani corporis fabric*, published posthumously in 1627.

11

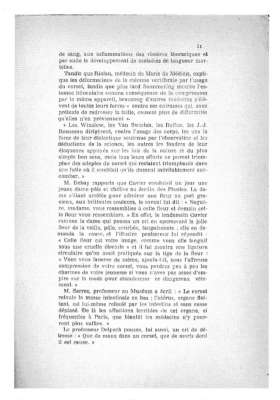

Figure 1.12 Page 11 in Chapter 1 of *Le Corset*.

Translation

blood, inflammation of the thoracic viscera, and as a result, the development of fatal languor-related diseases.

While Riolan,[23] Marie de Medici's physician, explained the deformities of the spine by the use of the corset, and later Soemmering[24] revealed the bilocular stomach to be a consequence of compression by the same apparatus, many other doctors railed with all their strength "against those breastplates which, under the pretext of straightening the waist, cause more deformities than they prevent."

"The Winslows,[25] the Van Swietens,[26] the Buffons,[27] the J-J. Rousseau[28] directed, against the use of corsets, some of the strength of their dialectic supported by the observation and deductions of science, others the wrath of their eloquence based on the laws of nature and the simplest common sense, but all their efforts could not triumph over the followers of the corset who remained triumphant in a struggle where it seemed that their critics inevitably had to succumb."

Mr. Debay[29] reports that Cuvier[30] once led a pale and frail young lady to the Jardin des Plantes. The lady, having stopped to admire a gracefully planted flower, brilliantly colored, the scholar said to her: "Once, madam, you looked like this flower, and tomorrow this flower will look like you." Indeed, the next day Cuvier brought the lady back, and she uttered a cry when she saw the pretty flower of the previous day, now pale, drooping, languid; she asked for the cause, and the illustrious teacher replied: "This flower is your image; like you, it languishes under a cruel embrace," and he showed her a circular ligation that had been placed on its stem: "You will also fade," he added. "Under the awful compression of your corset, you will gradually lose the charms of your youth if you do not have enough empire[31] on fashion to abandon this dangerous garment."

Mr. Serres,[32] a professor at the Museum,[33] wrote: "The corset pushes back at the intestinal mass, downward; the uterus, a floating organ, is itself repressed by the intestines and constantly displaced. Hence the terrible ailments of this organ, so frequent in Paris, that soon doctors will no longer be sufficient."

Professor Delpech[34] also uttered a cry of distress: "What evils in a corset, what deaths of which it is the cause."

23 Jean Riolan (Ioannis Riolani; 1577–1657). I am unable to find the source referred to by O'Followell: it is not listed in the bibliography to *Le Corset*, and even articles and other sources that mention both Riolan the younger and corsets do not mention them in connection with each other.

24 Samuel Thomas von Soemmering (1755–1830). *Uber Schœdichkeit der Schnürbrüdte* (Leipzig: 1788). Despite many of his works surviving, this source is no longer extant.

25 Jacques Bénigne Winslow (1669–1760). *Sur les mauvais effets de l'usage du corps à baleine.* Mémoires de l'Académie des Sciences (1741). This source ostensibly exists in digitized form on Gallica (http://visualiseur. bnf.fr/CadresFenetre?O=NUMM-3539&I=272&M=tdm), but the section in question does not mention corsets/corps/stays—it is instead talking about the preparation of cochineal dye.

26 Without a first name, it is impossible to tell which Van Swieten O'Followell is referring to (and this source is not listed in the bibliography), but it is most likely Gerard van Swieten (1700–72), a Dutch physician who attended Empress Maria Theresa of the Holy Roman Empire. His only extant digitized work is his anti-vampire treatise "Vampyrismus" (1768).

27 This is most likely Georges-Louis Leclerc, Comte de Buffon (1701–88). This source is not listed in the bibliography, though his extant work consists of his many-volumed natural history, which is available in its entirety on Project Gutenberg.

28 Jean-Jacques Rousseau (1712–78). *Oeuvres de J.J. Rousseau de Genève*, Volume 8, "Émile ou de l'éducation," p. 23 (1762). "On fait que l'aisance des vêtemens qui ne gênoient point le corps, contribuoit beaucoup à lui laisser dans les deux sexes ces belles proportions qu'on voit dans leurs statues, & qui servent encore de modele à l'art, quand la nature défiguré a cette de lui en fournir parmi nous. De touts ces entraves gothiques, de ces multitudes de ligatures qui tiennent de toutes parts nos membres en presse, ils n'en avoient pas une seule. Leurs femmes ignoroient l'usage de ces corps de baleine par lesquels les nôtres contrefont leur taille plutôt qu'elles ne la marquent. Je ne puis concevoir que ce tabus poussé en Angleterre à un point inconceivable, n'y fasse pas à la fin dégénérer l'espece, & je soutiens même que l'objet d'agrément qu'on se propose en cela est de mauvais gout. Il n'est point agréable de voir une femme coupée en deux commen une guêpe; cela choque le vue & fait soffrir l'imagination. La finesse de la taille a, comme toute le reste, ses proportions, sa mesure, passé laquelle elle est certainment un défaut: ce défaut seroit même frappant à l'oeil sur le nû; pourquoi seroit-il une beauté sous le vêtement?"

Trans.: "That means that the ease of the clothes which do not obstruct the body, contributed much to there remaining in the two sexes those beautiful proportions which one sees in statues of them, and which still serve as a model for art, when nature disfigures it, it has the power to provide it among us. Of all these Gothic shackles, of these multitudes of ligatures which keep our members pressed in on all sides, there was not a single one. Their women were unaware of the use of these whalebone corps by which ours counterfeit their size rather than mark it. I cannot conceive that this taboo, pushed to an inconceivable point in England, does not cause the species to degenerate there in the end, and I even maintain that the object of approval that is proposed in this is in bad taste. It is not pleasant to see a woman cut in two like a wasp; it shocks the sight &

tempts the imagination. The fineness of the cut has, like everything else, its proportions, its measure, beyond which it is certainly a defect: this defect would even be striking to the eye on the nude; why would she be a beauty under the garment?"

29 Auguste-Hyacinthe Debay (1804–65). *Hygiène Vestimentaire, Les Modes et Les Parures Chez Les Français Depuis L'Établissement de la Monarchie Jusqu'à Nos Jours Précédé d'un Curieux Parallèle Des Mods Chez Les Anciennes Dames Greques et Romaines* (1857). The quote is accurate (pp. 173–4), but may be apocryphal. Cuvier himself did not publish the quote, but (see footnote 30) the two men did overlap in time and location, and Cuvier may indeed have said this or something like it.

30 Jean Léopold Nicolas Frédéric, Baron Cuvier, known as Georges Cuvier (1769–1832). Cuvier was a naturalist—someone who collected studied plants and animals in order to understand the world around him. He is considered the father of French comparative anatomy, particularly for his work with fish: his *Histoire naturelle des poissons* (*c.* 1828) was the definitive assessment of types of fish for the time. Unfortunately for various indigenous peoples around the world, Cuvier's fascination with the comparative did not stop at the non-human animal, and his work to begin the Musée de l'Homme involved "collecting" examples of people of color, either himself or by directing other naturalists such as Serres (see footnote 32) to do so, and he even published a "helpful" guide to skeletonizing them on the way back to France, so as to have them ready to be displayed in his museum as soon as possible (Cuvier, N.D.). Cuvier was also responsible for the body cast, dissection, skeletonization, and display of Saartje Baartman, the Khoikhoi woman known as the Hottentot Venus.

31 This makes no sense but also does not seem to be an idiom.

32 Antoine Étienne Renaud Augustin Serres (1786–1868). This source is not listed in the bibliography, and targeted searches for the quoted text do not reveal which of Serres' many publications contain the quote. Serres was particularly influential in "collecting" "specimens" for the Musée de l'Homme under Cuvier's instruction. See Gibson *The Corseted Skeleton: A Bioarchaeology of Binding* (2020), for a full discussion of the lack of ethics in Cuvier's collection practices.

33 The Musée de l'Homme, now a division of the Muséum national d'Histoire naturelle.

34 With no first name, there is no way to determine which Delpech this refers to, but it is most likely Jacques Mathieu Delpech (1777–1832). This source is not listed in the bibliography, and none of the available lists of his works indicates which, if any, this quote would originate from. However, he was a noted surgeon and wrote extensively on both plastic-surgery techniques and the complications of treating aneurysm. There was also a François-Séraphin Delpech (1778–1825) who was an art critic and gallery/studio owner, who supervised certain corset-related caricatures, but I rather think it was the former.

12

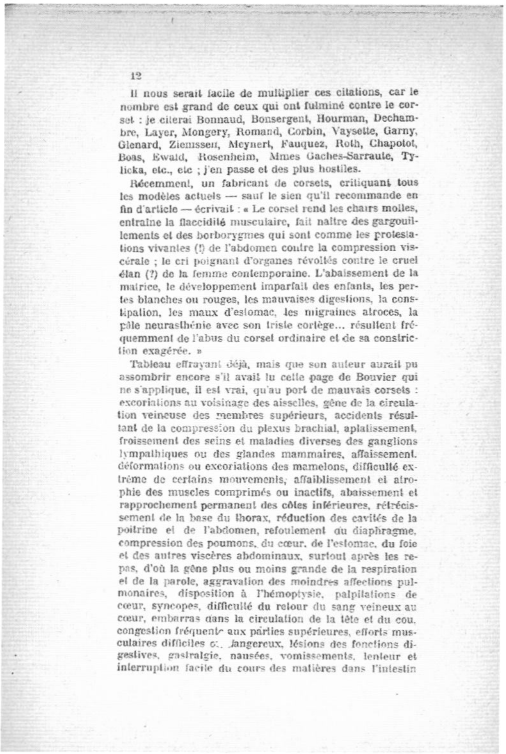

Figure 1.13 Page 12 in Chapter 1 of *Le Corset*.

Translation

It would be easy for us to multiply these quotes, because the number of those who have fulminated against the corset is large: I will quote Bonnaud,[35] Bonsergent,[36] Hourman,[37] Dechambre, Layer,[38] Mongery,[39] Romand,[40] Corbin,[41] Vaysette,[42] Garny,[43] Glenard,[44] Ziemssen,[45] Meynert,[46] Fauquez,[47] Roth,[48] Chapotot,[49] Boas,[50] Ewald,[51] Rosenheim,[52] Mrs. Gaches-Sarraute,[53] Mrs. Tylicka,[54] etc., etc.: I do not include the most hostile.

Recently, a corset manufacturer criticizing all current models—except his own, which he recommends at the end of the article—wrote: "The corset makes flesh soft, causes muscle flaccidity, gives rise to gurgling and borborygmus that are like living protests (!) of the abdomen contra visceral compression; the poignant cry of organs revolted against the cruel impulse (?) [both punctuation marks in parentheses are sic.] of contemporary women. The lowering of the womb, the imperfect development of children, white or red discharge, poor digestions, constipation, stomach upset, excruciating migraines, pale neurasthenia with its sad procession . . . frequently result from the abuse of the ordinary corset and its exaggerated constriction."[55]

A frightening picture already, but the author could have darkened it even further if he had read the page of Bouvier[56] which applies, it must be admitted, only to those who wear bad corsets: cuts into the flesh near the armpits, poor blood circulation in the upper limbs, accidents resulting from the compression of the brachial plexus, flattening, crumpling of the breasts and diverse maladies of the lymph nodes or the mammary glands, sagging, deformities or cuts on the nipples, extreme difficulty of certain movements, weakening and atrophy of compromised or inactive muscles, lowering and permanent overlapping of the lower ribs, restriction of the lower part of the thorax, reduction of the cavities of the chest and the abdomen, repression of the diaphragm, compression of the lungs, the heart, the stomach, the liver, and the other abdominal viscera, above all after a meal, more or less difficulty with breathing and speech, and aggravation of the slightest ailment of the lungs, disposition to coughing up blood, palpitations of the heart, syncope, circulatory difficulty returning the blood to the veins of the heart, embarrassment in the circulation of the head and the neck, frequent congestion in the upper genitals, difficulty using the muscles which have become languorous, digestive lesions (ulcers), indigestion, nausea, vomiting, slowness and easy interruption of the matter in the shrunken intestine,

35 This could be one of two people: Jacques Phillippe Bonnaud, sometimes listed as Bonneau (1757–97), who was a general in the French army. He does not appear to have written anything regarding the corset, or indeed anything at all. There is another potential, however: Jacques Jules Bonnaud, a Jesuit priest stationed in Haiti, and killed during the September Revolution of 1792, a martyr to the cause, and subsequently beatified by the Roman Catholic Church. His listed works also do not include anything about corsets, and the frontispiece of the book on corsets does not list a middle name—neither Phillippe nor Jules—simply Jacques Bonnaud. The full bibliography entry is *Dégradation de l'espèce humaine par l'usage des corps à baleine* (Paris: 1770). This piece is extant, and available in its entirety for free download on Google Books.

36 J.-E. Bonsergent, *Réflexions sur les inconvénients de corsets*, 1816. This source is not extant, nor could I find any biographical information about Bonsergent.

37 Hourman et Dechambre, "Maladies des organes, de la respiration chez les vieillards," *Ach. gen. de médecine* (1835). Without first names, there is no way to determine the authors of this piece, which is no longer extant—all searches for more information have ended up becoming recursive, referring me back only to the bibliography for *Le Corset*.

38 While listed in the bibliography as "Layer," this source is actually M. A. Layet, *Dangers de l'usage des corsets et des buscs* (1827). It is fully digitized and available for download on Google Books. No biographical information is available for Layet.

39 Louis Mongery/Louis Mongéri/Luigi Mongeri (1815–82) is considered the father of modern psychiatric medicine in the Ottoman Empire of Turkey. *Le corset et ses dangers* (Paris: 1893). The bibliography entry is Mongeri. The work on the corset appears to have been published posthumously, and is no longer extant.

40 This source is not listed in the bibliography, and the author (Romand) is never mentioned again in the full text of *Le Corset*.

41 Corbin, "Des effets Produits par les corsets sur les organes de l'abdomen," *Gazette médicale de Paris* (1830). Due to no first name for the author, and the fact that this publication is no longer extant, there is no further information about this source.

42 Paul Vaissette/Vaysette, birth listed as before 1820, no death date. *L'Usage Prémature et Abusif du Corset.* Paris, 1875. This source can be found, digitized, in the BnF: https://gallica.bnf.fr/ark:/12148/bpt6k840141n.image

43 A. Garny, no birth/death dates. *Du corset* (Paris: 1854). This source is not extant, and no biographical information is available about Garny.

44 Frantz Glénard (1848–1920). Many of these sources are available online. *Les Ptoses viscérales, diagnostic et nosograpgie* (1899).

Glénard. – Dyspepsie nerveuse, Détermination d'une espèce. De l'entéroptose, 1885.

Glénard. – Du rein mobile. Société de médecine de Lyon. Mars 1885.

Glénard – Neurasthénie gastrique, 1887.

Glénard. – Traitement de l'enréroprose, 1887.

Glénard. – Le vêtement féminin et l'hygiène. Condérence à l' Asspc. franç. Pour l'avancement des sciences. Paris 1902.

Glénard. – Mouvements diaphragmatiques des viscères abdominaux in Revue des maladies de la nutrition, 1905.

45 Hugo Wilhelm von Ziemssen (1829–1902), listed in the bibliography as Ziemmsen. *Über die physikalische Behandling chronischer Magen* (1888). A full analysis of this source can be found here: https://edoc.ub.uni-muenchen.de/6184/1/Pierson_Angelika.pdf

46 This source is not listed in the bibliography, and the author Meynert is never mentioned again in the full text of *Le Corset*.

47 This source is not included in the bibliography, and the author Fauquez is never mentioned again in the full text of *Le Corset*.

48 Roth, no birth/death dates. De la guérison et de la prophylaxie des maladies par le mouvement, 1870. I am unable to confirm any other information about this source due to lack of information, and the source itself not being extant.

49 Eugène Chapotot (1863–1947). *Estomac et corset* (Thesis, Lyon, 1891). This source is fully digitized on French Wikipedia: https://fr.wikisource.org/wiki/L%E2%80%99Estomac_et_le_Corset

50 Ismar Isidor Boas (1858–1938), said to be the father of modern gastroentrology. *Allgemeine diagnostik und thérapie der Magenkrankeiten* (Berlin, 1890). This source is available for purchase, but not digitized.

51 Ewald. "Entéroptose et rein mobile," in *Berl. Klin Wich* (March 24, 1890). No first name or other data on the author, and this source is not extant.

52 Theodor Rosenheim (1860–1939). *Über die Verdauungskrankheiten* (Vienna: 1891). This source is not extant, and is not listed in his biographical informaiton.

53 Inès Gaches-Sarraute, born Adélaïde Clotilde Joséphine Victoire Gaches (1853–1928). *Le Corset: Etude physiologique et pratique* (Paris: Masson 1900). Dr. Gaches-Sarraute was an extraordinary woman, writing extensively on the topic of the corset, publishing several books, and creating her own health corset. This source is digitized in its entirety on French Wikipedia: https://fr.wikisource.org/wiki/Le_Corset_:_%C3%A9tude_physiologique_et_pratique

54 Justyna Budzińska-Tylicka (1867–1936), *Les méfaits du corset* (Thesis, Paris, 1899). Dr. Budzińska-Tylicka was a powerhouse, actively arguing for women's autonomy across Europe, opening hospitals, and maintaining a private practice. None of her works are currently extant.

55 It would be quite helpful to know the identity of this corset-maker; alas, however, O'Followell does not include that, despite quoting them. Despite the fact that such quotation without attribution was common practice at the time, it completely decontextualizes the quote, leaving the reader (whether contemporaneous to 1908 or today) without a reason to take the quoted corset maker seriously—what were their credentials apart from making the corset? Whence did they learn to identify such maladies and their origins? We do not know; O'Followell does not tell us.

56 Sauveur-Henri-Victor Bouvier (1799–1877). "Etude historique et médicale sur l'usage des corset," in *Bulletin de l'Académie de médecine* (vol. XVIII, 1852–3). Held only in Paris; not available digitally. No further biographical information available.

13

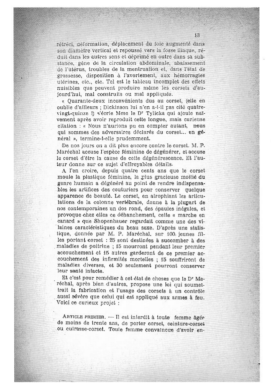

Figure 1.14 Page 13 in Chapter 1 of *Le Corset*.

Translation

deformation, displacement of the liver and swelling in the vertical dimension abutting the iliac fossa, reduction of the other senses and depression moreover in substance, discomfort in abdominal circulation, prolapse of the uterus, menstrual problems and, in the state of pregnancy, disposition towards abortion (miscarriage), with uterine hemorrhage, etc., etc. Such is the incomplete picture of the harmful effects that one can produce with the same corsets of today, badly constructed and badly applied.

"Forty-two disadvantages due to the corset," (she forgets besides that; didn't Dickenson mention ninety-five of them!) exclaims Mrs. Dr. Tylicka who naively adds after reproducing this long but curious quote: "We could not have counted so many, we who are declared opponents of the corset . . . in general," she concludes cautiously.

Nowadays, even more has been said against the corset. Mr. P. Maréchal[57] accuses the female species of degenerating, and accuses the corset of being the cause of this degeneration. And the author gives appalling details on this subject.

According to him, for the four hundred years that corset has molded the wax of the woman, the most graceful half of the human race has degenerated to the point of making the artifices of the couturiers indispensable to preserve some appearance of beauty.[58] The corset, by atrophying the joints of the vertebral column, gives most of our contemporaries a rounded back, uneven shoulders, and causes them to sway, in a "duck walk" that Schopenhauer regarded as one of the ugly characteristics of the fair sex. Based on a statistic given by Mr. P.

Maréchal, out of 100 girls wearing corsets: twenty-five are destined to succumb to chest diseases; fifteen will die during their first experience of childbirth and fifteen others will suffer fatal infirmities as a result of that labor; fifteen will suffer from various diseases, and only thirty will be able to maintain their health intact.

And it is to remedy this state of affairs that Dr. Maréchal, following many others, proposes a law[59] that would subject the manufacture and use of corsets to a control as severe as that applied to firearms. Here is this curious project:

Article 1.—It is forbidden for any woman under thirty years of age to wear a corset, a corset belt, or a corset breastplate. Any woman found to have endorsed

57   This source is not in the bibliography, but refers to Dr. Philippe Maréchal, who proposed a law restricting women from corseting, which will be discussed in footnotes 59 and 60 below. There appears to be no biographical information available for Maréchal, a search for which was complicated by the fact that "Maréchal" means "marshal," a rank in the French army, and often used as a nickname for men of that rank.

58   Here we have a classic catch-22: the corset has caused degeneration in women's natural forms, which requires women to resort to the corset to preserve their beauty. By this point in time, Lamarckian theories of proximal-cause physical changes being passed down from parent to child had been largely challenged by Darwinian evolution, but the flawed logic of the same had not passed out of common discourse.

59   This proposed (but unenacted) law regarding only bodies that have been gendered female sets a precedent for the tone of the book—women need to be (legally, medically) protected from the damage that they do to themselves by the abuse of the corset. For further discussion of laws effecting the gendered female body, both from the era of corsets and from the twenty-first century, see Chapters 4 and 5 of this book.

14

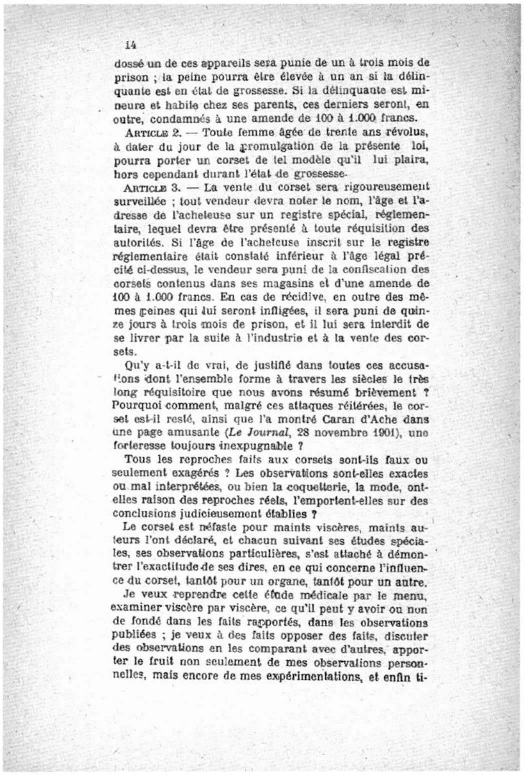

Figure 1.15 Page 14 in Chapter 1 of *Le Corset*.

Translation

one of these devices shall be punished by one to three months' imprisonment; the sentence may be increased to one year if the offender is pregnant. If the offender is a minor and lives with her parents, the latter will also be fined between 100 and 1,000 francs.

Article 2.—Any woman who has attained the age of thirty years, from the day of the promulgation of this law, may wear a corset of such model as she pleases, except, however, during pregnancy.[60]

Article 3.—The sale of the corset will be strictly monitored; any seller must note the name, age, and address of the buyer on a special, regulatory register, which must be presented at the request of the authorities. If the age of the buyer written in the regulatory register is found to be lower than the legal age mentioned above, the seller will be punished by the confiscation of the corsets contained in his stores and a fine of 100 to 1,000 francs. In the event of recidivism, in addition to the same penalties that will be imposed on him, he will be punished from fifteen days to three months in prison, and he will be prohibited from engaging thereafter in the industry and the sale of corsets.[61]

What is true, justified in all these accusations, the whole of which forms over the centuries the very long indictment that we have summarized briefly? Why, despite these repeated attacks, did the corset remain, as Caran d'Ache[62] showed in a comic sheet (*Le Journal*, November 28, 1901), an impregnable fortress?

Are all the reproaches made to corsets false or only exaggerated? Are the observations accurate or misinterpreted, or are coquetry, fashion, the right reason for real reproaches? Do they prevail over judiciously established conclusions?

The corset is harmful to many viscera, as many authors have stated, and each according to his special studies, his particular observations, has endeavored to demonstrate the accuracy of his words, with regard to the influence of the corset, sometimes for one organ, sometimes for another.

I want to take up this medical study with no particular agenda, examine viscera by viscera, what there may or may not be founded in the facts reported, in the published observations; I want to put facts in opposition to facts, to discuss observations by comparing them with others, to bring the fruit not only of my personal observations, but also of my experiments, and finally

60   Pregnant women are an additionally "protected" class, being seen as a "vessel" for the child rather than as fully realized sovereign citizens with the right to control their own bodies. This attitude extends much further back than O'Followell, as demonstrated by an examination of law-making around childbirth and gestation (Wilson 1993). Under legal debate, and therefore under its purview, were such things as time of conception, length of gestation, claims to paternity, and to whom the resulting child "belonged," and could therefore inherit from. In all of this discussion, while women were considered to be the authority on their own bodies on the whole—being mostly believed about conception, quickening, and gestation duration—they were also seen as not "whole" citizens (citizenship being highly defined and delimited, even in Republican France).

These ideas around women as womb first and foremost above all other functions have followed us to the present day, with restrictions on Human Subjects Research (HSR) conducted on pregnant people. Institutional Review Boards, which oversee HSR for university-based research projects among others, will nix everything from procedures and medications that can potentially harm a fetus, up to interview or survey questions that might upset a gestating person. This can be beneficial—for example, when new drugs go to the human trial phase, there is a benefit to ensuring that any abortifacient qualities discovered in previous phases are not expressed in the research population. However, dehumanization is inherent in the idea of protected classes. When an adult human being is not allowed to participate in a procedure, behavior, or event based on their status as someone who is or could gestate a fetus, even after they have been made aware of the potential for pregnancy-related complications and would like to consent to it, they are not being seen or treated as equal to other adult human beings.

Occasionally the lack of fully human status is inherent in the circumstances—ther protected classes involve children, which cannot legally consent for themselves before eighteen years old (though their parents can consent for them . . .); the institutionalized mentally ill, and the incarcerated, both of whom are seen as default-coerced by their circumstances—you cannot consent if you cannot voluntarily leave the room. But pregnant people, who (for the moment) can execute consent over their own bodies, are often "protected" away from participation. For extensive further discussion of medical misogyny against pregnant women, and laws pertaining to the same, see Chapter 4 of this book.

61   The 1902 newspaper coverage of Marèchal's law ends with the following: "These figures, according to Dr. Marechal (sic), can be fully proved. Dr. Marechal's law is causing considerable amusement," (*Evening News*, February 26, 1902). Additional coverage from 1901 in the *International Herald Tribune* quotes Marèchal as stating "The fair sex has degenerated in a most woeful fashion within the four hundred years since Catherine de Médicis introduced the corset. Constricting shoes have produced misshapen feet, tight gloves deformed the finger joints, and bulky hats reduced the feminine brain" (*NYT*, 2001).

62   Caran d'Ache, the pen name of Emmanuel Poiré (1858–1909).

15

rer des conclusions impartiales que j'appuierai alors mais alors seulement, de l'opinion des auteurs qui tolèrent ou qui recommandent le corset.

Les recherches nécessitées par la rédaction de la partie historique de mon ouvrage *Le Corset*, ont constitué une lourde tâche, je ne me dissimule pas que cette partie médicale et physiologique sera plus difficile encore, mais l'attrait du sujet fera paraître le labeur léger.

S'il est indispensable, pour mener à bien ce travail, de procéder avec une grande méthode et de diviser son étude avec soin, il est non moins indispensable pour juger avec exactitude la valeur des faits, des observations, des raisonnements, de connaître anatomiquement les régions du corps étudiées, et de les connaître non pas superficiellement, non pas minutieusement, mais de les connaître d'une façon à la fois très simple et très précise.

« Le corset est la seule pièce du vêtement féminin qui ait une influence sur la position des viscères, sur leur fonctionnement, et par suite sur la santé.

Ceux qui le confectionnent devraient avoir des notions exactes d'anatomie et de physiologie qui leur font toujours défaut; les corsetières, recrutées généralement parmi des ouvrières sans instruction spéciale, ne suivent et ne connaissent d'autres lois que celles de la mode . . . et si l'on découvre dans un corset bien étudié d'un type nouveau, des qualités qui lui assurent un succès avantageux, on s'ingéniera à le copier plus ou moins adroitement, mais sans chercher à se rendre compte des mobiles qui ont guidé l'inventeur, de telle sorte que les indications données sont maladroitement suivies et que les résultats obtenus ainsi par à peu près sont plutôt nuisibles qu'utiles.

Qu'on ne s'y trompe pas; pour qu'un corset devienne un vêtement inoffensif, il faut qu'il soit extrêmement bien adapté, qu'il ne gêne aucun de nos organes, aucun de nos mouvements; c'est en cela que réside la grande difficulté de son application, et c'est ce qui nécessite les connaissances spéciales dont j'ai parlé plus haut. »

Il est impossible, actuellement, d'exiger des corsetières des diplômes ou des licences officielles; cependant lorsqu'on sait le mal qu'elles ont fait et qu'elles peuvent faire aux femmes, on en arrive à souhaiter que, à la technique de leur art, à leur adresse professionnelle, elles s'efforcent d'ajouter ces connaissances élémentaires de splanchnologie (splanchnologie ou description des viscères), dont

Translation

to draw impartial conclusions that I will support then, but only then, from the opinion of the authors who tolerate or recommend the corset.

The research required by the writing of the historical part of my book *Le Corset*[63] was an arduous task, and I do not hide that this medical and physiological part will be even more difficult, but the attraction of the subject will lessen the load.

If it is indispensable, in order to carry out this work, to proceed with a robust method and to divide its study carefully, it is no less indispensable to accurately judge the value of facts, observations, and reasoning, to know anatomically the regions of the body studied, and to know them not superficially, not meticulously, but to know them in a way that is at once very simple but very precise.[64]

"The corset is the only piece of women's clothing that has an influence on the position of the viscera, on their functioning, and consequently on their health.

Those who make it should have a proper understanding of anatomy and physiology that they still lack; the corset-makers, usually recruited from among non-specialist workers, do not follow and know other laws than those of fashion . . . and if one discovers, in a new type of popular corset, qualities which ensure its success, manufacturers will engineer to copy it more or less skillfully, but without seeking to realize the motives which guided the inventor, so that the indications given are followed clumsily and the results thus obtained are overall more harmful than useful.

Make no mistake; for a corset to become a harmless garment, it must be extremely well adapted [to the body; ed.], that it does not interfere with any of our organs, none of our movements; this is where the great difficulty of its application lies, and this is what requires the special knowledge I mentioned above."[65]

It is currently impossible to require corset-makers to have official diplomas or licenses;[66] however, when we know the harm they have done and that they can do to women, we come to hope that, after developing professional techniques and skills, they will try to add this elementary knowledge of splanchnology (splanchnology or description of the viscera of which

63 Rather than 1908 being a republication of 1905, they are in fact two separate books; 1905 covers art history and culture, whereas 1908 addresses the aforementioned subtitle "medicine, history, and hygiene." Due to the fact that the 1908 book is the one that has been publicized and reproduced by corset historians, and the fact that they bear the same name but slightly different subtitles, there has been an erroneous tendency to conflate the two, a tendency to which I, unfortunately, have contributed.

Yet the above sentence "The research required by the writing of the historical part of my book *Le Corset* was a heavy task" is disingenuous. A perusal of the table of contents shows that the first four chapter foci were lifted directly—if not word for word, then concept for concept—from the table of contents of a book by William Berry Lord (1825–84) the 1868 book *Freaks of Fashion: The Corset and the Crinoline*.

I have reproduced them here, and highlighted the similarities:

Lord: Chapter I: The Corset:—Origin. Use amongst Savage Tribes and Ancient People. **Slenderness of Waist** esteemed in the East, Ceylon, Circassia, Crim Tartary, Hindustan, Persia, China, **Egypt, Palestine**.

O'Followell: Chapitre Premier: L'Histoire du corset a été divisée en cinq époques. Il y a lieu distinguer une sixième période: l'époque médicale. **Vestiges du corset chez les Egyptiens, les Hébreux.** (Translation: Chapter One: The History of the corset which has been divided into five epochs. A sixth period must be distinguished: the medical period. Vestiges of the corset among the Egyptians, the Hebrews.)

Lord: Chapter II: The Corset according to Homer, Terentius. **The Strophium of Rome, and the Mitra of Greece. The Peplus.** A Roman Toilet, Bath, and Promenade. General Luxury. Cleopatra's Jewels. Tight-lacing on the Tiber.

O'Followell: Chapitre II: Première époque de l'histoire du corset, époque de l'antiquité. **Le Corset des Grecques et des Romaines.** Le corset annamite. **Capitium**, fascia, zona, **strophium**, etc. (Translation: Chapter II: First epoch in the history of the corset, epoch of antiquity. The Corset of the Greeks and Romans. The Annamite corset. Capitium, fascia, shingles, strophium, etc.)

Lord: Chapter III: **Frankish Fashions. The Monks and the Corset**. Corsets worn by Gentlemen as well as Ladies in the Thirteenth Century. The Kirtle. Small Waists in Scotland. **Chaucer on Small Bodies. The Surcoat**. Long Trains. Skirts. Snake-toed Shoes. High-heeled Slippers.

O'Followell: Chapitre III: Deuxième époque de l'histoire du corset. **Le costume des femmes sous les dynasties des Mérovingiens et des Carlovingiens. Les Capétiens, apparition des robes justes au corps. La cotte-hardie.** Le corset. (Translation: Chapter III: Second epoch in the history of the corset. The costume of women under the Merovingian and Carolingian dynasties. The Capetians, appearance of dresses on small bodies. The surcoat. The corset.)

After this point, Lord gets more specific, dividing up the eighteenth century into various periods, whereas O'Followell covers its entirety in one chapter, but the themes remain similar until O'Followell veers off into medicine in Chapter 10.

Lord was contemporary to Auguste Racinet, to whom I will return in Chapter 5 of this book. Racinet published six volumes giving a thorough overview of fashion across the world, across history, in exquisite colored drawings and paintings; Lord's line drawings, as well as his classifications and the divisions of them, are taken from his work.

At this point in French history, authors had the exclusive right to print and distribute their own work as long as that work was certified by the government—what we now consider copyright—and thus no one other than Racinet in this particular plagiarist triumvirate comes out clean, yet O'Followell was clearly the most wrong. We all build our research on the work of those who come before us, but we also acknowledge that we must not steal from them outright. O'Followell quotes and paraphrases plenty in *Le Corset*, and yet was also extremely willing to cut corners if he could.

64   Yet he does not do this. While the anatomical descriptions are mostly accurate and reflect the knowledge of the human body available in 1908 (I will address any inaccuracies in subsequent chapters, as they come up) the diagnostics are often not, as they are made up of suppositions, flawed differential diagnostic procedures, reductio ad absurdum arguments, appeal to authority arguments, etc. O'Followell takes that "very simple and very precise" knowledge of anatomy, and extrapolates it to more complicated medical arguments—if done without agenda, this indeed is how one makes a medical diagnosis. However, O'Followell does have an agenda, which becomes clear as we move further into the book.

65   There is no indication to whom this quote should be attributed.

66   While corset-makers did not hold diplomas or licenses, neither did many doctors during the early 1900s (despite a law requiring it being on the books since 1803 (Crosland 2004; Pinell 2011)), making O'Followell's desire highly hypocritical; why not concentrate on making sure that people who merely set out a shingle proclaiming themselves "doctor," were being taken to task for it, instead of coming for the corsetiers, who were, after all, mostly only making clothing not medical devices (Boulle 1982; Huard and Imbault-Huart 1975; Léonard 1966; Porter 1993; Ramsey 1977; Weisz 1978 and 2003)?

67   One must give O'Followell this: the book is readable, and understandable, by people with no medical knowledge. However, this is problematic given that so much of what he writes is riddled with inaccuracies. These errors are not just incorrect in the light of modern medical knowledge, but had actually been disproven in O'Followell's era, and will be discussed as they occur.

68   Not further defined—maybe centuries? This would be the 1700s and 1800s, as the book was published in 1908.

16

nous devrions tous être instruits en vue de notre propre conservation.

C'est pourquoi je ferai précéder l'étude des rapports du corset avec un organe d'une étude anatomo-physiologique de cet organe, et cette étude, illustrée de figures nombreuses et simples, permettra aux gens de l'art de me suivre facilement, aux corsetières de me comprendre entièrement. J'estime, en effet, que ce livre n'est pas écrit seulement pour des médecins s'installer corsetières, que je ne songe à obliger toutes les corsetières à se faire recevoir médecins.

Dans les pages que vont suivre, et dans lesquelles je vais étudier successivement l'influence du corset sur les systèmes respiratoire, circulatoire, digestif et génito-urinaire, il sera toujours sous-entendu, sauf mention spéciale (date ou désignation), que les faits ou les observations consignés ont trait à des cas où les femmes portaient un des corsets des époques moderne ou médicale, c'est-à-dire des deux dernières époques de l'histoire du corset.

[Fin.]

Translation

we should all be educated for our own preservation.

That is why I will precede the study of the relations of the corset with an organ with an anatomo-physiological study of this organ, and this study, illustrated with numerous and simple figures, will allow the people of art to follow me easily, the corset-makers to understand me fully. I believe, in fact, that this book is not written only for medical people to [use when they; ed.] set up to become corset-makers, but also that I do not contemplate forcing all corset-makers to become doctors.[67]

In the pages that will follow, and in which I will study successively the influence of the corset on the respiratory, circulatory, digestive, and genitourinary systems, it will always be implied, unless mentioned in particular (by date or designation) that the facts or observations recorded relate to cases where women wore one of the corsets of the modern or medical eras, that is, the last two epochs[68] of the history of the corset.

[End.]

REFERENCES

Balch, E. (1904). "Savage and Civilized Dress," in the *Journal of the Franklin Instituteo of the State of Pennsylvania, for the Promotion of the Mechanic Arts*, 157 (5).

Berlanstein, L. (1984). *The Working People of Paris, 1871–1914*, Baltimore, MD: The Johns Hopkins Press.

Boulle, L. (1982). "La Médicalisation Des Hopitaux Parisiens Dans La Première Moitié Du XIXème Siècle," in *Historical Reflections*, 9 (1/2): 33–44.

Bruna, D. (2015). *Fashioning the Body*, New York, NY: Bard Graduate Center, Yale.

Crosland, M. (2004). "The *Officiers de Santé* of the French Revolution: A Case Study in the Changing Language of Medicine," in *Medical History*, 48: 229–44.

Cunningham, P. (2003). *Reforming Women's Fashion, 1850–1920: Politics, Health, and Art,* Kent, Ohio: Kent State University Press.

Cuvier, G. (n.d.) *Note Instructive sur les Recherches à Faire Relativement aux Différences Anatomiques des Diverses Races d'Hommes,* ed. Maurice Girard and François Péron.

Debay, A-H. (1857). *Hygiène Vestimentaire, Les Modes et Les Parures Chez Les Français Depuis L'Établissement de la Monarchie Jusqu'à Nos Jours Précédé d'un Curieux Parallèle Des Mods Chez Les Anciennes Dames Grecques et Romaines.*

Edwards, L. (2017/2018). *How to Read a Dress: A Guide to Changing Fashion from the 16th to the 20th Century*, London: Bloomsbury Academic.

Evening News. (1902). Corsets in France.

Flood, C., and S. Grant (2014). *Style and Satire: Fashion in Print 1777–1927*, London: V&A Publishing.

Gaches-Sarraute, I. (1900). *Le Corset: Étude Physiologique et Pratique,* (no publisher given).

Galen. (2nd century). *Des causes des maladies.*

Gibson, R. (2020). *The Corseted Skeleton: A Bioarchaeology of Binding*, Cham, Switzerland: Palgrave Macmillan.

Gullickson, Gay. 1996. *Unruly Women of Paris*, Ithaca, NY: Cornell University Press.

Huard, P., and M. J. Imbault-Huart (1975). "La Clinique Parisienne Avant Et Apres 1802," in *Clio Medica,* 10 (3): 173–82.

Hunt, L. (2004). *Politics, Culture, and Class in the French Revolution*, Berkeley, CA: University of California Press.

Kunzle, D. (1982). *Fashion and Fetishism,* London: George Prior Associated Publishers Ltd.

Lancet. No author. (1887.) "Corsets and Tight-Lacing," 129 (3330): 1296–7.

Lancet. No author. (1887.) "Mercurial Injections," 129 (3330): 1296.

Lancet. No author. (1887.) "Dysacusis," 129 (3330): 1299.

Léonard, J. (1966). "Les Etudes Médicales en France Entre 1815 Et 1848," in *Revue d'Histoire Moderne & Contemporaine*, 13 (1): 87–94.

Lord, W. B. (1868/1870). *[Freaks of Fashion] The Corset And the Crinoline*, London: Ward, Lock, and Tyler.

Moore, J., and J. Buckberry. (2016). "The Use of Corsetry to Treat Pott's Disease of the Spine from 19th Century Wolverhampton, England," in the *International Journal of Paleopathology*, 14: 74–80.

No author. (1910). An Anatomical Vindication of the Straight Front Corset, *Current Literature* Vol. XLVIII, No. 2: 172–4.

NYT. (2001) "1901: Corset Crimes: In Our Pages: 100, 75, and 50 Years Ago."

O'Followell, L. (1905). *Le Corset: Histoire, Médecine, Hygiène, Étude Historique*, Paris: A. Maloine.

Paré, A. (1598/1632). *Des Oeuvres.*

Pinell, P. (2011). "The Genesis of the Medical Field: France, 1795–1870," in *Revue Française de Sociologie*, 52 (5): 117–51.

Porter, D. (1993). "Medicine and Industrial Society: Reform, Improvement, and Professionalization," in *Victorian Studies*, 37 (1): 129.

Ramsey, M. (1977). "Medical Power and Popular Medicine: Illegal Healers in Nineteenth-Century France," in *the Journal of Social History*, 10 (4): 560–587.

Ribeiro, A. ([1986] 2003). *Dress and Morality*, Oxford: Berg.

Rousseau, J.-J. (1762). *Oeuvres de J.J. Rousseau de Genève, Volume 8, "Émile ou de l'éducation,"* p. 23.

Schwarz, G. (1979). "Society, Physicians, and the Corset," in the *Bulletin of the New York Academy of Medicine,* 55 (6): 551–90.

Steele V. (2001). *The Corset: A Cultural History*, New Haven, CT: Yale University Press.

Vaissette, P. (1875). *L'Usage Prémature et Abusif du Corset*, Paris, FR: A. Derenne.

Weisz, G. (1978). "The Politics of Medical Professionalization in France 1845–1848," in *Journal of Social History*, 12 (1): 3–30.

Weisz, G. (2003). "The Emergence of Medical Specialization in the Nineteenth Century," in *Bulletin of the History of Medicine*, 77 (3): 536.

Wilson, L. 1993. *Women and Medicine in the French Enlightenment: The Debate over* Maladies des Femmes. Baltimore, MD: Johns Hopkins University Press.

Figure 1.16 Corset number I.27.60 and 60A from the Bath Fashion Museum, exterior view. Brilliant red silk, no heavy wear patterns, with gussets on both top and bottom. Measurements: front 37cm; back 36cm; sides 35cm; bust 100cm; waist 41cm; hips 87cm. Ratio of bust/waist/hips: 1:.41:.87. Dated between 1890 and 1900. Photo © Rebecca Gibson, 2023.

Figure 1.17 Corset number I.27.60 and 60A from the Bath Fashion Museum, interior view. Photo © Rebecca Gibson, 2023.

2

THE UPPER TORSO
Covering Chapters 2–4 of *Le Corset*, on the Topics of the Lungs, Thoracic Cage, Circulation, and Lactation

CHAPTER 2

23

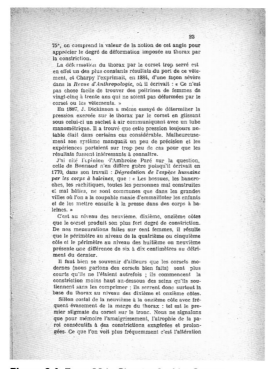

Figure 2.1 Page 23 in Chapter 2 of *Le Corset*.

Translation

The deformation of the chest caused by the too-tight corset is indeed one of the most constant results of wearing this garment. Charpy[1] expressed this severely in 1884 in the *Revue d'Anthropologie*, where he wrote: "it is not easy to find chests of women from twenty-five to thirty years old that are not deformed by the corset or clothes."

In 1887, J. Dickenson[2] even tried to determine the pressure exerted on the chest by the corset by sliding under it an air bag linked to a gauge tube. He found this constant and noticeable pressure to be considerable in some cases. Unfortunately his system was not overly precise, and the experiments focused on too few cases for the results to be particularly useful.

I quoted the opinion of Ambroise Paré[3] on the question, Bonnaud's[4] view is much the same since he wrote in 1770, in his work "*Degradation* of the human species by whale bone corps," that: "The hunchbacks, the bandylegs, the rickets,[5] all the poorly constructed and poorly built people, are common only in the big cities where one has the guilty quirk to swaddle children and to put them subsequently in the press of the Baleine corps."

It is at the level of the ninth, tenth, and eleventh ribs[6] that the corset produces its highest degree of constriction. From our measurements made on 100 women, it follows that the perimeter at the level of the fourth or fifth rib and the perimeter at the level of the eighth or ninth rib has a difference of six to ten centimeters to the detriment of the latter.

It must also be remembered that modern corsets (by which I mean well-made corsets) are shorter than they once were;[7] they begin constriction lower below the breasts that they support without compressing; they therefore squeeze in particular the base of the thorax at the level of the tenth and eleventh ribs.

1 Adrien Charpy, "De l'angle xiphoidien," *Revue d'Anthropologie* (1884). This source is digitized on Google Books: https://books.google.com/books?id=EHMrAQAAIAAJ&pg=PA268&source=gbs_toc_r&cad=4#v=onepage &q&f=false

2 This source is not listed in the bibliography, but I own a copy of it. While O'Followell attributes it to J. Dickenson, the copy I own, purchased from a reprinter of out of print books, lists the author as Robert Latou Dickinson, American gynecologist, 1861–1970. Titled *The Corset: Questions of Pressure and Displacement—Illustrated Edition*, it was indeed published in 1887.

In his assessment of Dickenson/Dickinson, O'Followell and I are in complete agreement: the experiment lacked precision (which Dickinson admits) and does not have a sufficiently high amount of data to provide results that have scientific validity. However, one of the points that he makes in this pamphlet is "[W]ithin half a minute after hooking the corset such an adjustment occurs that a distinct fall in pressure results," (36), thus indicating that while putting on a corset creates high physical pressure on the body, it does not create long lasting pressure differentials—the body adjusts to its new shape.

3 See Chapter 1 of this book for the full Paré quote discussion.

4 Bonnaud, *Dégradation de l'espèce humaine par l'usage des corps à baleine* (Paris: 1770), see Chapter 1, footnote 35.

5 This is an example of correlation not being equal to causation. Certainly, metabolic disorders, birth defects, and other types of deformities were "common" in large cities by virtue of their having more people in general, and more resources to serve those people, leading to higher levels of everything: pollution, birth rates, death rates, and doctors, meaning that people whose birth defects were not life threatening stood a better chance of living in general and being at least mostly self-sufficient if they reached adulthood. In a small country town of a dozen families, there might not be resources for a person who was unable to work, but in London a person could fall back on begging to bring in income.

Several studies discuss the prevalence of rickets in England during this time period, and implicate multiple factors for the overrepresentation of it in cities, citing coal dust, lack of adequate food resources, and the "city fashions" which often included long sleeves (Paterson and Darby 1926; Benson et al. 1963; Newton 2021; O'Riordan 2006; Gibbs 1994). Rickets is a metabolic disorder caused by low levels of vitamin D, which inhibits calcium deposition and retention in the bones, making them soft and malleable. While corseting, or any pressure on calcium-deficient developing bones, can exacerbate the effects of rickets, even without a corset the thoracic cage can take on what is called a "pigeon-breasted" look, due to the pressure of the arms on the ribs.

6 According to my own research where data was available, the circumference of the fifth and sixth was equivalent or slightly smaller than the circumference of the ninth or tenth rib. The full data table can be accessed by digital download on the Springer Nature website.

7 This is incorrect, based not only on what was being advertised at the beginning of *Le Corset* (see the ad illustrations in Chapter 1 of this book, which show corsets that cover the entire torso from the top of the breasts/thoracic cage to the bottom of the pelvis), but also on my own research on corsets from this time period. Most of the corsets I examined for my 2020 publication, *The Corseted Skeleton*, were not underbust, but instead included the bust in their construction, and covered some, if not all, of the hips. They did not have the long, pointed fronts of the eighteenth-century stays, but they were not short.

24

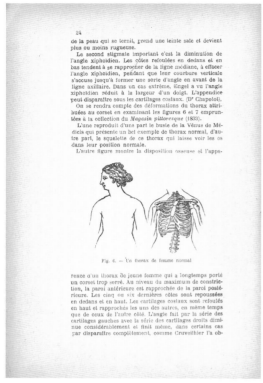

Figure 2.2 Page 24 in Chapter 2 of *Le Corset*.

Translation

The deformations of the chest attributed to the corset can be seen by examining Figures 6 and 7 borrowed from the collection of the *Magasin pittoresque* (1833).

One reproduces on the one hand the bust of the Venus de Medici that presents a beautiful example of a normal thorax,[8] and on the other hand, the skeleton of this thorax which shows the bones in their normal position.

The other figure shows the bone arrangement and the appearance [2.2][9] of the chest of a young woman who has an overly tight corset for a long period. When maximum constriction is reached, the anterior wall is brought closer to the posterior wall. The last five or six ribs are pushed back in and up. The costal cartilages are pushed back at the top and close to each other, as are those on the other side simultaneously. The angle made by the series of left cartilages with the series of right cartilages decreases considerably, and even ends, in some cases by disappearing completely, as Cruveilhier[10] observes

8 Here we have the first discussion of ideal forms, comparing the human body to artwork. I will explore how this is problematic later in this chapter, where O'Followell himself expands on the topic.

9 Captioned "the thorax of a normal female," this drawing shows a breastless silhouette of a woman, beside an internal/skeleton-only representation of a similar form. The woman's hair is done in a classical Greek style. Both figures are slightly canted so that the rib cage in the figure on the right is shown in not quite frontal view. This is a fairly accurate drawing—certainly accurate for 1908—of an anatomically normal thoracic cage, clavicles, the upper ends of the humerus, and the lumbar vertebrae, but it is just that: a drawing. I strongly question O'Followell's use of drawings where photographs would have better illustrated his points. While drawings can be accurate and photographs can lie, one can literally draw *anything* and leave the casual viewer who has no medical knowledge with no way to check the accuracy.

This is particularly cogent when paired with his use of photographs in later chapters—Chapters 10 and 13–15, for example, are rife with photographs, though these are, respectively, of the genitalia, and of children and exotic women. What is absent completely from the main chapters of *Le Corset* are any photographs of the patients who form his main evidentiary case studies. And let us not think that drawings could show more than photographs—as shown by the radiographs later in this chapter, O'Followell either had experience or knew someone experienced with the ability to layer images in order to create composites.

10   Cruveilhier. *Traité d'anatomie*, tome Ier, art. thorax. This is largely correct, according to my own research, in that the corset rounds the ribcage, altering the angle of the cartilage and the proximal location of the ribs to each other.

[no page number]

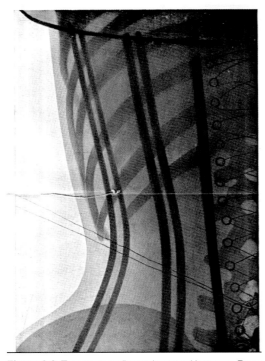

Figure 2.3 Two-page radiograph spread between Pages 24 and 25, Chapter 2, of *Le Corset*, no page number.

Translation

Annotations page[11]

11   Coming as it does between pages 24 and 25, this is the first non-hand-drawn, non-photographic image in the book—this is the first radiograph, upon which O'Followell hangs his major argument, that corseting deforms (and harms, although we must be careful to avoid conflating the two) the body through extreme changes in the rib cage. And it is a falsification—the 1908 equivalent of performing alterations in Adobe Photoshop or a similar program.

This radiograph is meant to show a corseted woman, with the top of the corset lined with metal, the laces replaced with metal wire. Most things about this image look as they should—for example, you can see the ribs, the metal bones of the corset, and the curve of the iliac crest, all where they should be. However, there are four things represented in this image that are immediately identifiable as being falsified: the slackness of the laces, the way the upper edge of the corset overlaps both the metal corset boning and the outline of the body, the lack of internal organs, and the placement of the vertebrae. I will deal with each individually.

The slackness of the laces: one thing about radiographs that stands out from candid photos or images taken by amateurs is that they are often (almost always) posed in such a way as to produce exactly the image that is desired. If a radiograph technician needs a certain angle, or to emphasize a certain body feature, they can move the subject of the radiograph to show the relevant angle or feature. Here, purportedly, is a corset laced with wire, so that the wire shows up strongly on the radiograph. The corset is, again purportedly, laced tight to show how the body of the woman changes when she "abuses" the corset. But the top four eyelets show slack and irregular lacing. This type of lacing is certainly possible when a person dresses themselves, but this radiograph is meant to show the doctors having dressed her and tight-laced her.

The metalized upper edge of the corset: O'Followell states that metal was added to the upper and lower edges of the corset to (again) make them stand out in the radiographs. In a normal corset, these edges are formed by hemmed and stitched fabric. In the image, we can clearly see the boundaries of the person's body—the fat/muscle layer that creates the curves of the thoracic area and the hip. At the top of the image, you see the metal "in" the corset. Yet this metal overlaps the exterior edge of the body. When a corset is worn and tightened, the rear upper edge curves around to the front to create the front part of the corset. This is visibly not making that curve. Furthermore, it overlaps the metal boning of the corset. In corsets from O'Followell's time period, his so-called "good" corsets, the boning did not go all the way to the top seam, and thus would not be overlapped by the metal put in place for the radiograph.

The lack of internal organs: this is partially exacerbated by the poor quality of the image (though it is the clearest of all the radiographs—more on that below), however, personal correspondence with a radiography expert at Indiana University South Bend (Langton 2022) indicates that although this is ambiguous (the shadow beginning about an inch and a half from the left edge of the body could be internal organs), it is certainly not definitive, and taken with the fourth point of falsification below, the shadow was almost certainly manufactured by stuffing the rib cage with something to keep the shape.

The placement of the vertebrae: beginning just below the head of the twelfth rib, we can see what is meant to be the L1, the first lumbar vertebra. When viewed via radiograph from the posterior, as this purports to be, lumbar vertebrae should have one short transverse process on each side, angled very slightly downward (if at all). Experimentally, I have found that the corset does not affect the angles of the transverse processes (Gibson 2020). The posterior or spinous processes should be visible in a clear, modern radiograph, but only as knobbly bits on the midline of the radiograph—they should not be seen off to the side at all. The superior and inferior articular facets meet each other between the main vertebral bodies, where they articulate in an interlocking mortise and tenon type joint. This joint should be visible, and should fully (in L1–L2) or partially (in L3–L5) obscure the intervertebral disc—the pad of cartilage which sits between the vertebrae as a buffer and to improve the motion of the vertebrae. Instead, in this radiograph, the transverse processes begin at L1 angled downward, but abruptly switch to angled upward at L4. The spinous processes are able to be seen pointed down and to the left—they would not be clearly seen at all in a radiograph (of this quality—modern radiographs taken in 2022 would visualize them clearly as the aforementioned knobbly bits, though not at this angle) of a living human. There are no visible superior and inferior articular facets, because what is visible at the mid-line of the vertebrae in this image is the vertebral foramen—the hole through which the spinal cord passes—which is notably larger, rounder, and more regularly shaped than the gaps between the superior and inferior articular facets. The set of all vertebral foramen in the body forms a vertical tube which begins at the foramen magnum in the skull, just below the brainstem, and ends at the base of the sacrum. Nerves branch off of the spinal cord via smaller foramen or intercostal grooves all down the length of the spinal cord, and were a person to suddenly find one of the vertebral foramen facing backward/horizontally, as they do in L1–L5 shown here on this radiograph, they would instantly be paralyzed by spinal cord compression. Furthermore, Langton states: "…the vertebra definitely seem to be misaligned/misplaced/artificial. It also appears that this is either a radiograph of a deceased patient or phantom (radiography term used when we image an artificial body part)." This radiograph was not taken on a living human being, nor on a whole human being; it is a creation intended to present a certain story, not a representation of an actual occurrence.

Now that this falsification has been established, let us consider why O'Followell (or the doctors he quotes) would rely on such methods.

I will discuss this further with other radiographs from this chapter, but I contend that the late nineteenth-century doctors were not seeing the results they desired. Yes, the ribs changed form—I have addressed this elsewhere in this book and in *The Corseted Skeleton* (Gibson 2020)—but they were not seeing the wide-scale organ damage that they attributed to the misuse and abuse of the corset. Having combed through 3,815 death records from St. Bride's Parish in Fleet Street, London, for the period of time between 1770 and 1849 (ibid) not only were none directly attributed to corsets—the words "corset," "corseting," "stays," and "tightlacing" do not appear once in nearly 100 years—none of the causes of death are traceable to damage by corsets without any other possible cause. In every case that might have been influenced by the corset (injuries like broken ribs, burst blood vessels, and bowel obstructions), there was always one or more alternative influences or causes, in most cases including simply bad health, bad luck, or bad timing. This one parish may or may not be representative, but that is immaterial—when O'Followell, other doctors, and pundits cry "death by corseting!," they do not show proof—there are no autopsy photos, no death records from the parishes, no mention of any disease or deformity that could not be attributed to something other than the corset. However, even today, no one wants to publish a study that states that all patients are fine and the radioscopy showed no adverse effects. To keep publishing and remain relevant, O'Followell and his contemporaries needed results.

Additionally, as I previously mentioned, O'Followell hangs his arguments about corsets on these images. Most of the rest of the images in *Le Corset* are drawn or photographs, here is where you can see the (lack of) guts, pun very much intended, of his assertions. If these images did not show what he wanted them to, then they had to be manipulated. This particular radiograph, as mentioned above, is the clearest of all the ones included in *Le Corset*. It is the largest, with a full unnumbered double-set of pages dedicated to it. It shows the ribs without the confusion of the interior side of the anterior aspect showing through. This emphasizes the possibility that the rib cage was stuffed ith a material to hold its shape—were this a radiograph on a living person, the interior portion of the anterior side of the rib cage would show through, creating interference on the clear pattern of the posterior of the ribs. Depth is impossible to read in this radiograph, but that shadow persists down to the pelvis, and the lumbar vertebrae appear to have been lain on top of whatever material was used.

In fairness to all who have discussed O'Followell's radiographs and pictures previously (Steele 2001; Stone 2012; Kunzle 1982), this particular falsification—and a few others discussed below—are easy to miss. I missed it myself during my first few read-throughs of *Le Corset*. Cultural historians (Steele 2001; Kunzle 1982) are generally working without detailed anatomical knowledge and understanding of the skeleton, and thus would not see the wrongness of the positioning of the lumbar vertebrae. Even trained biological anthropologists (Gibson 2015; Gibson 2020; Stone 2012), will miss this if we are not thoroughly interrogating not only the radiographs, but also the text of O'Followell's book. He had an agenda, clearly laid out, exhaustively defended, which hinged on two principles: women were abusing their corsets, which in turn caused myriad types of damage to their skeletal system, internal organs, and overall health. In cases where self-abuse was not present, women were wearing the wrong corset, causing same. I must be completely clear about this: this agenda is *not immediately apparent* without close, careful examination of both the text and the images contained within *Le Corset*. If a scholar uses the images alone, particularly if they give them a superficial reading and take them at face value, they are likely to miss the agenda and see only the damage "caused" by the corset.

To answer the question I asked above: O'Followell and the other doctors used falsified radiographs, radiographs not performed on living people, or even on whole skeletons, because they were pushing the agenda of women self-harming with their corsets, and creating and disseminating these images furthered that agenda. This is particularly fascinating in light of the fact that people who wore corsets often used padding to create their silhouette—far from tight-lacing to injury and illness, they would sew false hips and breasts into their corset where needed, especially once ready-made corsets were available and thus not tailored directly to the person (Bendall 2022; Summers 2001; Waugh 2018).

Figure 2.4 Page 25 in Chapter 2 of *Le Corset*.

Translation

in an elderly woman who, since the age of puberty, had squeezed into her corset.

M. Brouardel's report on a memoir by M. Hamy.[12] *Contribution à l'étude des déformations du thorax,* which was read at the session of the Academy of Medicine on December 31, 1901, describes as follows thoracic deformities related to the wearing of the corset: the lady who is the subject of the observation was born in 1753; she belonged to a bourgeois family and had suffered, like her contemporaries, the extravagant fashions that then regulated women's clothing. She had to mold her body into the narrow and elongated cone of one of the baleine busk and bodies whose examples can be seen in old fashion journals (and the

[2.4][13]

original in some museums), and it is the chest narrowed by this artificial deformation that constitutes the characteristic feature of the subject discussed by Mr. Hamy.

12 Neither Paul Camille Hippolyte Brouardel (1837–1906), nor Ernest-Théodore Hamy (1842–1908) are in the bibliography, and the source (Contribution à l'étude des déformations du thorax) is not extant.

13 In the preceding sentence, "bodies" refers to the "corps" which was the term for pre-corsets/early stays.

This image, captioned "Thorax of a woman restricted by the corset," this is a drawing of a breastless, wasp-waisted woman with a Greek hairstyle, next to a drawing of a partial upper torso showing the thoracic cage, clavicles, and upper humeri. The same objection as above can be made here: why use a drawing? O'Followell uses radiographs and photographs of women throughout *Le Corset*, but chooses the unverifiable line drawings as his primary illustration of the phenomenon of the corseted torso.

26

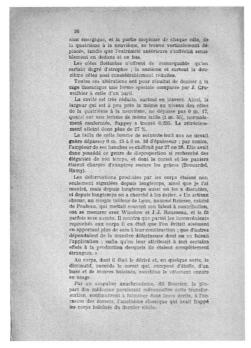

Figure 2.5 Page 26 in Chapter 2 of *Le Corset*.

Translation

The floating ribs show no remarkable change other than a certain degree of atrophy; the eleventh and especially the twelfth ribs are considerably reduced.

All these alterations result in giving the rib cage a special shape, compared by J. Cruveilhier to that of a barrel.[14]

The cavity is very small: jn particular, the width, which is about the same level of the fourth to the ninth ribs, does not exceed 0.17 m.,[15] when on a woman of the same height (1 m. 55 cm.), un-corseted and conforming to anatomically normal, Sappey recorded a width of 0.235 m. The shrinkage therefore is more than 27%.

The size of this sixty-eight-year-old woman's rib cage[16] should ideally be 0 m. 15 cm to 0 m. 16 cm; on the other hand, the size of her hips were 27 or 28 cm. She therefore possessed the proportions so sought after by the elegant women of her time, and whose corset and panniers were charged with further exaggerating her graces (Brouardel, Hamy).

The deformities produced by the bodies have been known for a long time, as I have shown, but they also been discussed for similar period, during which time we doctors have sought to avoid them. "An obscure craftsman, a simple tailor from Lyon, named Reisser, esteemed by Pouteau, who often put his talent to work, dared to compete with Winslow and J.-J. Rousseau, and sometimes did so successfully. He showed that among the disadvantages attributed to the bodies, that deformity was easily avoided by taking more care in their construction; that others depended on the faulty way in which it was applied; and that they were wrongly attributed certain effects to the production of which they were completely alien."[17]

14 Judging by the line drawing, an amphora is a more accurate comparison.

15 What I found in the course of my research on skeletons from the Museum of London's St. Bride's Lower Churchyard collection and the Musée de l'Homme's collection was that regardless of height, the width of the rib cage ranged between 21 and 17 cm. Unlike Sappey, I could not determine their dimensions prior to corseting, but the smallness of the women is not nearly as drastic as he describes.

16 In the preceding sentence, "panniers" refers to basket-like structures that provided the under-structure and support for wide and shapely skirts.

Without having analyzed this woman for osteoporosis, it is difficult to know how much bone loss can be attributed to the corset, versus to aging. Osteoporosis was first defined in the early 1800s by the pathologist Jean Georges Chrétien Frédéric Martin Lobstein (1777–1835).

17 Here we have the advent of the idea of a "bad" corset—the construction is to be blamed—but also of the "bad" woman applying the well-made corset incorrectly.

32

Pour suppléer au silence des anatomistes, sur la largeur comparative de la portion abdominale du thorax, Bouvier a mesuré à différentes hauteurs le diamètre transversal de cette cage osseuse sur cent clinquantes sujets des deux sexes, de différents âges, placés dans des conditions sociales diverses. Ce diamètre a été constamment moindre au niveau de la onzième côte, que dans l'espace compris entre la quatrième et la huitième, où se rencontrait, tantôt plus haut, tantôt plus bas, la plus grande étendue transversale du thorax. Il existait, terme moyen, entre ce grand diamètre et le diamètre inférieur près de la onzième côte, une différence de deux à quatre centimètres.

Déjà Hourman et Dechambre mesurant la poitrine dans un autre but, avaient trouvé chez la femme adulte et dans leur seconde catégorie de vielles femmes, près de trois centimètres de moins au niveau de la huitième côte qu'à la hauteur des seins.

Voici, d'après l'analyse des observations de Bouvier, les conditions principales des différences que présente l'écartement des côtes abdominales, d'un côté à l'autre :

1° Sexe : Les fausses côtes sont un peu plus rapprochées dans le sexe féminin comme l'avait vu Soemmering. La différence moyenne des deux diamètres transverses indiqués plus haut, s'est trouvée plus forte, de près d'un demi-centimètre, chez les femmes que chez les hommes.

2° Age : La conformation propre à la jeunesse, aug-

Translation

To compensate for the silence of the anatomists on the comparative width of the abdominal portion of the chest, Bouvier measured at different heights the transverse diameter of the thoracic cage on 100 flashy[18] subjects of both sexes, of different ages, and hailing from different social conditions. This diameter was constantly smaller at the level of the eleventh rib[19] than in the space between the fourth and the eighth, where the largest transverse extent of the thorax met, although this diameter varied. There was, on average, a difference of two to four centimeters between the upper and lower measurements of the eleventh rib.

Hourman and Dechambre had already been measuring the chest for another purpose and had found in the adult woman (and in their second category of the older woman) nearly three centimeters less width at the level of the eighth rib than at the height of the breasts.

Here are the main conditions of the differences in the spacing of the abdominal ribs, from one side to the other, according to an analysis of Bouvier's observations:

1. Sex: The false ribs are a little closer in women, as Soemmering had observed. The average difference of the two transverse diameters indicated above was found to be larger, by almost half a centimeter, in women than in men.

2. Age: The conformation to the appropriate-sized body during youth increases

18 *OED* defines "clinquant" as flashy, gilded, or decorative, though I cannot see what that has to do with anything in this sentence.

19 The eleventh rib is one of the floating ribs, and does not connect to the cartilage in the front. This makes it both more susceptible to the pressure of the corset, and also de facto of smaller diameter than that of the eighth rib.

33

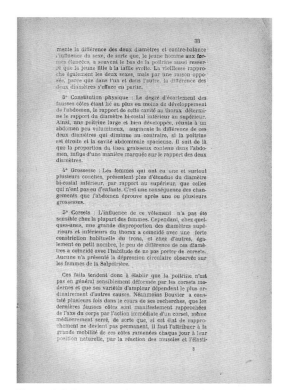

Figure 2.6 Page 33 in Chapter 2 of *Le Corset*.

Translation

the difference of the two diameters and counterbalances the influence of sex, so that a slender young man might have a lower chest as narrow as a slender-waisted girl.[20] Old age also brings the two sexes closer together, but for the opposite reason: in both, the difference between the two diameters is partly erased.[21]

3. Physical constitution: The degree of spacing of the false ribs being related more or less to the development of the abdomen, the ratio of this cavity to the thorax determines the ration of the bi-costal diameter from the lower to the upper. Thus, a wide and well-developed chest, combined with a small abdomen, increases the difference of these two diameters, which then (to the contrary) decreases if the chest is narrow and the abdominal cavity wide. It follows from this that the proportion of fatty tissue contained in the abdomen has a marked influence on the ratio of the two diameters.

4. Pregnancy: Women who have had one or especially several deliveries, have a wider lower bi-costal diameter (compared to the upper) than those who have not had children. This is a consequence of changes to the abdomen after one or more pregnancies.[22]

5. Corsets: The influence of this garment has not[23] been noticeable in most women. However, in a few, a large disproportion of the upper and lower diameters of the thorax usually coincided with strong constriction of the trunk; in others, also in small numbers, the small difference in these diameters coincided with the habit of not wearing corsets. None presented with the circular depression observed on the women of the Salpétrière.

20 It is unfortunate that O'Followell (or rather Hourman and Dechambre) does not note the ages in question. The similarity between a mid-teenage girl and boy is quickly erased by skeletal and muscular development in early adulthood, so that by their early twenties the difference is pronounced (White et al 2011).

21 During the first forensic anthropology class I took as an undergraduate, my professor (now colleague) Dr. Jay VanderVeen stated that your last bone fuses at approximately age twenty-seven, and then you start to die. His cheerfully morbid pronouncement returns to me here, to make explicit what O'Followell only hints at: once the skeleton stops growing, the two processes for bone remodeling take over as the main way the skeleton changes over time—bone repair when repair is needed (osteoblast activity) and bone resorption when, through lack of use or through the degenerative processes of osteoporosis/osteopenia, the calcium deposits and cartilage substrates are removed and repurposed elsewhere (osteoclast activity). Therefore as we age, all skeletons lose bone mass through degenerative processes, meaning that older people of all sexes resemble each other more than they resemble a different sex as a young person (White et al 2011).

22 This is very accurate: the changes due to pregnancy spread the rib cage, producing a wider diameter—and this could be confirmed not only medically, but also by pregnant people themselves. However, it also draws attention to the fact that despite all the changes discussed in *Le Corset* which are directly attributable to pregnancy and childbirth, many of which are considerably more immediately dangerous (see Berthiaud 2012) than any concretely attributable to corseting, becoming a mother is repeatedly and unwaveringly held up as the pinnacle of womanhood, the ultimate goal, and the most desirable aspiration of women. Having a fetus shift around your insides (ibid), potentially more than once, or over and over again throughout your life, is something a woman is meant to bear without complaint and to see as natural and normal. Having a corset (purportedly) do the same thing, however, is product of a vain, coquettish, egotistical, wanton woman abusing herself. See Chapter 4 of this book for a full discussion on pregnancy and childbirth.

23 This appears to directly contradict what was said earlier. It is here in Chapter 2 of *Le Corset* that we first begin to understand the problem with using O'Followell's drawings, photos, and radiographs without the context of his written text: unless you read the text, and take it in context with whomever he is quoting at any given

time, it is remarkably easy to miss where he includes contradictions, plays devil's advocate, or uses an image or a quote to illustrate a point he is arguing against. In this numbered list, of which the influence of corsets is the fifth point, he is paraphrasing Bouvier's "Etude historique et médicale sur l'usage des corset," in *Bulletin de l'Académie de médecine* (vol. XVIII, 1852–3). Does he agree with Bouvier? Not entirely. See the next page, where he says that he does not have the proper data to invalidate the figures, indicating that the veracity of Bouvier's analysis is in question, but not immediately falsifiable. This type of logical/linguistic switchback where he quotes someone only to disagree with or attempt to disprove them is rife throughout the entirety of *Le Corset*, because the harm done to the body is not his primary focus: rather, his main goal is to place that harm firmly in the hands of the women who wore corsets. In chapter after chapter, we see him present alternate causes for every ailment that the corset *might* have engendered, only to end on the note of "but it is the woman who abuses the corset who does this to herself with the corset."

34

Pour infirmer ces chiffres donnés comme mesure des diamètres thoraciques, il faudrait mesurer cent femmes de 17 à 60 ans, n'ayant *jamais* porté de corset, et trouver des mesures sensiblement différentes des précédentes.

Translation

To invalidate these figures given as a measurement of chest diameters, it would be necessary to measure 100 women ranging in age from seventeen to sixty years old who had never worn a corset, and find that the measurements were significantly different than the previous ones.

43

Figure 2.7 Page 43 in Chapter 2 of *Le Corset*.

Translation[24]

In his treatise on radiography (from which I extract Fig. 23) Mr. Foveau de Courmelles[25] writes that as soon as X-rays became available, the Queen of Portugal wanted to see the effect of the corset on the organs it encloses. The quality newspapers themselves reported in 1897 on the Queen's scientific curiosity. Later, Mrs. Dr. Gaches-Sarraute presented to the Society of Public Hygiene and Professional Medicine, a corset

24   The drawing on this page depicts the set-up of an X-ray table.

25   François Victor Foveau de Courmelles (1862–1943), a radiographic specialist and electrotherapist. Traité de radiographie médicale et scientifique. This source is not listed in the bibliography, but is held digitally in the BnF in Paris and available for download. There is no such radiograph in Foveau de Courmelles' work, and Figure 23 in O'Followell's *Le Corset* is the drawing discussed in footnote 27 below.

44

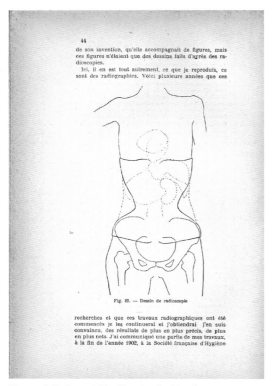

de son invention, qu'elle accompagnait de figures, mais
ces figures n'étaient que des dessins faits d'après des ra-
dioscopies.
Ici, il en est tout autrement, ce que je reproduis, ce
sont des radiographies. Voici plusieurs années que ces

Fig. 23. — Dessin de radioscopie

recherches et que ces travaux radiographiques ont été
commencés je les continuerai et j'obtiendrai j'en suis
convaincu, des résultats de plus en plus précis, de plus
en plus nets. J'ai communiqué une partie de mes travaux,
à la fin de l'année 1902, à la Société française d'Hygiène

Figure 2.8 Page 44 in Chapter 2 of *Le Corset*.

Translation

of her invention, which she accompanied with figures, but these figures were only drawings made based on X-rays.
Here, however, I am reproducing X-rays. It has been several years now, that this [2.8][26]
research and this radiographic work were started; I will continue them and am convinced that I will obtain ever more precise results, ever more clarity. At the end of 1902, I communicated part of my work to the French Society of Hygiene

26 This is the drawing of a radiograph, as presented by Mrs. Dr. Gaches-Sarraute.

45

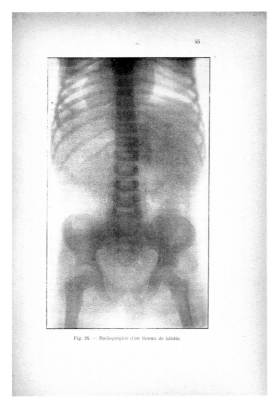

Fig. 24. — Radiographie d'un thorax de fillette.

Figure 2.9 Page 45 in Chapter 2 of *Le Corset*.

Translation

Annotations page[27]

27 This image appears to be exactly what is stated: a radiograph of the thorax of a young girl. We can contrast the fuzziness of the image with the clarity of the one discussed in footnote 11. Here on page 45, the ribs are not delimited umambiguously clearly, nor is the outline of the body. The short, stubby transverse processes of the lumbar vertebrae can be clearly seen (or as clearly as this incredibly low-quality image allows. . .) jutting off to each side, and not angled down or up. There is a shadow for the heart and for the liver, and there are shadows for the bowels and the kidneys. The iliac crest, sciatic notch, sacrum, the posterior rim of the acetabulum, the obturator foramen, and the posterior side of the pubic symphysis are all able to be visualized. This was taken on a living woman, who had not begun corseting yet, from the back.

46

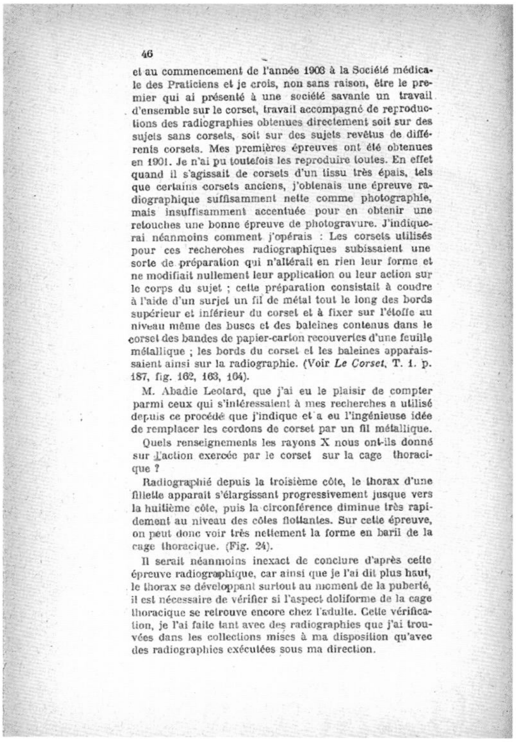

Figure 2.10 Page 46 in Chapter 2 of *Le Corset*.

Translation

and informed the Medical Society of Practitioners of it in early 1903. I believe myself to be, not without reason, the first person to present to a learned society an extensive work on the corset, work accompanied by reproductions of X-rays obtained directly either on subjects without corsets, or on subjects clothed with different corsets. My first radiographic proofs were obtained in 1901. However, I have not been able to reproduce them all. Indeed, when it came to corsets of a very thick fabric, as used on some old versions, I obtained an X-ray print clear enough as a photograph, but was unable to obtain a good photoengraving proof even with retouching. I will nevertheless indicate my methods. The corsets used for these radiographic research experiments underwent a kind of preparation that neither altered their form in any way nor modified the application or their action on the body of the subject; this preparation consisted of sewing with an over-stitch a metal thread all along the upper and lower edges of the corset and fixing on the fabric, at the same level of the buscs and whalebones contained in the corset, strips of paper and cardboard covered with a metal sheet. This allowed the edges of the corset and the whalebones to appear on the X-ray. (See *Le Corset*, T. 1. P. 187, figs 162, 163, 164).[28]

Mr. Abadie Leotard, whom I have the pleasure of counting among those who were interested in my research, has since used this process, and had the ingenious idea of replacing the corset cords with a metal wire.

What information did X-rays give us about the action exerted by the corset on the rib cage?

X-rayed from the third rib, the chest of a girl appears to be gradually widening to the eighth rib, after which the circumference decreases very quickly at the level of the floating ribs. On this test, we can therefore see very clearly the barrel shape of the rib cage. (Fig. 24).

It would nevertheless be inaccurate to form a conclusion from this radiographic test alone, because as noted above, the chest develops considerably during puberty, and thus it is necessary to check if the doliform [sic] aspect of the rib cage is still found in adults. I did this verification both with X-rays that I found in the collections made available to me and with X-rays performed under my direction.

28   Here we have O'Followell describing his process for creating a corset that would show up on the radiographs. In an effort to have this book be cogent, relevant, and as brief as possible while still addressing the subject adequately, I have removed several pages of O'Followell praising and explaining the radiographic technique. Undoubtedly what he suggests here would have made the radiographs more clearly indicate the presence of the corset, yet as discussed above in footnote 11, and below in regard to other radiographs, his technique was not the issue in the veracity of the prints thus acquired.

47

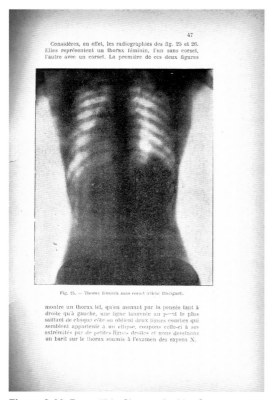

Figure 2.11 Page 47 in Chapter 2 of *Le Corset*.

Translation

Consider, in fact, the X-rays of Figs. 25 and 26. They represent a female chest, one without a corset, the other with a corset. The first of these two figures, Figure 2.11,[29]

shows such a thorax, that by conducting a thought experiment, both to the right and to the left, creating a tangent line to the most prominent point of each rib, we obtain two curved lines that seem to belong to an ellipse, cut it at its ends by small straight lines and we draw a barrel shape on the image of the thorax subjected to X-rays.

29 O'Followell's Figure 25, female thorax without corset. This image is so muddy as to be practically unusable, but I can see that there is a heart shadow and a liver shadow. In personal correspondence with a radiology expert, we reached the conclusion that the woman pictured here was had very little body fat, thus the iliac crests appear to protrude outside the bounds of the body's shadow. The photo appears to have been taken with the subject's arms held out to the side, which would account for the fact that the shadows of the scapulae are shifted further to the lateral aspect than if seen with arms down.

49

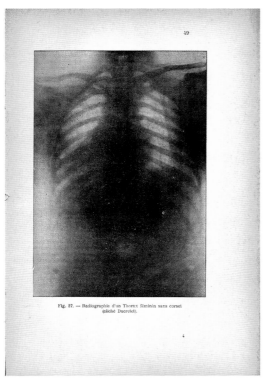

Fig. 27. — Radiographie d'un Thorax féminin sans corset
(cliché Ducretet).

Figure 2.12[30] Page 49 in Chapter 2 of *Le Corset*.

Translation

Annotations page

30 O'Followell's Figure 27 is much like Figure 25 discussed in footnote 28. Another radiography of a woman without a corset, there are visible heart and liver shadows, but everything else is just too indistinct to be of any use.

50

toute la région située au-dessus des deux œillets métalliques supérieurs, on voit que déjà les trois côtes situées immédiatement au-dessus de ces œillets commencent un mouvement d'inclination en dedans qui va s'accentuant brutalement sous la pression des baleines et du lacet.

Cette épreuve prouve, en outre, qu'en se serrant dans son corset une femme peut modifier singulièrement et dangereusement sa cage thoracique, et je tiens à mettre ceci en évidence, car si je veux établir qu'un corset bien mis et bien fait ne peut troubler la fonction respiratoire, je veux prouver aussi et la suite le démontrera que la constriction exagérée d'un corset modifie profondément l'expansion et la capacité des poumons.

Translation

[. . .in] the whole region located above the two upper metal eyelets, we can see that the three ribs located immediately above these eyelets having begun to incline, a process that will be sharply accentuated under the pressure of whalebones and lacing.

This test proves, moreover, that by squeezing into her corset, a woman can singularly and dangerously[31] modify her rib cage. I want to highlight this, because if I want to establish that a well-set and well-made corset cannot disturb respiratory function, I also want to prove, as the following will demonstrate, that the exaggerated constriction of a corset profoundly modifies the expansion and capacity of the lungs.

31   As I have previously demonstrated (Gibson 2020), the modification of the rib cage is not dangerous, in that it does not measurably shorten life or endanger the woman. The negative connotations of the word "dangerous" are here deliberately and explicitly assigned to the woman—she is modifying her rib cage, she is squeezing into her corset, her actions are, as seen in the latter part of the sentence, constricting her chest and profoundly modifying expansion and capacity of the lungs. O'Followell again relies on demonizing the woman, and exonerates a "well-set and well-made corset." If the corset is good, the woman who misuses it is bad. If the corset is bad, the woman should not have been using it in the first place.

52

> Pour en revenir à la dernière radiographie reproduite ci-dessus, j'ajouterai que le modèle en question étant revêtu d'un corset tout moderne et fait sur mesure par un de nos meilleures corsetières fut examinée à l'écran radioscopique et le thorax n'apparut pas modifié. Mais tandis que l'on continuait l'examen radioscopique, les lacets du corset étaient progressivement serrés jusqu'à provoquer un gêne très grande de la respiration du sujet, on voyait alors la base du thorax se rétrécir sous l'influence de la constriction exagérée.
>
> Une fois de plus, je pouvais conclure que le corset sagement appliqué ne modifiait pas les contours thoraciques, mais qu'employé d'une façon abusive, il devenait dangereux, puisqu'il diminuait le diamètre inférieur de la cage thoracique. Cette conclusion, l'étude que je fais plus loin de l'influence du corset sur la fonction respiratoire, la mettra davantage en lumière.
>
> . . . .
>
> Dans son étude sur *Le Corset Ligne,* brochure publiée chez Naud en 1904 je trouve aussi des radiographies de corsets ; j'en choisis quatre qui représentent une femme vêtue du corset-ligne, invention de l'auteur et un autre vêtue du corset cambré, les deux radiographies sont vues chacune de face et de dos. Les contours de ces épreuves fig. 31, 32, 33, 34 ont toutefois été accentués pour la reproduction.

Translation

Returning to the last X-ray reproduced above, I would add that the model in question wore a made-to-measure modern corset created by one our best corset-makers. The chest did not appear modified when first viewed on the X-ray screen. As the X-ray examination continued, however, the laces of the corset were gradually tightened until the base of the chest was seen to narrow as a result of exaggerated constriction, and the wearer found it difficult to breathe.[32]

Once again, I could conclude that while a wisely applied corset did not alter the chest contours, if used in an abusive way, the garment became dangerous since it decreased the lower diameter of the rib cage. My further study on the influence of the corset on respiratory function will shed more light on this conclusion.

. . . .

In his study on *Le Corset Ligne*, a pamphlet published by Naud in 1904, I also found X-rays of corsets; I chose four that show a model wearing the straight corset (invented by the author), and another dressed in the arched corset, the two X-rays of which are shown from the front and back. However, the contours of these tests, Figures 31, 32, 33, 34 have been accentuated for reproduction.[33]

32 This experiment uses acute and sudden constriction to push a woman who was not used to such to the point of pain. The only thing that this proves is that if you change a study's parameters mid-experiment, you get drastically different results—it says nothing about the long-term effects of tight constriction. However, it brings to the fore an interesting thing I have observed in modern popular-culture representations of corsetry and in the mainstream discussions of discomfort caused by corsets: actors who experience discomfort from

their corsets, or people who do corset challenges and find the garment less than comfortable are often a) wearing corsets not made for them; b) wearing garments that are the wrong size; c) corseting too tightly or in ways that would induce pain; d) wearing corsets that are poorly made/of cheap construction; and/or e) may be predisposed to pain under compression. Let us take these points one at a time:

a) While there are several bespoke corset-makers that can be found online or at Renaissance fairs, buying bespoke is extremely expensive, and inconvenient due to long production times. The majority of corset purchases are pre-made to a particular desired waist size, but do not take into account issues like bust/breast cup size, torso length, or hip size. All of these measurements are important for ensuring a proper fit that will not rub, pinch, or dig into the body uncomfortably (see for example Orchard Corset (https://www.orchardcorset.com/), which are premade, vs. Lucy's Corsetry (https://lucycorsetry.com/measurements/), which allows for proper measuring). While the horizontal measurements are almost assuredly done by wardrobe people for actors wearing corsets, there are still the issues of the vertical measurements, and the overtightening.

b) As mentioned in point a, size matters. Many corseting videos on YouTube or corset manufacturers online give tutorials and instructions on how to find your proper size, how to convert that measurement to a corset size, and how to place your corset on your body and season it when it arrives (see Orchard Corset: https://youtu.be/sOQMJaRAPHI; Lucy's Corsetry for Timeless Trends Corsets: https://youtu.be/jdWSRHOO-C4; or The Closet Historian's video on how to draft your own pattern: https://youtu.be/ilNTOeGdUQ4). However, not all corseting manufacturers cover this, and it is all too easy to buy a corset on amazon.com, or to purchase one at a lingerie store, and not be fitted properly.

c) Corsets are supposed to compress no more than two inches from your natural waist, and are meant to be worn over an undergarment or chemise (see Dark Garden Corsetry's video, here: https://youtu.be/nCkh33R51M8). As in points a and b, while this knowledge is commonplace among people who seek out knowledge about corsets, it is easy to purchase and wear one without being aware of the ways one should be wearing it. If wearers tighten their corset more than a few inches, particularly on the first wearing or without any preparation, they will be out of breath, and have trouble eating and drinking. If they wear it on bare skin, it will rub, pinch, and hurt.

d) Modern corsets run the gamut from exquisite and expensive bespoke corsets made from high-quality fabric and steel boning, to mass-produced garments of flimsy material and plastic boning. Based on "common sense" thinking, we might assume that less rigidity would be more comfortable, but the opposite is true for a corset: the more rigid and supportive the garment, the less it moves around. The less movement, the less friction and pinching. A steel-boned corset supports much more thoroughly and effortlessly than a plastic-boned one (see V. Birchwood's Historical Fashion video, here: https://youtu.be/3NNKBmFYSH0).

e) And here we do venture into medical territory, though not very far: there are several conditions that could be made more painful by compression. Everything from intestinal gas to gall stones might not respond too well to even a small reduction in waist size. However, this issue is not unique to corseting, being seen in people who wear skinny jeans, have tight waistbands, or wear clothing too small for them. Compression itself is not the problem, the problem is that there is an underlying, untreated condition which does not react well to compression.

33 O'Followell's drawing our attention to the accentuation of the contours here is a clever bit of sleight of hand—if we are concentrating on the contours of the *corset*, we are not looking at the skeletons themselves, as demonstrated by the radiographs (see discussion below).

53[34]

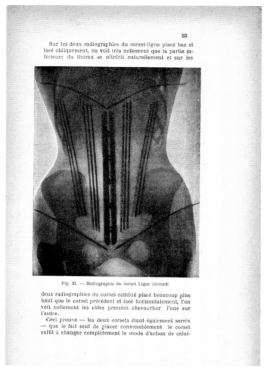

53

Sur les deux radiographies du corset-ligne placé bas et lacé obliquement, on voit très nettement que la partie inférieure du thorax se rétrécit naturellement et sur les

Fig. 31. — Radiographie du corset Ligne (devant)

deux radiographies du corset cambré placé beaucoup plus haut que le corset précédent et lacé horizontalement, l'on voit nettement les côtes pressées chevaucher l'une sur l'autre.

Ceci prouve — les deux corsets étant également serrés — que le fait seul de placer convenablement le corset suffit à changer complètement le mode d'action de celui-

Figure 2.13 Page 53 in Chapter 2 of *Le Corset*.

Translation

On the two X-rays of the straight corset placed low and laced obliquely, it is very clear that the lower part of the chest narrows naturally; on the
[2.13]
two X-rays of the arched corset, placed much higher than the previous corset and laced horizontally, we clearly see the pressed ribs overlapping each other.

This proves—the two slender corsets laced equally tight—that putting the corset on correctly in the first place is enough to completely change the garment's effect on the wearer.

34   Here again we see a very muddy radiograph. This makes interpretation harder, and the radiology expert I consulted had a different take on it than I (Langton 2022). What remains incontrovertible, however, is the fact that the metalized top and bottom of the corset are not wrapped around the body—they are laid on top of it. The corset is also, at first glance, backward.

This backward placement is quite easy to spot, as the mid-section of the corset—a metal busk containing a hook-and-eye closure—is the "front" part of the corset, yet is purportedly on the posterior of the woman's body, according to O'Followell's caption, "Fig. 31—Radiographie du corset Ligne (devant)" (Figure 31, radiography of the straight corset (from the rear)). In fact, the reason that the hook-and-eye-containing busk is used in the front of corsets is because it is impossible to do up oneself from the back. You need a full range of hand and shoulder motion to insert the hooks into the eyes. It would also catch at any hair that had not been done up. Laced busks with eyelets, as seen in the falsified radiograph discussed in footnote 11, can be done up from the back with no assistance, whereas hook-and-eye busks were never used for the back of the corset. On all styles of corset, the top of the back does not slope down into a V-shape, but rather is cut straight across. Yet we can see that the *ribs* are can be seen from the back—that is, a posterior view of the rib cage, underneath a front view of a corset.

However, it is not a posterior view of the pelvic girdle. In personal correspondence, Langton asserted that he could not visualize the heart and liver, but the density of the thoracic cavity did not rule out the presence of internal organs. Furthermore he could not tell the angle from which the radiograph had been taken, and therefore could not verify the location or rotation of the corset itself. Yet there are many things wrong with the pelvic girdle; so many, in fact, that it is only able to be explained by a 180° rotation from the rest of the torso.

As established, we can visualize the posterior view of the ribs. The pelvic girdle, however, appears as an anterior view, as we can see more depth of field in this radiograph than in the previous ones. The thick front edge of the iliac crests can be seen curving toward the viewer. The obturator foramina are unobstructed, and appear very clearly in the foreground of the image. The anterior edge of the acetabula are just able to be visualized, and the sacrum and coccyx are completely obscured by the structure of the corset, as they would be were the corset on correctly. This is the front view of a pelvis. This is a radiograph that has been manipulated extensively.

The importance of this lies in the fact that for the first three years of the official bioarchaeology of corseting (from Stone's publication of her piece "Binding women: Ethnology, skeletal deformations, and violence against women" in the *International Journal of Paleopathology* in 2012, until my publication of "Effects of Long Term Corseting on the Female Skeleton: A Preliminary Morphological Examination" in *NEXUS* in 2015), this very image was used to demonstrate "damage" done by and "violence" perpetrated against women by the corset. Any use of this image, or bioanthropological work derived from it, rests on evidence that was quite clearly a falsification, using at least two images to make a composite.

Again, we must return to the fact that the way O'Followell and his contemporaries spoke about women has directly influenced the medical interpretation of women to this day. Use of these radiographs as evidence of corseting "damage" perpetuates that prejudice.

54

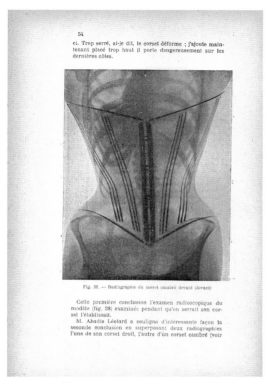

Translation

As I have said, the corset distorts if too tight; I now add that if placed too high, it is places dangerous pressure on the lower ribs. (See Figure 2.14.)

35 Comparing O'Followell's Figure 32 (this image) to Figure 31 (the image referenced in footnote 34), a few interesting similarities and differences stand out. The corset once again overlaps the body of the radiograph subject, although this is done more subtly. The top is almost convincing (apart from once again forming a V, and being on backward), except we can see where the top right of the image has been slightly scrubbed or blurred to remove the overlap of the metal part of the corset from the place where the body is not. This scrubbing/blurring can be seen at the bottom right of the corset as well, though it has not been done very thoroughly. The internal cavity shows what Langton identifies as a discernable heart shadow, and indications of bowel activity. Yet the fact remains that the pelvis is on backwards.

This is evident due to the fact that there is clear indication of depth of frame in this radiograph—a clear back and front of the image are visualizable, with the corset overtop the spine, which is in itself in front of the heart shadow, the anterior portions of the ribs, and the rib cartilage. However, the bottom edge of the corset sits much higher in this radiograph, and the front edges of the pelvic girdle are easily visualized. The thick top edge of the iliac crest curves forward toward the viewer, and the top edge of the pubis is not obscured by the sacrum as it would be if the image were taken from the posterior view, but can be seen at the very bottom and front of the image. Here again the pelvis is rotated almost a full 180° from the rib cage. Here again too, this radiograph has been manipulated to portray what O'Followell needed. It is a falsification, a composite of at least two images.

As a biological anthropologist, I generally hold to the principle that bones do not lie. Unfortunately, people do, and often—they make things up, they falsify, they manipulate data and evidence to demonstrate a point or uphold an argument. Composite images that are represented as being one image are a way of lying to the reader, and one which we do not expect. We assume that when we see a photograph or radiograph in a medical textbook, with a caption clearly stating the contents of that image, we will be able to trust it. The issue here is not just that O'Followell broke that trust, but the lasting ramifications of that breach. These can be seen in how O'Followell and others who wrote negatively about the corset have changed the way we discuss it—for example, this very radiograph is quoted as late as 2020 in a chapter on structural violence and bioarchaeology (Stone 2020). O'Followell, as discussed in the preface to this book, is now the de facto representative of what a radiograph of a woman in a corset looks like—and yet, most of the radiographs he uses are falsifications.

[No page number—between 56 and 57]

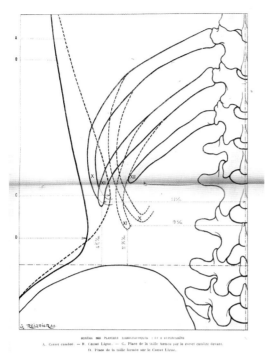

Figure 2.15 Two-page drawings spread based on X-ray between Pages 56 and 57 of *Le Corset*, no page number.

Translation

Annotations page[36]

36 This is a drawing of the overlap of the two types of corsets, abstracted from the radiographs.

64

Quant aux corsets d'aujourd'hui, on n'a fait, sous ce rapport, que redire à leur égard ce que l'on avait dit des corps. C'est ainsi que l'on prétend, comme autrefois, déduire l'influence de ce vêtement sur les déformations du rachis, de leur plus grande fréquence chez les femmes que chez les hommes, chez les habitants des villes que dans les campagnes, dans la classe riche que dans les familles pauvres, parmi les peuples de la vieille Europe que dans beaucoup de colonies européennes, comme si les individus

Translation

As for today's corsets, in this respect, we have only said about them what was said about the whalebone body. Thus it is claimed, as in the past, to deduce the influence of this garment on the deformities of the spine, from their greater frequency in women than in men, in the inhabitants of the cities than in the countryside, in wealthier than poorer families, among the inhabitants of Europe than many European colonies, as if individuals

65

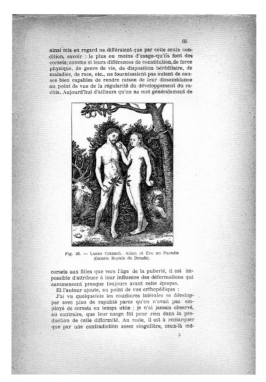

Figure 2.16 Page 65 in Chapter 2 of *Le Corset*.

Translation

thus compared differed only by this single condition, namely that: the more or less use they make of corsets; as if their differences in constitution, physical strength, type of life, hereditary disposition, diseases, race, etc., did not provide so many causes well capable of justifying their dissimilarity from the point of view of the regularity of the development of the spine. Today, moreover, given that we do not usually put

[2.16]

corsets on girls until around the age of puberty, it is impossible to attribute deformities that almost always begin before this time to corsets.[37]

And the author[38] adds, from an orthopedic point of view:

I have sometimes seen the lateral curvatures develop more quickly because corsets had not been used early enough; I have never observed, on the contrary, that their use did not contribute to the production of this deformity. Moreover, it should be noted that by a rather singular contradiction, these same [people]

37 Scoliosis is a congenital deformity of the spinal column, which results in a side-to-side curvature—being congenital, it can be seen as early as birth, and at least in the US, is now screened for during yearly health assessments both in and out of school. The diagnosis of idiopathic scoliosis is seen as far back as Hippocrates in the fourth century BCE, and much was written about how to treat it both before and during O'Followell's time. When diagnosed early enough, medical braces—or in the nineteenth century, corsets—are used to treat the malformation. I find it odd that Naud and O'Followell are equating the childhood deformity of scoliosis with the adulthood potential for corseting damage, particularly considering that long history of identification, discussion, and treatment (Fassoux et al 2009; Elsaesser and Butler 2014).

38 He is still paraphrasing Naud here—Naud is not listed in the bibliography.

66

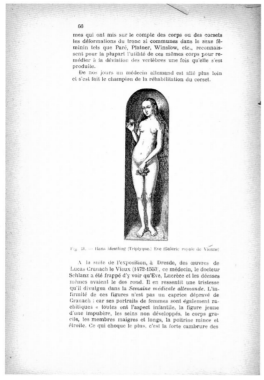

Figure 2.17 Page 66 in Chapter 2 of *Le Corset*.

Translation

who have blamed corps or corsets for the trunk deformities so common in the female sex, such as Paré, Planter, Winslow, etc., mostly recognize the usefulness of these same corps in remedying the deviation of the vertebrae once it has occurred.[39]

A German doctor has now gone further and championed the rehabilitation of the corset.

(See Figure 2.17.)

Following the exhibition in Dresden of the works of Lucas Cranach the Elder (1472–1553), this doctor, Dr. Schlanz, was struck to see that Eve, Lucretia, and the goddesses themselves had round backs.[40] He felt a sadness about it, which he disclosed in the *German Medical Weekly*. The infirmity of these figures is not a depraved whim of Cranach,[41] for his portraits of women are also rickety: "all have the infantile appearance, the young figure of an impubère,[42] the undeveloped breasts, the graceful body, the skinny and long limbs, the thin and narrow chest. What shocks most is the strong arch of the

71

Si donc quelque déformation de la cage thoracique est produit par un corset, « elle résulte de l'abus que les femmes ont fait du corset ordinaire serré d'une manière exagérée et appliqué sur le thorax dès l'enfance » ; c'est ce que je traduirai encore avec Mme Gaches-Sarraute, qui ne peut être suspectée de tendresse pour le corset moderne (je ne parle pas du type qu'elle a créé) ; la constriction de la cage thoracique a une importance capitale sur la direction du développement osseux, et ce sont les femmes qui se sont *serrées pendant longtemps sur une grande étendue, depuis la taille jusque sous le bras,* qui présentent un thorax dont la circonférence est très amoindrie, la région dorsale bombée, la région pectorale aplatie et des côtes incurvées vers le bas. Ce sont les corsets hauts et trop serrés qui en déformant le thorax amènent forcément un arrêt dans le développement normal des poumons qui deviennent ainsi plus sensibles aux influences pathogènes.

. . . .

Toutes réflexions, on le voit, qui incriminent non l'usage, mais l'abus des corsets.

Translation

If, therefore, some deformation of the rib cage is produced by a corset, "it results from the abuse that women have made of the ordinary corset tightened in an exaggerated way and applied to the chest from childhood"; this is what I will relate to you from Mrs. Dr. Gaches-Sarraute,[49] who cannot be suspected of warm feelings for the modern corset (I am not talking about the type she created); the constriction of the rib cage is of paramount importance to the direction of bone development, and it is women who have *tightened over a long period of time over a large area, from the waist to under the arm,* who have a thorax whose circumference is greatly reduced, as well as a bulging dorsal region bulging, flattened pectoral region and ribs curved downwards.[50] It is the high and too tight corsets that, by deforming the chest, necessarily bring a stop to the normal development of the lungs, which thus become more sensitive to pathogenic influences.

. . . .

All reflections, as we can see, which incriminate not the use, but the abuse of corsets.[51]

49 And he is back to using those same experts to blame the women, while simultaneously returning to holding the artwork up as an ideal—the artwork is "natural," the woman who abuses the corset is deformed.

50 This is, of course, anatomically accurate: I confirmed as much in my 2020 study. What it does not speak to (yet—he will get there) is anything regarding quality of life, or whether the changes in the internal organs produced any noticeable differences or painful conditions.

51 This is really distinction without a difference land. O'Followell states that lacing the corset tight is abusing it, but does not define tight, does not define the duration, and does not show any understanding of the idea that as the body changes, the woman will lace to accommodate the changing body, which will then change more.

77

Un corps à baleine enserrant toute la poitrine et étant très rigide, est néfaste pour la fonction respiratoire puisqu'il entrave considérablement l'expansion thoracique, cela me paraît un fait trop net pour que l'on s'y arrête, c'est donc en même temps accepter qu'un corset qui monte très haut sur la poitrine gêne la respiration.

Je veux seulement indiquer ce qui peut se produire avec un corset actuel ayant de justes proportions.

Ce corset, je l'ai montré par les radiographies qui précèdent, entoure en général le thorax seulement à sa base.

Si la femme a un type respiratoire qui met en jeu surtout les parois thoraciques supérieures, un corset moderne—à moins que trop serré il ne refoule fortement les viscères abdominaux sous le diaphragme,—ne saura gêner l'expansion des poumons. Si au contraire le type respiratoire féminin est abdominal, un corset, quelque peu serré soit-il, sera gênant du moment qu'il produira une compression quelconque.

Pilson déclare qu'il y a une diminution de l'expansion pulmonaire même avec les corsets des enfants ou avec la compression la plus légère.

Quel est le type respiratoire féminin ? Il semblerait que la plupart des femmes civilisées respirent surtout, d'après les auteurs, en dilatant la partie supérieure du thorax, ayant ainsi une respiration à type costo-supérieure.

Si ce dernier type de respiration prédomine chez ces femmes, la faute, dit M. Butin, en est au corset que le détermine par l'opposition qu'il apporte à la libre dilatation de la partie inférieure du thorax.

Translation

A whalebone corps that rigidly encloses the entire chest is harmful to the respiratory function since it considerably hinders chest expansion. With this in mind, we must also accept that a corset that rises very high on the chest hinders breathing.

I just want to indicate what can happen with a corset currently in use and which has the right proportions.

This corset, I have shown by the X-rays above, surrounds the chest only at its base.

If the woman has a respiratory type that involves mainly the upper chest walls, a modern corset—unless it is too tight, it strongly represses the abdominal viscera under the diaphragm—will interfere with the expansion of the lungs. If, on the contrary, the female respiratory type is abdominal, a corset, however tight it may be, will be annoying as long as it produces any compression.

Pilson[52] states that there is a decrease in lung expansion even with children's corsets or with the lightest compression.

What is the female respiratory type? It would seem that most civilized[53] women breathe by, according to the authors, dilating the upper part of the chest, thus having a costo-superior breathing.

If the latter type of breathing predominates in these women, the fault, says Mr. Butin, is the corset that determines it by impeding the free dilation of the lower part of the chest.

52 Pilson is not listed in the bibliography, and without a first name or initial, I can find neither any biographical information, nor the title of this work.

53 I have briefly mentioned previously that there is a civilization discourse held during this time period which prioritizes white western European men, then white western European women, then everyone else, in terms of who is considered civilized vs. savage—a discourse O'Followell would have been well aware of in his time, due to Balch (1904), whom he quotes. In fact, O'Followell himself goes on to address this below, by saying it would be necessary to compare women from different races to see if this differentiation is accurate, however, he does not do this, nor does Butin.

79

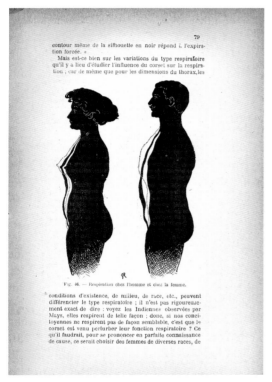

Figure 2.20 Page 79 in Chapter 2 of *Le Corset*.

Translation

But it is the variations of the respiratory type that require study in order to gauge the influence of the corset on breathing; for as well as for the dimensions of the thorax, the

[2.20]

conditions of existence, environment, race, etc., can have an effect on the respiratory type. It is not strictly accurate to say: "look at the Indian women observed by Mays, they breathe in such a way." So if our fellow citizens do not breathe in a similar way, it is because the corset has come to disturb the respiratory function? What would be needed, in order to make a fully informed decision, would be to choose women of various races, from

80

divers pays, de diverses conditions, d'en former deux groupes, l'un n'ayant jamais porté de corset, l'autre en faisant usage et de comparer alors les résultats entre eux, groupe à groupe.

Translation

various countries, of various conditions, to form two groups, one having never worn a corset, the other making use of it, and then to compare the results between them, group to group.[54]

54   He does not do this, though, which makes the majority of the rest of the experiments in this chapter baseless supposition.

81

Le problème à résoudre, est en effet le suivant :

1° Etant [sic.] donné une femme faisant usage du corset rechercher quelle est sa capacité pulmonaire : et lorsque son thorax est vêtu d'un corset et lorsqu'elle ne porte pas de corset.

2° Etant [sic.] donné plusieurs femmes, rechercher si l'action du corset est analogue sur chacune d'elles.

La première expérience consiste à faire respirer la femme qui a revêtu son corset selon ses quotidiennes habitudes, je mesure alors sa capacité respiratoire ; puis la femme ayant serré son corset, je mesure un deuxième fois cette capacité. Enfin, je mesure sa capacité pulmonaire, lorsque dans la troisième expérience la femme a enlevé son corset.

Les trois chiffres obtenus permettront de juger mathématiquement l'influence du corset sur la respiration.

Translation

The problem to be solved is, in effect, the following:

1. Given that a woman regularly wears a corset, we need to study her lung capacity: both when she is dressed in the item and when not.

2. Studying several women, to investigate whether the action of the corset is analogous to each of them.[55]

The first experience consists in making the woman who has put on her corset breathe as she would do normally, after which I measure her respiratory capacity; I measure that capacity once more after the woman has tightened her corset,[56] and then repeat the process for the final time once she has removed it.

The three results obtained make it possible to judge mathematically the influence of the corset on breathing.

55 Again, this is problematic—there are too many unknown variables here, and he addresses none of them.

56 The issue with this is that he changes the parameters of the study to unnatural tightness. If the woman comes in dressed in her corset, not tight-laced but the way she normally dresses, then *that* is the measurement that is relevant. A person who is not used to tightlacing, who is then made to tightlace, will be uncomfortable, short of breath, and have lower respiratory capacity.

84

Ces recherches ont été poursuivies de la façon suivante :

1° Mesure de la capacité respiratoire de la femme vêtue de son corset, tel qu'elle le portait en entrant dans mon cabinet et sans qu'elle ait été prévenue des expériences auxquelles elle se prêterait (colonne I).

2° Mesure de la capacité respiratoire du même sujet dont le corset a été fortement serré (colonne II).

3° Mesure de la capacité respiratoire de la femme ayant enlevé son corset (colonne III).

Afin de diminuer les chances d'erreur, l'expérience était répétée trois fois pour chaque cas et ce sont les moyennes des trois chiffres obtenus qui ont été comparées entre elles.

Soixante pour cent des personnes examinées portaient des corsets confectionnés, les autres des corsets sur mesure. Pour presque toutes, la forme du corset était droite devant en tous [sic.] cas peu cambrée ; il faut toutefois ne pas prendre de vue que le corset droit cambre d'autant plus qu'il est plus serré et qu'alors à la gêne de la respiration produite par les cambrures latérales vient s'ajouter la gêne de la pression abdominale.

Translation

This research was continued as follows:

1. Measure of the respiratory capacity of the woman dressed in her corset, as she wore it when entering my office and without her having been informed of the experiences to which she would lend herself (column I).

2. Measurement of the respiratory capacity of the same subject whose corset has been tightened strongly (column II).

3. Measurement of the respiratory capacity of the woman who removed her corset (column III).

In order to reduce the chances of error, the experiment was repeated three times for each woman and the averages of the three figures obtained were compared with each other.

Sixty percent of those examined wore ready-made corsets; the rest wore custom-made versions. For almost all, the corset was straight at the front and in all cases a little arched;[57] however, it should not be seen that the straight corset arches, especially since it is tighter, and that then the discomfort of breathing produced by the lateral arches exacerbates the discomfort of abdominal pressure.

57 This appears to be contradictory as he is still discussing the front of the corset, though the next sentence seems to clarify that it is a result of the "abuse" of the corset.

85

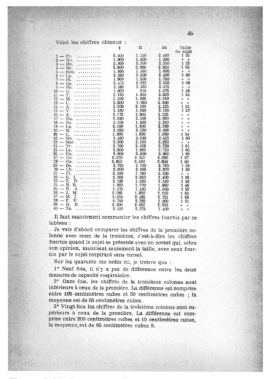

Figure 2.21 Page 85 in Chapter 2 of *Le Corset*.

Translation

Here are the figures obtained:

[2.21]

It is now necessary to comment on the figures provided by this table:

I will first compare the numbers in the first column with those in the third, that is, the numbers provided when the subject presents herself with a corset that, in her opinion, maintains only the size of the breathing subject without a corset.

Of the forty cases noted here, I find that:

1. On nine occasions, there is no difference between the two measures of respiratory capacity.

2. On eleven occasions, the figures in the third column are lower than those in the first. The results vary between 105 cubic centimeters and 30 cubic centimeters; the average is 55 cubic centimeters.

3. On twenty occasions, the digits in the third column are higher than those in the first. The results vary between 200 cubic centimeters and 10 cubic centimeters; the average is 65.5 cubic centimeters.

86

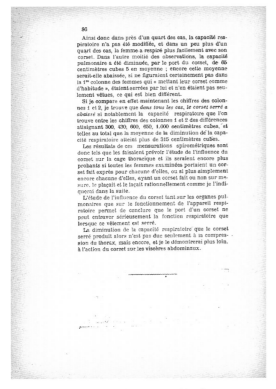

Figure 2.22 Page 86 in Chapter 2 of *Le Corset*.

Translation

Thus, in almost a quarter of the cases, the respiratory capacity was not affected, and in a little more than a quarter of the cases, the woman breathed more easily while wearing her corset. In the other half of the observations, the lung capacity was decreased by wearing the corset by 65 cubic centimeters 5[58] on average; this average would be lower still, if it did not appear in the first column of women who certainly "put on their corset as usual," but if instead the corset were tightened by them and instead of them merely dressing in it, which is very different.[59]

If I compare the figures in columns 1 and 2 now, I find that in any case the tight corset has so significantly lowered the respiratory capacity that we find between the figures in columns 1 and 2 differences reaching 300, 430, 600, 1,000 cubic centimeters, and such in total that the average decrease in respiratory capacity reaches more than 315 cubic centimeters.

The results of these spirometric measurements are therefore in line with predictions made in the study of the influence of the corset on the rib cage, and they would be even more convincing if all the women examined wore a corset that had been custom made for them, or if even more simply each of them placed and laced their corset (custom made or not) correctly, as I will indicate in the following chapters.

The study of the influence of the corset both on the pulmonary organs and on the functioning of the respiratory system leads to the conclusion that wearing a corset can seriously impede respiratory function only when the garment is tight.

The decrease in respiratory capacity produced by the tight corset is not only due to the compression of the chest, but also, and I will demonstrate this later, to the action of the corset on the abdominal viscera.

[End.]

58 65.5 cm.

59 This shows that women who corset "as usual" are…fine. They breathe easily, have the same or better lung capacity, and have no ill effects. This would go far toward proving his point that women who "abuse" the corset have both pain and decreased lung capacity, as he goes on to say about column 2, except that none of the women in the study *were* abusing their corset—instead, the changed parameters of the study subjected them to sudden and abnormal compression, which is a) traumatic, b) as mentioned, abnormal, and c) not long term.

This type of misinterpretation is a fundamental attribution error, attributing the results of column 2 to the behavior of the women, rather than to the actions of the experimenter.

92

est autrement lorsque le corset est trop serré. Alors par la gêne de la circulation veineuse, résultant de cette constriction exagérée, le cœur gauche, c'est-à-dire la partie du cœur composée de l'oreillette gauche et du ventricule gauche, doit faire des efforts anormaux, la dilatation cardiaque peut en résulter. Si le cœur est déjà hypertrophié, le corset vient aggraver la situation (Dr. Butin).

Il est de pratique courante que les palpitations et les syncopes peuvent se produire chez les jeunes filles et les femmes surtout quand elles sont trop serrées dans leur corset. A l'époque de Louis XV où cette constriction était de règle, ces syncopes ou vapeurs étaient d'une extraordinaire fréquence. De nos jours, à la fin des dîners de cérémonie, dans les soirées, dans les théâtres, la syncope est également fréquente ; mais là encore, il s'agit de cas où par coquetterie, les femmes ont voulu se faire très fine taille, cas dans lesquels vient encore s'ajouter à cette constriction exagérée, le manque d'aération et souvent le travail de la digestion. Le simple délacement [sic.] du corset fait presque toujours tout rentrer dans l'ordre.

Le corset peut donc produire des troubles de la circulation par compression et ces troubles de circulation font que le sang s'oxygène moins dans les poumons, il en résulte que la femme trop serrée réalise les conditions nécessaires à la production de certaines maladies de l'appareil circulatoire, de la chloro-anémie en particulier. Mais je tiens à bien le répéter en terminant, il ne s'agit là que de femmes faisant un abus du corset serré, un corset bien fait et bien placé, s'il répond aux desiderata que j'indiquerai plus tard, ne pourra avoir aucune influence dangereuse sur le cœur en particulier et sur le système circulatoire en général.

[End]

Translation

different when the corset is too tight. So by the discomfort of the venous circulation, which results from this exaggerated constriction, the left heart—that is to say the part of the heart composed of the left atrium and the left ventricle—must work harder than normal and cardiac dilation can ensue. If the heart is already enlarged, the corset aggravates the situation (Dr. Butin).[68]

Palpitations and syncopes commonly occur in young girls and women, especially when their corsets are too tight. At the time of Louis XV when tightlacing was the rule, these syncopes or "vapors" occurred with extraordinary frequency.[69] Nowadays, at the end of ceremonial dinners, in the evenings or at the theatre, syncope is also frequent; but here again, these are cases where by coquetry, wanting to show their figures to best effect, women wanted to have the smallest possible waists. A lack of air or lacing tightly too close to a meal add to this problem. Simply unlacing the corset almost always solves the problem.[70]

The corset can therefore produce circulation disorders by compression. These circulation disorders cause the blood to oxygenate less in the lungs, which results in those women in overly tight corsets laying themselves open to the conditions[71] necessary for the production of certain diseases of the circulatory system, chloro-anemia in particular. But I want to repeat in closing, that I am referring here only to those women whose corset is too tight: a well-made and well-placed corset, if it meets the requirements that I will indicate later, cannot have any dangerous influence on the heart in particular and on the circulatory system in general.

[End.]

68 This seems reasonable, but perhaps he should then try to get to the bottom of the epidemic of enlarged hearts?

69 Syncope, or fainting, is an acute response usually, often idiopathic, and generally benign (Jeanmonod et al. 2022; Grossman and Badireddi 2022), meaning it can just happen, and often doctors do not know why, but the patient is fine afterward and has no lasting effects. This, however, remains one of the most common myths about corset-wearing—that people fainted because of the corset, and that it caused the attendant syncope-related issues, such as spikes or dips in blood pressure, high or pale color, languor, listlessness, lack of appetite, etc. Some people have conditions that provoke these symptoms as a chronic response (ibid), but then the condition is at issue, not the corset, and were you to use all of the above symptoms in a differential diagnosis (a practice that was already well in use by O'Followell's time), you would get results ranging from anemia to cancer to anorexia to Postural Orthostatic Tachycardia Syndrome, as all produce similar symptoms on occasion. That is to say that although the narrative was firmly established by 1908 that the cause of fainting was the corset, even then doctors knew of underlying syndromes and illnesses which could also cause it, and to automatically attribute all fainting to coquetry via the use of the corset was incredibly lazy doctoring.

70 There is no indication as to where he is getting this information. We can assume that O'Followell hears these complaints in his role as a doctor and extrapolates outward, but these are broad sweeping generalizations backed up with only an aggregated anecdote—mere gossip, what the modern French would term "on-dit" or "one says." Furthermore, during the era of coal-gas lighting, toxic gas fumes, including carbon dioxide and methane, could replace much of the oxygen in theatres, leading to palpitations, vapors, and syncope.

71 Here again the woman is blamed. This occurs at the end of every chapter, and again highlights the need to take the text in addition to the illustrations, and to pick apart where O'Followell's medical knowledge is accurate, and remains accurate even now, *but* is filtered through his misogyny. We cannot separate the misleading images from the reliance on biased medical sources from the misogyny of O'Followell repeatedly blaming the woman for any ailment that *might* even possibly been caused by the corset. The root of the medical dismissal of women's pain which can be seen in study after modern study (Samulowitz et al. 2018—this is a meta-analysis) is the leveraging of medical authority against the female body and psyche.

From birth to death, our bodies are created as medical subjects—when we are born, a doctor signs off on the birth certificate and declares our sex, and when we die a doctor certifies that death and may investigate its cause. This had been a stable of the French medical system for centuries, and was codified more firmly with the law of 1803 that certified the fitness of practicing doctors (Crosland 2004; Pinell 2011). In between, we are conditioned by society to go yearly for a check-up, as well as contacting a doctor in cases of injury, illness, or conception of a child. As medical subjects, a good subject would follow the doctor's recommendations—take prescribed medicine, do suggested exercises, undergo surgeries and other procedures—because the doctor has more knowledge than we do about how our bodies work. Yet this presupposes a level of other-interest in the doctor, that the doctor is seeing us as a person, seeing our individualities, quirks, and life history, rather than reducing us to an algorithm of data, one of which is the check-box of our sex assigned at birth. In O'Followell, and subsequently in modern medicine, the answer to the question of "what can be done to cure what ails this patient?" is "this patient needs to stop acting like a woman," and what it means to be "acting like a woman" is in many cases based on the erroneous and sexist assumptions of the doctor.

CHAPTER 4

93

En 1792, Bernard-Christophe Faust adressa à l'Assemblée nationale un mémoire *Sur un vêtement libre unique et national à l'usage des enfants,* où il écrit : « La manière de s'habiller de nos femmes est très défectueuse..., les habillements serrés des hanches, partagent pour ainsi dire le corps en deux..., la chaleur de la partie supérieure amollit, affaiblit et gâte les mamelles ; la compression qu'éprouvent les seins dans l'enfance, non seulement les affaiblit, mais en détruit les bouts, une infinité d'enfants nouveaux-nés périssent parce que les mamelles de leur mère en sont dépourvues, dans les cas où les bouts ne sont pas absolument détruits, ils sont au moins en si mauvais état, si petits et si faibles, que la plupart des mères qui allaitent souffrent considérablement des inflammations et des abcès (*sic*) des mamelles. »

Bouvier, dans son *Etude* [sic.] *sur l'usage des corsets,* parue en 1853, accuse un mauvais corset de produire les accidents suivants, parmi d'autres : aplatissement, froissement des seins et maladies diverses des ganglions lymphatiques ou des glandes mammaires, affaiblissement, déformations ou excoriations des mamelons.

Le Dr. Butin écrit en 1900 : « Sur la question des seins, l'hygiène et l'usage du corset ne se rencontrent pas davantage. Ce n'est certainement pas le corset qui les fait naître quand il n'y en pas, et lorsqu'il y en a, il les compromet en ne les laissant pas à leur place naturelle. »

Dans son réquisitoire contre le corset, Mme le Dr. Tylicka affirme que « l'usage prématuré du corset avant que les glandes mammaires aient atteint leur développement parfait, nuit beaucoup au développement des seins, lesquels s'atrophient sous la compression du corset ; les religieuses réussissent souvent à produire cette atrophie à un âge plus avancé. »

Translation

In 1792, Bernard-Christophe Faust[72] sent a memorandum "On a Unique and National Free Garment for the Use of Children" to the National Assembly, where he wrote: "The way of dressing of our women is very defective..., the tight clothing of the hips, divides so to speak the body in two..., [punctuation is sic.] the heat of the upper part softens, weakens, and spoils the breasts; the compression that the breasts experience in childhood, not only weakens them, but destroys the tips, an infinity of newborn children perish because the breasts of their mother are devoid of them,[73] in cases where the ends are not absolutely destroyed, they are at least in such poor condition, so small and so weak,[74] that most nursing mothers suffer considerably from inflammations and abscesses of the breasts."

Bouvier, in his "Etude sur l'Usage des Corsets," published in 1853,[75] accuses a bad[76] corset of producing the following side-effects, among others: flattening, wrinkling of the breasts and various diseases of the lymph nodes or mammary glands, weakening deformities, or abrasions to the nipples.[77]

Dr. Butin wrote in 1900: "On the question of breasts, hygiene, and the use of the corset do not meet either. It is certainly not the corset that gives birth to them when there are none, and when there are, it compromises them by not leaving them in their natural place."[78]

In her indictment against the corset, Mme. Dr. Tylicka states that "the premature use of the corset before the mammary glands have reached their perfect development greatly harms the development of the breasts, which atrophy under the compression of the corset; nuns often experience this atrophy at an older age."[79]

72   Bernard Christophe Faust (1755–1842), "Sur un vêtement libre, unique et national à l'usage des enfants" (1792). This source is digitized and held at the BnF in Paris.

73   Presumably here he is referring to mastitis, but there are other things that could cause the nipples to be destroyed. I do think we can rule out the corset, however, given that temporary uniform pressure (therefore, not pressure that pinches off a section of skin) does not cause necrosis or gangrene. The list of things that could, though, includes cancer, syphilis, leprosy, the aforementioned mastitis, and cellulitis, among others.

74   Nipple size and shape do not contribute to mastitis, which is a clogging of the milk ducts, nor does it contribute to a lack of milk (mastitis does, as in that case the milk *is* there but the blockage may prevent it from being expressed, while nipple size and shape do not). It may make it difficult for a child to latch on, which is one reason nipple covers were often used.

75   Sauveur-Henri-Victor Bouvier (1799–1877). "Etude historique et médeicale sur l'usage des corset," *in Bulletin de l'Académie de médecine* (vol. XVIII, 1852–3). Held only in Paris; not available digitally. No further biographical information available.

76   Again, the "bad" corset.

77   The danger with ascribing such things as "wrinkling," "diseases of the lymph nodes," and "excoriations of the nipples" to the corset is that these are all symptoms of breast cancer. Pitting of the skin, like the skin of an orange, swollen lymph nodes, and sores on the breast, including the areola or nipple, are indications of potential breast cancer, and physicians were aware of this long before O'Followell's writing. An 1878 article in *Scientific American* (Vol. 39, anonymous) describes new patent treatments for breast tumors using percussion (regrettably, this most likely did not work at best and potentially made things worse…) indicating that not only were doctors knowledgeable about breast cancer, but that it had also gone mainstream in the manner of patented inventions.

78   The same argument has been lodged against bras in the twentieth and twenty-first centuries, but has been proven false (Chen et al. 2014).

79   Again, this appears to be apocryphal: as non-medical changes to breast tissue are incredibly under-studied, I am unable to find information for or against Dr. Tylicka's conclusions about childhood breast development or the flattening of nun's breasts. Potentially, and hopefully, with the prevalence of out trans people, we may see studies in the future that have gathered such data. Often when I am contacted by a friend or acquaintance going through their own transition, or asking for a friend, I am asked if such studies exist; they do not, as of yet, and I must redirect them to my own work on corsets and the lack of evidence of compression changing the breast tissue in any meaningful way.

94

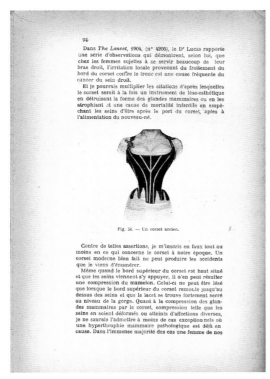

94.

Dans *The Lancet*, 1904, (n° 4205), le D' Lucas rapporte une série d'observations qui démontrent, selon lui, que chez les femmes sujettes à se servir beaucoup de leur bras droit, l'irritation locale provenant du frottement du bord du corset contre le tronc est une cause fréquente du cancer du sein droit.

Et je pourrais multiplier les citations d'après lesquelles le corset serait à la fois un instrument de lèse-esthétique en détruisant la forme des glandes mammaires ou en les atrophiant et une cause de mortalité infantile en empêchant les seins d'être après le port du corset, aptes à l'alimentation du nouveau-né.

Fig. 51. — Un corset ancien.

Contre de telles assertions, je m'inscris en faux tout au moins en ce qui concerne le corset à notre époque. Un corset moderne bien fait ne peut produire les accidents que je viens d'énumérer.

Même quand le bord supérieur du corset est haut situé et que les seins viennent s'y appuyer, il n'en peut résulter une compression du mamelon. Celui-ci ne peut être lésé que lorsque le bord supérieur du corset remonte jusqu'au dessus des seins et que le lacet se trouve fortement serré au niveau de la gorge. Quant à la compression des glandes mammaires par le corset, compression telle que les seins en soient déformés ou atteints d'affections diverses, je ne saurais l'admettre à moins de cas exceptionnels où une hyperthrophie mammaire pathologique est déjà en cause. Dans l'immense majorité des cas une femme de nos

Figure 2.24 Page 94 in Chapter 4 of *Le Corset*.

Translation

And I could multiply the quotes according to which the corset is both an instrument of injury-aesthetics by destroying the shape of the mammary glands or by atrophying them, and a cause of infant mortality by preventing the breasts from being, after having worn such a garment, suitable for feeding the newborn.

[2.24]

I disagree[80] with such assertions, at least as far as today's corset is concerned. A well-made modern corset cannot produce the problems I have just listed.

Even when the upper edge of the corset is high and the breasts come to support it, it can not [sic] result in the compression of the nipple. This can be damaged only when the upper edge of the corset goes up to the top of the breasts and the lace is tightened strongly at the level of the throat.[81] As for the compression of the mammary glands by the corset, compression such that the breasts are deformed or affected by various ailments, I cannot accept this unless there are exceptional cases where pathological mammary hypertrophy is already involved.[82] In the vast majority of cases, a modern woman,

80 Here again we have O'Followell disagreeing with the experts he has brought in to support his own medical assessments.

81 This line is confusing—corsets do not lace to the throat. There was a short period (from 1880–1910, approximately) where collars were extended from the garment all the way up the neck to the chin, and some did have boning in them, but they were not part of the corset (Edwards 2017; Waugh 1954).

82 Here he and I are in agreement—the corset does not cause these lesions, deformations, or atrophies. However, we can see that this is obviously leading up to the repeated accusation of "abuse" of the corset.

95

Fig. 52. — Un corset ancien.

Figure 2.25 Page 95 in Chapter 4 of *Le Corset*.

Translation

even though her corset may be poorly adjusted, does not compress her breasts strongly, first because this compression would be painful and intolerable, and also because current corsets have gussets that cover the breast but do not crush it. One can see this by considering a woman wearing a corset and leaning back, and you will always find that there is space between the mammary glands and the fabric of the upper part of the corset.

What is true is that the corset can be harmful to pregnant women and to wet nurses; for women in a state of pregnancy, because their breasts (see Figure 2.25) gradually increase in size and that the corset that would not be purposefully created for their condition, when it might hinder the glandular development of the breasts; it may be problematic for breastfeeding women because the volume of their glands, and the obligation to present them several times a day to the infant, would prohibit them from wearing a corset that is not adapted expressly for this function.[83]

As for the girls and young women, the brassières that are put on when younger, the corsets that the older ones wear, must be absolutely intended only to support the clothes and even moderate constriction being absolutely

83 O'Followell skips over several logical steps in his urge to jump to blaming the corset and the woman wearing it, including the practice of confinement where a heavily pregnant woman stayed at home and saw very few visitors during her late pregnancy and birth process, thus allowing her to go lightly or un-corseted. There are also pregnancy corsets/pregnancy stays, including one I would like to focus on, N.P.05-984/A.1905.984 from the National Museum of Scotland—photos of which are included at the end of this chapter (see Figures 2.27 and 2.28, below).

N.P.05-984/A.1905.984 is made of linen and dates from the 1700s. In addition to the front-lacing holes, it contains two sets of internal hook-and-eye closures that make it adjustable. The ratios of the bust to the waist for each of the adjustments mean that when it is hooked closed on the smallest setting, the woman would have a very small waist: that ratio is 1:.67. The next step up is only a little larger, 1:.68. However, when laced with the full available space, the ratio is 1:.78, a larger than "natural" waist. The corresponding waist sizes are 55 cm., 60 cm, and 68.5 cm, meaning that this corset let a woman's waist size grow by 80% from the smallest to largest setting. This corset could be worn on the smallest setting at the beginning of a pregnancy, and hooked or laced progressively larger as the pregnancy moved toward confinement.

Due to its style, the corset can be dated to the 1700s. This, therefore, is one of the "old/bad" sets of stays that O'Followell says cannot ever be healthy or good, particularly not when compared to the modern well-made corset. Yet this is evidentially incorrect—women during this time were wearing corsets that could expand and be made more comfortable during a pregnancy, and would not pose an extreme risk to themselves or the fetus.

96

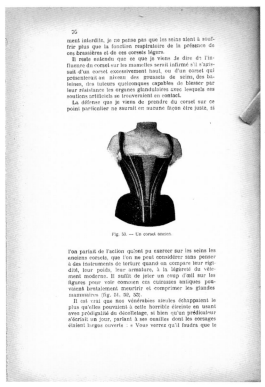

Figure 2.26 in the original contains the following French text and image:

> ment interdite, je ne pense pas que les seins aient à souf-
> frir plus que la fonction respiratoire de la présence de
> ces brassières et de ces corsets légers.
>
> Il reste entendu que ce que je viens de dire de l'in-
> fluence du corset sur les mamelles serait infirmé s'il s'agis-
> sait d'un corset excessivement haut, ou d'un corset qui
> présenterait au niveau des goussets de seins, des ba-
> leines, des tuteurs quelconques capables de blesser par
> leur résistance les organes glandulaires avec lesquels ces
> soutiens artificiels se trouveraient en contact.
>
> La défense que je viens de prendre du corset sur ce
> point particulier ne saurait en aucune façon être juste, si

Fig. 53. — Un corset ancien.

> l'on parlait de l'action qu'ont pu exercer sur les seins les
> anciens corsets, que l'on ne peut considérer sans penser
> à des instruments de torture quand on compare leur rigi-
> dité, leur poids, leur armature, à la légèreté du vête-
> ment moderne. Il suffit de jeter un coup d'œil sur les
> figures pour voir combien ces cuirasses antiques pou-
> vaient brutalement meurtrir et comprimer les glandes
> mammaires (fig. 51, 52, 53).
>
> Il est vrai que nos vénérables aïeules échappaient le
> plus qu'elles pouvaient à cette horrible étreinte en usant
> avec prodigalité du décolletage, si bien qu'un prédicateur
> s'écriait un jour, parlant à ses ouailles dont les corsages
> étaient larges ouverts : « Vous verrez qu'il faudra que le

Figure 2.26 Page 96 in Chapter 4 of *Le Corset*.

Translation

prohibited, I do not think that the breasts need more support that brassieres and light corsets, which do not affect the respiratory function.

It should be understood that what I have just said about the impact of the corset on the breasts would be invalidated if it the garment were excessively high, or one that would present at the level of the breast gussets, or include whalebones, or stakes of any kind capable of injuring by their resistance the glandular organs with which these artificial supports would be in contact.

The defense I have just made of the corset on this particular point cannot in any way be fair, if (see Figure 2.26) we were talking about the action that the ancient corsets may have exerted on the breasts, which we cannot consider without thinking of instruments of torture when we compare their rigidity, weight, and frame to the lightness of modern clothing. One only has to look at the figures to see how these ancient breastplates could brutally bruise and compress the mammary glands (Fig. 51, 52, 53).[84]

It is true that our venerable ancestors escaped this horrible embrace as much as they could by using these low-collared stays prodigiously, so much so that a preacher cried out one day, speaking to his flock whose bodices were wide open: "You will see that it will be necessary that the

84 This is the same type of corset mentioned in footnote 83, corset N.P.05-984/A.1905.984 from the National Museum of Scotland.

97

roi envoie ses mousquetaires par la ville matin et soir, afin de faire rentre nos coquettes dans le devoir et les gorges dans les corsets. »

L'influence néfaste du corset sur les seins a donc été exagérée ou mal interprétée. L'on ne saurait accepter que lorsqu'il est bien placé et fait sur mesure, notre corset moderne si léger puisse produire une atrophie des glandes mammaires, un déviation de la colonne vertébrale, une déformation du thorax. S'il amène quelque accident dans le fonctionnement des organes respiratoires et des glandes mammaires, c'est que ce corset est trop haut ou exagérément serré.

Je tirerai donc de ce début de mon étude médicale du corset, cette première conclusion pratique que le bord supérieur du corset doit être fait de telle sorte qu'en arrière, il atteigne l'angle inférieur des omoplates et que s'inclinant en avant il emprisonne légèrement les côtes flottantes laissant les seins dégagés et le thorax libre.

Si les seins sont volumineux et que l'on fasse le corset un peu plus haut, celui-ci présentera en avant deux goussets qui seront simplement des nids de repos et non des appareils compresseurs ; mieux vaudrait cependant une brassière spéciale pour soutenir les seins que de faire le corset trop montant.

[End.]

Translation

king sends his musketeers through the city morning and evening, in order to fit our coquettes into duty and their throats into the corsets."[85]

The harmful influence of the corset on the breasts has therefore been exaggerated or misinterpreted.[86] We cannot accept that when it is well placed and made to measure, our modern light corset can atrophy the mammary glands or cause a deviation of the spine or a deformation of the chest. If it does cause some accident in the functioning of the respiratory organs and mammary glands, it is because the corset is too high or excessively tight.

I will therefore draw from this start of my medical study of the corset, this first practical conclusion that the upper edge of the corset must be made in such a way that behind it reaches the lower angle of the shoulder blades; if it tilts forward, it slightly traps the floating ribs, leaving the breasts clear and the chest free.[87]

If the breasts are large and the corset is made a little higher, it will present forward two gussets that will simply be nests of rest and not compression devices; however, it would be preferable to have a special brassière to support the breasts than to make the corset too high.

[End.]

85　The corset pictured does not approach the throat in any way.

86　While it is a relief to have him finally say this outright, it has implications for the rest of *Le Corset*. If the corset does not harm the breasts, which are on the outside of the body, and are dense and therefore less squishily compressible than the internal body cavity, how can it be said to do harm to the organs inside? It does change the location of the ribs, and alters the angle of the spinous processes. It does make the thoracic cage more circular. My own work demonstrates the extent of those changes. But if O'Followell rejects injuries to the breasts, he should also reject internal injuries caused by the movement of the much softer, much more mobile, and much more spacious internal organs. Organs, which it again must be emphasized, that move and compress considerably (and predictably) during pregnancy.

87　He ends this chapter by saying what a better corset would look like, and he will return to this subject in later chapters.

REFERENCES

Anonymous (1878). "Treatment of Cancer by Pressure," in *Scientific American*, no other information given.

Balch, E. (1904). "Savage and Civilized Dress," in the *Journal of the Franklin Instituteo of the State of Pennsylvania, for the Promotion of the Mechanic Arts*, 157 (5).

Bendall, S. (2022). *Shaping Femininity: Foundation Garments, the Body, and Women in Early Modern England*, London: Bloomsbury Publishing.

Benson, P., et al. (1963). "Rickets in Immigrant Children in London," in the *British Medical Journal*, no other information given.

Berthiaud, E. (2012). "Le Vécu de la Grossesse aux XVIIIe et XIXe Siècles en France," in *Revue d'Histoire Sociale et Culturelle de la Médecine, de la Santé, et du Corps*, No. 2.

Birchwood, V. (2022). Why Bridgerton Actors Complain About Corsets (From a Daily Corset Wearer), https://youtu.be/3NNKBmFYSH0

Bonnaud, J. (1770). *Dégradation de L'espece Humaine par L'usage des Corps a Baleine : Ouvrage dans Lequel on Demontre que C'est Aller Contre les Loix de la Nature, Augmenter la Dépopulation, & Abâtardir, pour Ainsi Dire, L'homme, que de le Mettre a la Torture, des les Premiers Instans de son Existence, Sous Prétexte de le Former*.

Chandrasekhar, S. (1981). *"A Dirty, Filthy Book": The Writings of Charles Knowlton and Annie Besant on Reproductive Physiology and Birth Control and an Account of the Bradlaugh-Besant Trial*, Berkeley, CA: University of California Press.

Chen, L., et al. (2014). "Bra Wearing Not Associated With Breast Cancer Risk: A Population Based Case-Control Study," in *Cancer Epidemiol Biomarkers*, 23 (10): 2181–5.

Crosland, M. (2004). "The *Officiers de Santé* of the French Revolution: A Case Study in the Changing Language of Medicine," in *Medical History*, 48: 229–44.

Dark Garden Corsetry. (2020). Dark Garden Corsetry Self-Lacing Tutorial, https://youtu.be/nCkh33R51M8

Dickinson, R. (1887). "The Corset: Questions of Pressure and Displacement," in *New York Medical Journal*, no other information given.

Edwards, L. (2017/2018). *How to Read a Dress: A Guide to Changing Fashion from the 16th to the 20th Century*, London: Bloomsbury Academic.

Elsaesser, S., and A.R. Butler. (2014). "Nineteenth-Century Exercise Clinics for the Treatment of Scoliosis," in the *Journal of the Royal College of Physicians Edinburgh*, 44: 240–6.

Fayssoux, R., et al. (2010). "A History of Bracing for Idiopathic Scoliosis in North America," in *Clinical Orthopedics and Related Research*, 468 (3): 654–64.

Faust, B. C. (1792), "Sur un Vêtement Libre, Unique et National à l'usage des Enfants." Presented at the National Assembly of France.

Fouveau de Courmelles, F. (1897). *Traité de Radiographie Médicale et Scientifique*, Octave Doin, ed, Paris, FR.

Gibbs, D. (1994). "Rickets and the Crippled Child: An Historical Perspective," in the *Journal of the Royal Society of Medicine*, 87: 729–32.

Gibson, R. (2015). "Examining the Morphological Effects of Long Term Corseting on the Female Skeleton: A Preliminary Morphological Examination," in *NEXUS: The Canadian Student Journal of Anthropology*, 23 (2): 45–60.

Gibson, R. (2020). *The Corseted Skeleton: A Bioarchaeology of Binding*, Switzerland: Palgrave Macmillan.

Grossman, S., and M. Badireddy. (2022). "Syncope," in the *NCBI Bookshelf*: https://www.ncbi.nlm.nih.gov/books/NBK442006/?report=printable

Jeanmonod, R., et al. (2022). "Vasovagal Episode," in the *NCBI Bookshelf*: https://www.ncbi.nlm.nih.gov/books/NBK470277/?report=printable

Kunzle, D. (1982). *Fashion and Fetishism*, London: George Prior Associated Publishers Ltd.

Langton, R. (2022). Pers. Corrs.

Lawrensia, S., and Y. Khan. (2022). "Inferior Vena Cava Syndrome," in the *NCBI Bookshelf*: https://www.ncbi.nlm.nih.gov/books/NBK560885/?report=printable

Lord, W B. (1868/1870). *[Freaks of Fashion] The Corset And the Crinoline*, London: Ward, Lock, and Tyler.

Newton, G. (2021). "Diagnosing Rickets in Early Modern England: Statistical Evidence and Social Response," in *Social History of Medicine*, 35 (2): 566–88.

O'Followell, L. (1905). *Le Corset: Histoire, Médecine, Hygiène, Étude Historique*, Paris: A. Maloine.

Orchard Corset. (2017). Orchard Corset: Corset Sizing—How to Measure for a Steel Boned Corset, https://www.youtube.com/watch?v=sOQMJaRAPHI

O'Riordan, J. (2006). 'Perspective: Rickets in the 17th Century,' in the *Journal of Bone and Mineral Research*, 21 (10): 1506–10.

Patel, S., and S. Sharma. (2022). "Respiratory Acidosis," in the *NCBI Bookshelf*. https://www.ncbi.nlm.nih.gov/books/NBK482430/

Paterson, M.B., and R. Darby. (1926). "A Study of Rickets; Incidence in London," from *Archives of Disease in Childhood*, no other information given.

Pinell, P. (2011). "The Genesis of the Medical Field: France, 1795–1870," in *Revue Française de Sociologie*, 52 (5): 117–151.

Samulowitz, A., et al. (2018). "'Brave Men' and 'Emotional Women': A Theory-Guided Literature Review on Gender Bias in Health Care and Gendered Norms towards Patients with Chronic Pain," in *Pain Research and Management*, 2018: 1–14.

Steele V. (2001). *The Corset: A Cultural History*, New Haven, CT: Yale University Press.

Stone, P. (2012). "Binding Women: Ethnology, Skeletal Deformations, and Violence Against Women," in *International Journal of Paleopathology*, 2–3 (2): 53–60.

Stone, P. (2020). "Bound to Please: The Shaping of Female Beauty, Gender Theory, Structural Violence, and Bioarcheological Investigations," in *Purposeful Pain*, ed. Susan Sheridan, New York, NY: Routledge.

Summers, L. (2001). *Bound to Please: A History of the Victorian Corset*, Oxford: Berg.

Timeless Trends Corsets. (2015). Corset Sizing Help: How to Measure Yourself for Timeless Trends Corsets, https://youtu.be/jdWSRHOO-C4

Waugh, N. (1954/2018). *Corsets and Crinolines*, New York, NY: Routledge.

White, T., M. Black, and A. Folkens (2011). *Human Osteology*, 3rd edn, Burlington, MA: Elsevier Press.

Figure 2.27 N.P.05-984/A.1905.984 from the National Museum of Scotland, exterior view. "Woman's stays of linen and stiffening with the outside brownish-cream colored and the lower edge deeply dentated with tapering points. English 18th c." Space for a central back busk, but has been removed or fallen out. Front has adjustments for pregnancy: closed by laces, but a set of hook/eyes has been added on a bias, then shifted further across the bust. Dimensions: front 30.5cm; back 37,5cm; side 26cm; bust 87/88/81.5cm; waist 68.5/60/55cm. This is one of the so-called "bad" corsets (stays) that O'Followell mentions, because of the conical shape that tapers to the waist. Photo © Rebecca Gibson, 2023.

Figure 2.28 N.P.05-984/A.1905.984 from the National Museum of Scotland, interior view. Photo © Rebecca Gibson, 2023.

3

THE LOWER TORSO
Covering Chapters 5–9 of *Le Corset*, on the Topics of the Liver, Spleen, Kidneys, Stomach, and Intestines

CHAPTER 5

101

Figure 3.1 Page 101 in Chapter 5 of *Le Corset*.

Translation

The study of the displacements of the liver and its deformations by the corset have been the subject of many works, among which we can mention those of Murchison, Engel, Frerichs, Corbin, Charpy, Glénard, etc.[1]

For Dickinson, the more the corset is worn at a tender age, the more the liver is affected, since it is proportionally larger in children than in adults.[2]

Corbin claims that since the liver is fixed mostly backwards, it is its anterior part that under the influence of pressure can descend in such a way that its normally upper surface becomes anterior and vertical. This is, he says, a constant effect even with minimal constriction. He often saw the liver as cut in half by a vast furrow that Engel once found as wide as a hand; part of it was truly floating.

All those who have done—post-mortem—a number of examinations of viscera, have noted these furrows; during my most recent autopsies, I myself saw on the liver of a young woman deep furrows due to the pressure of ribs. However, I hasten to add that this patient had succumbed to the phenomena of alcoholism, and that her the liver was very considerably enlarged, such that the gland had come to print itself on the costal wall without it being compressed by a tight corset.[3]

The abnormal grooves observed on the liver were reported first by Cruveilhier and subsequently by several other anatomists, including Dr. Charpy, who made a detailed study, from which I extract the following lines, some concerning the costal furrows, the others concerning the so-called diaphragmatic furrows.

The costal groove sits on the lateral and anterior part of the right lobe. It is transverse or weakly oblique in the direction of the ribs, opaline in appearance, scarring, 5–10 cm long at least. It is usually flat, superficial, rarely deep and narrow. The groove is most often unique, or, if one or two others are observed above it, they are simple impressions that get smaller.

Leue,[4] who systematically examined 516 autopsy subjects in Kiel, noted this groove in 5 percent of male and 56% of female cadavers.[5] He never encountered it in subjects under the age of fifteen.

1   Jamaica-born Scottish physician Charles Murchison (1830–79), *Maladies du foie* (1877/1878). Digitized as "Clinical Lectures on Diseases of the Liver: Jaundice and Abdominal Dropsy."

　　Engel, "Influence de la structure du corset sur la position des viscères" in *Wiener med Wochenblatte* (1860). This source is not extant, and without a first name or initial, I can find no biographic information about Engel.

　　Friedrich Theodor von Frerichs (1819–85), German pathologist and doctor. *Maladie du foie* (3rd edn. Paris 1877)—not digitized, but available to purchase.

　　Corbin, "Des effets produits par les corsets sur les organes de l'abdomen," *Gazette médicale de Paris* (1830). Due to no first name for the author, and the fact that this publication is no longer extant, there is no further information about this source.

　　Adrien Charpy, "Article Foie" in *Traité d'anatomie* de P. Poirier, no date given—source extant but not digitized

　　Frantz Glénard, "Mouvements diaphragmatiques des viscères abdominaux," in *Revue des maladies de la nutrition* (1905). This source is not extant.

2   The quote from Dickinson is: "The earlier corsets are worn, the more the liver would be affected since it is proportionally much larger in the child than in the adult. Previous to puberty its weight may be as much as one thirtieth, or even one twentieth, of that of the entire body; in the adult it averages one fortieth," (1887: 32, in my copy). There is no evidence given for this, no studies cited, no autopsy photographs shown, or anything to indicate why having a proportionally larger liver would cause equally proportionally large effects.

3   Based on my own experimentation, and all of the extant "corseted livers" that exist in museums, corseting damage is not what was being described here (Gibson 2020).

4   Leue is not in the bibliography, and neither a first name nor a date is provided. A detailed search for any source matching this information yielded no results.

5   What else could account for this difference? It is such a grave discrepancy that surely there must be something to account for it, but there are no modern studies that indicate such a difference. Perhaps it is confirmation bias.

102

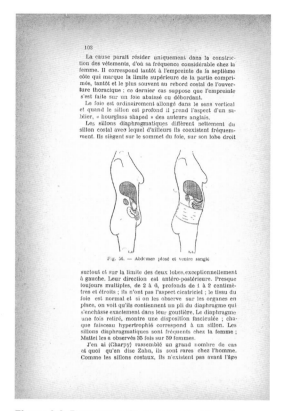

102

La cause paraît résider uniquement dans la constriction des vêtements, d'où sa fréquence considérable chez la femme. Il correspond tantôt à l'empreinte de la septième côte qui marque la limite supérieure de la partie comprimée, tantôt et le plus souvent au rebord costal de l'ouverture thoracique ; ce dernier cas suppose que l'empreinte s'est faite sur un foie abaissé ou débordant.

Le foie est ordinairement allongé dans le sens vertical et quand le sillon est profond il prend l'aspect d'un sablier, « hourglass shaped » des auteurs anglais.

Les sillons diaphragmatiques diffèrent nettement du sillon costal avec lequel d'ailleurs ils coexistent fréquemment. Ils siègent sur le sommet du foie, sur son lobe droit

Fig. 56. — Abdomen ptosé et ventre sanglé

surtout et sur la limite des deux lobes, exceptionnellement à gauche. Leur direction est antéro-postérieure. Presque toujours multiples, de 2 à 6, profonds de 1 à 2 centimètres et étroits ; ils n'ont pas l'aspect cicatriciel ; le tissu du foie est normal et si on les observe sur les organes en place, on voit qu'ils contiennent un pli du diaphragme qui s'enchâsse exactement dans leur gouttière. Le diaphragme une fois retiré, montre une disposition fasciculée ; chaque faisceau hypertrophié correspond à un sillon. Les sillons diaphragmatiques sont fréquents chez la femme ; Mattei les a observés 35 fois sur 59 femmes.

J'en ai (Charpy) rassemblé un grand nombre de cas et quoi qu'en dise Zahn, ils sont rares chez l'homme. Comme les sillons costaux, ils n'existent pas avant l'âge

Figure 3.2 Page 102 in Chapter 5 of *Le Corset*.

Translation

The cause seems to lie solely in the constriction of clothing, hence its considerable frequency in women.[6] It sometimes corresponds to the imprint of the seventh rib which marks the upper limit of the compressed part, sometimes and most often to the costal rim of the thoracic opening; the latter case assumes that the imprint was made on a descended or overflowing liver.

---

6 Correlation does not imply causation.

103

Dans son étude sur les sillons costaux du foie (thèse de Toulouse 1902) M. Soulé décrit les impressions costales sous forme d'empreintes, de sillons simples et de sillons cicatriciels. M. Dieulafé a observé sur une femme âgée présentant tous les désordres habituels de la constriction une incisure profonde du lobe droit du foie, située dans le voisinage du bord inférieur. Cette incisure longue de 25 millimètres, correspondait à l'extrémité antérieure de la onzième côte ; elle détachait du restant de l'organe une sorte de lobe accessoire qui représente le lobe de constriction de Soulé.

Dans les cas de constriction basse, sous-hépatique [sic.] (ceinturons, cordons de jupe, ceintures de corsages), le foie déplacé peut aller se soumettre directement, à l'action de l'agent constricteur ou présenter à l'action des dernières côtes une région élevée de l'organe. Sur une femme présentant de l'hépatoptose et un resserrement très marqué des rebords costaux, le foie était parcouru par un sillon transversal étendu sur tout la face antérieure. Ce sillon correspondait à l'impression du rebord costal sur le lobe droit et sur le lobe gauche, à celle de l'agent constricteur dont la ligne d'action devait prolonger la direction des fausses côtes. (Dr. Dieulafé, prof. agrégé à la Faculté de Toulouse.)

Mme Tylicka n'a pas manqué, dans sa thèse inaugurale, de relever les opinions et les observations relatives à l'action du corset sur le foie, mais pour rester fidèle à ce titre qu'elle avait choisi : *Les méfaits du corset*, elle a pris soin dans ce chapitre, comme dans d'autres, de ne citer que les cas extrêmes favorables à sa thèse, encore que ceux-ci soient pars leurs auteurs eux-mêmes rapportés

Translation

In his study on the costal furrows of the liver (1902), M. Soulé[7] describes costal impressions as having the form of imprints, simple furrows, and scar grooves. Mr. Dieulafé observed on an elderly woman with all the usual disorders of constriction a deep incision on the right lobe of the liver, located in the vicinity of the lower edge. The incision, which was 25 mm long, corresponded to the anterior end of the eleventh rib; it detached from the rest of the organ a kind of accessory lobe that represents the constriction lobe of Soulé.

In cases of low, subhepatic constriction (belts, skirt cords, bodice belts), the displaced liver can go in the direction of the action of the constrictor agent, or present with the action of the last ribs as an elevated region of the organ. On a woman with hepatoptosis and a very marked tightening of the costal edges, the liver was traversed by a transverse groove that extended over the entire anterior face. This groove corresponded to the impression of the costal rim on the right lobe and on the left lobe to that of the constrictor agent whose course of action extended in the direction of the false ribs. (Dr. Dieulafé, associate professor at the Faculty of Toulouse.)[8]

Mrs. Tylicka did not fail, in her inaugural thesis, to note the opinions and observations relating to the action of the corset on the liver, but remained faithful to the title that she had chosen: "The harms of the corset." She took care in this chapter, as in others, to cite only the extreme cases favorable to her argument,[9] although these are by their authors themselves reported

7 This source is not extant, and is listed in the bibliography as 1788 not 1902. Regardless, my own research on this matter (Gibson 2020) indicated that the ribs leave a very slight but distinct scoring on the liver, less than a millimeter deep, and they are in an orientation that is not indicated by the above discussion. Irrespective of the size of the liver, or constriction of the corset, the ribs do not protrude into the body cavity enough to make deep furrows on the liver, and the liver does not exceed the body cavity enough to be damaged by the ribs—there is a layer of fascia between the interior of the rib cage and the abdominal cavity that prevents this. An inflammation or infection of this fascia may be responsible for a foreign-body protrusion into the abdominal cavity, but again, that is not due to corseting.

8 It is extremely telling that there are no photos of this particular intrusion provided by O'Followell. Paul Georges Dieulafé (1839–1911), "Influence du corset sur la rate" in *La Presse médicale* and in *Toulouse médical* (1900, 1901, 1904).

9 Every author in this book, O'Followell included, has cherry-picked their data to support their own agenda.

104

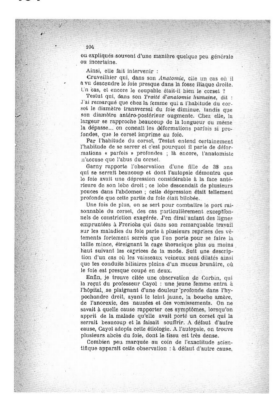

Figure 3.3 Page 104 in Chapter 5 of *Le Corset*.

Translation

or often explained in a somewhat general or uncertain way.

For example:

Cruveilhier who, in his Anatomy, cites a case where he saw the liver descend almost into the right iliac fossa. One case, and still the culprit was the corset?[10]

Testut[11] who, in his *Treatise on Human Anatomy*, says: "I have noticed that in women who are used to the corset the transverse diameter of the liver decreases, while its antero-posterior diameter increases. In her, the width is very close to the length or even exceeds it. . . we know the deformities sometimes so deep, that the corset prints on the liver."

By the habit of the corset, Testut certainly means the habit of tightening and that is why he speaks of "sometimes" deep deformations; again, the anatomist places the blame squarely on abuse of the corset.

Garny[12] reports the observation of a thirty-eight-year-old girl[13] who tightlaced frequently and whose autopsy showed that the liver had considerable depressions on the anterior side of the right lobe; this lobe descended several inches into the abdomen. Indeed this depression was so deep that this part of the liver was bilobed.

Once again, we propose to fight for the reasonable wearing of the corset,[14] particularly those of exceptionally exaggerated constriction. I will say the same about the lines borrowed from Frerichs[15] who, in his remarkable work on liver diseases, speaks several times of the extremely tight clothing that one wears to make one's waist thin, hugging the rib cage at various height according to the whims of fashion. His text contains a description of a case when the venous vessels are dilated as are the bile ducts, which are full of brownish mucus,[16] where the liver is almost cut in half.

Finally, I find quoted an observation by Corbin, who received it from Professor Cayol: a young woman entered the hospital complaining of deep pain in the right hypochondrium, and displaying a yellow complexion, a bitter taste in her mouth, anorexia, nausea, and vomiting. It was not known to what cause these symptoms relate, when it was learned from the patient that she had worn a corset that compressed a good deal and caused her pain. In the absence of any other cause,[17] Cayol[18] adopted this etiology. At autopsy, there were several abscesses of the liver, whose tissue is very dense.

And one finds, at the boundaries of scientific accuracy, this small observation: in the absence of another cause,

10   Here he argues against Cruveilhier—this is French anatomist and pathologist, Jean Cruveilhier (1791–1874), whose *Anatomie Descriptive* runs to a staggering 1,100 pages. The quote is "J'ai rencontré plusiers fois, chez les femmes qui usent de corsets fortement serrés, le rein droit dans la fosse iliaque du même côté. Ce déplacement arrive lorsque, par la pression exercée par le corset sur le foie, le rein est chassé de l'espèce de loge qu'il occupe à la face de cet organe, à peu près comme un noyau entre les doigts que le pressent" (1837: 824).

      Translated, it reads: "I have seen several times, in women who use tight corsets, the right kidney in the iliac fossa of the same side. This displacement occurs when, by the pressure exerted by the corset on the liver, the kidney is driven out of the kind of lodge it occupies in the face of this organ, almost like a nucleus between the fingers that presses it."

   Here we can see that Cruveilhier is actually talking about the kidney, not the liver.

11   French physician and anatomist Leo Testut (1849–1925), *Traité d'anatomie* (1893). This source has not been digitized.

12   Agustin Garny, *Du corset* (Paris: 1854). This source is not extant, and no biographical information is available about Garny.

13 The text uses "fille," so although we do not consider people "girls" when they are thirty-eight years old, the translation is accurate.

14 O'Followell does not propose to eliminate the corset, merely the abuse of it—this is a recurring theme, never fully developed. What is that abuse? Lacing too tightly. What constitutes lacing too tightly? Whatever causes the damage. This recursive thought process places the blame on the woman, and allows O'Followell and others to decide that any practice, even moderate or "reasonable" corseting as defined by the woman, is harmful, abusive, or dangerous, the damage determining the diagnosis regardless of any other possible explanation for damage or disease.

He goes on to say, in the second half of that sentence, that he thinks there are reasonable ways to wear a tightly constricting corset. However, again, this suffers from a lack of definition (or perhaps a definition that would have been understood by his contemporaries, but not ours.) What does he consider tightly constricting? We do not know. What does he consider reasonable wearing practice? We do not know. I can make an assumption, however, based on my knowledge of garment construction—that a tightly constricting corset was one that was designed to be laced closed—for example, a bodice or dress that had a built-in corset and was meant to lace completely closed in the back, giving no flexibility to how a person would wear it.

Despite the fact that many sources exist that *discuss* tightlacing, they do not *define* tightlacing. While the argument can be made that people of the time period would understand what is meant, we are once again entering the realm of *on-dit*—rumor, say-so, etc.—which does not provide any meaningful starting point for understanding.

One issue with the lack of definition is that it rests on many assumptions—not only that people would know what was meant, but that tightlacing was the most common of practices instead of women just using the corset to live their lives. However, we have far more evidence of that than we do of miniscule anatomically abnormal waists. This can be seen in the majority of the corsets I examined for 2020's *The Corseted Skeleton*, including T.96&A-1984 from the Victoria and Albert Museum. In the late 1800s/early 1900s, the most prevalent corset came in two pieces (a right side and a left side) and fastened with a hook-and-eye busk in the front, and lacing in the back. While the hook and eye closed to form an unbroken front to the garment, the laces could be drawn as tight, or as loose, as the wearer wanted. Furthermore, this is one of the larger corsets I examined, with the bust to waist to hips ratio coming in at 1:.92:.81, and the respective sizes being 84cm, 77cm, and 68cm. See Figures 3.18 and 3.19 below.

15 This is listed in the bibliography as Freruchs, not Frerichs. Frederick Theodore Frerichs, *Maladie du foie* (3rd edn, Paris: 1877), as in footnote 1 above.

16 I am unable to find either a contemporary or modern medical example of brown bile in the liver's ducts apart from the formation of gallstones, or as a result of infection (Trotman and Soloway 1975), both of which also can be the cause of the symptoms found in the next paragraph. I did, however, find a fascinating and disgustingly unscientific experiment on constriction on the production of bile in guinea pigs (Collins 1888).

17 When a cause is unknown, the general practice is to label the disease or disorder "idiopathic," meaning of unknown origin. However, as the body was autopsied, as mentioned in the next sentence, liver abscess should have been recorded as the cause of jaundice, the taste of bile in the mouth, and nausea/vomiting. Abscesses are generally caused by infections, and those infections may or may not stem from injured/lacerated tissue, but there is no mention of injury to the liver, just the abscesses—which, if pressed upon by a corset, may indeed have been painful. Much of medical inquiry is circular in terms of determining the proximate (or proximal) cause of a symptom, yet in this particular case it is in no way clear that the corset was the cause, not merely an exacerbating presence. O'Followell goes on to address this in the next paragraph, deriding Corbin's logic.

18 Cavol is not listed in the bibliography, and although Corbin is ("Des effets produits par lescorsets sur les organesde l'abdomen," *Gazette Médicale de Paris* (1830)), no information is available about this source.

105

accusons le corset ! Et cette autopsie qui montre plusieurs abcès au foie, d'où ces abcès ? mais du corset !!

. . . .

M. F. Glenard pense que des causes multiples peuvent, sans le secours du corset, déformer, abaisser le foie ; si j'admets parfaitement, dit-il, les déformations du foie par ce vêtement, il n'en est pas de même de son abaissement qu'on trouve toutes les fois que cet organe a été le siège de fréquentes congestions. Le lobe droit se déforme et s'abaisse, on trouve ce signe en particulier chez un grand nombre d'uricémiques [sic.]. Je ne crois pas que l'action du corset sur le foie soit pathogène sauf en ce qui concerne le lobe gauche ou épigastrique, celui qui recouvre l'estomac ; il force les malades à quitter le corset après le repas lorsque leur foie est congestionné à l'épigastre.

Le Dr. Faure, dans sa thèse de 1892 sur l'appareil suspenseur du foie : *L'hépatoptose et l'hépatopexie*, [sic.] soutient la même opinion : les corsets de tout genre et de tout mode, dit cet auteur, s'appliquent par leur point le plus rétréci, très exactement à la taille, immédiatement au-dessus de la hanche, c'est-à-dire de la crête iliaque, au-dessous du rebord costal. La constriction de l'abdomen, lorsque le corset est serré, se fait donc en avant, tout au-dessous des côtes et, par conséquent, au-dessous du foie. Il tend donc à soutenir le foie, à le soulever même et non à l'abaisser. Il ne peut avoir cette dernière influence que lorsque le foie est déjà descendu et c'est dans ces cas qu'on rencontre sans doute sur sa surface l'empreinte du corset, empreinte qui ne saurait évidemment se transmettre à travers la cuirasse costale. Il est donc probable que les cas assez nombreux où l'on a signalé une déformation du foie sous l'influence du corset étaient, eux aussi, des cas d'hépatoptose mal observés.

Je n'ajouterai, pour conclure, que peu de chose à ces lignes ; j'estime qu'une constriction très forte exercée sur le plastron costal peut produire sur le foie des empreintes costales, mais il faut alors que le corset exerce cette constriction très haut, ce qui n'a pas lieu avec les corsets modernes, même avec le corset cambré ; la cambrure

Translation

let's blame the corset! And this autopsy that shows several abscesses in the liver, wherefore these abscesses? But it must be the corset!![19]

. . . .

M. F. Glenard thinks that multiple causes can, without the help of the corset, deform or cause the liver to descend; if I admit, he says, that this garment has deformed the liver, its descent is not the same as that which is found often when this organ has been the seat of frequent congestion. The right lobe deforms and descends as a result of congestion and this sign is found especially in a large number of uricemia. I do not believe that the action of the corset on the liver is pathogenic except with regard to the left or epigastric lobe, the one that covers the stomach; it forces those who are ill to remove the corset after eating when their liver is congested at the epigastrium.[20]

Dr. Faure,[21] in his 1892 thesis on the suspensory apparatus of the liver, Hepatoptosis and hepatopexy, supports the same opinion: corsets of all kinds and fashions, says this author, apply pressure at their narrowest point, very precisely at the waist, immediately above the hip, that is, the iliac crest, below the costal rim. The constriction of the abdomen, when the corset is tightened, is therefore done forward, all below the ribs and, therefore, below the liver. It therefore tends to support the liver, even to lift it rather than to cause it to drop down.[22] It can only have this last influence when the liver has already descended and it is in these cases that we will probably encounter on its surface the imprint of the corset, an imprint that obviously cannot be transmitted through the costal cuirass. It is therefore likely that the fairly numerous cases where liver deformation was reported under the influence of the corset were also poorly observed cases of hepatoptosis.[23]

To conclude, I will add little to these lines; I believe that a very strong constriction exerted on the costal plastron can produce costal imprints on the liver, but then the corset must exert this constriction very high on the body, which does not take place with modern corsets, even with the arched corset; arch

19   Here we have an instance of O'Followell distinctly disagreeing with his source material, yet if one only relies on the illustrations in *Le Corset*, one would not catch this implication.

20   This is a fascinating distinction, in that even though the cause of discomfort is said to be the corset, there is an underlying illness that is *not* attributed to the corset. Those who are *already ill* are forced to leave off the corset after meals.

21   Jean-Louis Faure (1863–1944), noted gynecological surgeon. *L'appareil suspenseur du foie* (1892), is not listed in the bibliography, and is not digitized. Faure's brother, Jacques Élie Faure (1873–1937), was also a doctor.

22   As there is no consensus on which direction the corset pushes the liver, with Murchison suggesting three different directions (1877: 8), let us return to three facts: corsets were not worn twenty-four hours a day; internal organs are mobile regardless of what fascia/ligament support they have; and pregnancy involves much more organ displacement over longer durations of time.

23   Hepatoptosis, or wandering liver, was documented as early as 1754 by Heister: *Acta Phys. med. naturæ Curiosorum* (Nuremberg, 1754 (not extant)), but again is a syndrome that could have been benign or incidental, not a product of the corset or other constriction or pathology. My own genetic disorder, Ehlers-Danlos Syndrome—a full-body systemic disabling disease where certain variant genes code for malformed or otherwise faulty collagen—can result in the (usually benign, though often painful) movement of otherwise stable organ systems.

106

coïncidant presque toujours avec la partie du tronc que l'on peut le plus facilement serrer, c'est-à-dire la partie située entre l'os de la hanche et les fausses côtes ; or, comme normalement le foie ne doit pas dépasser ce rebord costal, il s'ensuit que le laçage du corset étrangle le tronc au niveau des intestins mais au-dessous du foie, il faut donc, pour que celui-ci se trouve dans la région de constriction maxima des lacets, ou que le corset soit trop haut placé, ou que le foie soit déjà affecté d'une tare pathologique : déplacement, hypertrophie, etc.

C'est ce qu'exprime, sous une forme différente, le Dr. Glénard : La constriction par les vêtements et spécialement par le corset, ne me paraît pas suffisante à elle seule pour abaisser le foie, car j'ai observé plusieurs fois que l'organe très déformé était resté en place ou même était surélevé et rétroversé [sic.]. Il est très vrai que dans la majorité des cas, on trouve le bord inférieur bien au-dessous des côtes et même dans la fosse iliaque ; mais, outre que dans ces case l'abaissement est compliqué d'antéversion et d'allongement vertical du viscère, ce déplacement n'est rendu possible que par la détension [sic.] abdominale qui accompagne ordinairement la constriction. L'intestin grêle prolabé [sic.], le côlon transverse vide ou abaissé, l'estomac plus ou moins disloqué ne fournissent plus au foie le coussin élastique qui le maintenait en place. Il fuit du côté de la moindre résistance.

[End.]

Translation

almost always coinciding with the part of the trunk that can most easily be tightened, that is, the part between the hip bone and the false ribs. However, the liver must not exceed this costal edge normally, it follows that the lacing of the corset strangles the trunk at the level of the intestines but below the liver. It is therefore necessary for it to be in the region of maximum constriction of the laces, or that the corset is too highly placed, or that the liver is already affected by a pathological tare: displacement, hypertrophy, etc.[24]

This is what Dr. Glénard expresses in a different form: constriction by clothing (and especially by the corset) does not seem to me sufficient on its own to make the liver descend, because I have observed several times that the very deformed organ had remained in place or was even raised and reversed. It is very true that in the majority of cases, the lower edge is found well below the ribs and even in the iliac fossa; but, apart from the fact that in these cases the lowering is complicated by the anteversion and vertical elongation of the viscera, this displacement is made possible only by the abdominal relaxation which usually accompanies constriction. The prolapsed small intestine, the empty or lowered transverse colon, the more or less dislocated stomach, no longer provide the liver with the elastic cushion that held it in place. It leaps aside at the slightest resistance.

[End.]

24   In this, we are in agreement.

CHAPTER 6

109

Les auteurs qui ont étudié la question du corset n'ont point signalé beaucoup de cas dans lesquels la rate ait eu à souffrir du port de ce vêtement.

. . . .

Cependant la loge splénique correspond à la zone thoracique qui s'étend de la 9ᵉ à la 11ᵉ cote, zone de compression thoracique possible par le corset.

Il est donc bon de consacrer ce livre quelques lignes à la rate et d'étudier par sa situation dans l'hypochondre gauche cette gland peut ou non se soustraire à la compression du thorax.

Translation

The authors who studied the question of the corset did not report many cases in which the spleen suffered as a result of wearing this garment.

. . . .

However, the splenic lodge corresponds to the thoracic area that extends from the 9th to the 11th rib, the area of chest compression possible by the corset.

It is therefore good to devote in this book a few lines to the spleen and to study its situation in the left hypochondrium, as this gland may or may not escape the compression of the chest.

112

Comment peuvent se produire ces déformations ? Leur mécanisme est assez facile à expliquer. Tout d'abord nous remarquons que, dans tous les cas, elles coexistent avec des traces indélébiles de la compression extérieure sur le thorax et les viscères sous-jacents ; il est tout naturel de les rapporter à la même cause, puisque la rate occupe une situation topographique qui l'expose aux effets de cette compression.

Dans aucun cas la rate n'a subi de déplacement notable ; dans plusieurs observations nous l'avons vue redressée, se rapprochant de la verticale par son grand axe ; comme elle est normalement située, de la neuvième à la onzième côte, son grande axe étant presque parallèle à la direction oblique des côtes, le relèvement de cet organe est nécessaire pour que ces dernières marquent leur empreinte sous forme de sillons transversaux. Dans ce mouvement de la rate, le pôle supérieur s'éloigne de la

Translation

How do these deformations occur? The mechanism for deformation is quite easy to explain. First of all we notice that, in any case, they coexist with indelible traces of external compression on the thorax and underlying viscera;[25] it is only natural to relate them to the same cause, since the spleen occupies a topographical situation that exposes it to the effects of this compression.

In no case has the spleen undergone any noticeable displacement; in several observations we have seen it straightened, approaching the vertical by its main axis; as it is normally situated, from the ninth to the eleventh rib, its major axis being almost parallel to the oblique direction of the ribs, the raising of this organ is necessary for the latter to mark their imprint in the form of transverse furrows.[26] In this movement of the spleen, the upper pole moves away from the

25   He states elsewhere that not all compression is visible and not all visible compression produces disease or damage.
26   There is no evidence presented for this.

113

colonne vertébrale ; en effet, le thorax comprimé diminue tous ses diamètres, la loge splénique est rétrécie, l'organe qu'elle contient est déplacé, mais, arrêté en dedans par le rein, il se porte forcément en dehors.

Translation

spine; indeed, the compressed chest decreases all its measurements, the splenic lodge is narrowed, the organ it contains is displaced but, stopped on the interior side by the kidney, it is necessarily forced toward the outside.

114

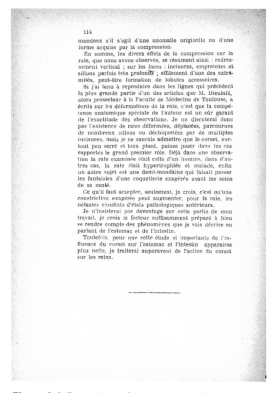

Figure 3.4 Page 114 in Chapter 6 of *Le Corset*.

Translation

. . . .I will therefore not discuss the existence of deformed, displaced spleens traversed by many furrows or shredded by multiple incisures, but I cannot admit that the corset, especially if it is well placed and not overly tight, can play in the cases reported the most vital role.[27] In one observation the spleen examined was that of a man, in other cases the spleen was enlarged and diseased, finally another subject was a half-socialite who put the fantasies of exaggerated coquetry above her health.[28]

What we have to accept, only, I believe, is that exaggerated constriction can increase, for the spleen, the harmful results of previous pathological conditions.[29]

I will not discuss this part of my work further: I believe the reading sufficiently prepared the reader to recognize the phenomena that I will describe when talking about the stomach and intestine.

However, in order for this important study of the influence of the corset on the stomach and intestine to be as clear as possible, I will begin by looking at the action of the corset on the kidneys.

[End.]

27   Here he is arguing against the doctors he has brought in as experts—this is easy to miss if one relies only on the illustrations in *Le Corset*, as he uses this rhetorical tactic often in the text, while using the illustrations without differentiating them via the captions as to whether he is agreeing or disagreeing with what they demonstrate.

28   This negative appeal to women's vanity will be repeated throughout this section of *Le Corset* as he continues to blame the woman for her own discomfort.

29   This seems logical and obvious—pressure and constriction can indeed exacerbate previous underlying conditions. This does not, however, make the corset the cause of those conditions.

CHAPTER 7

118

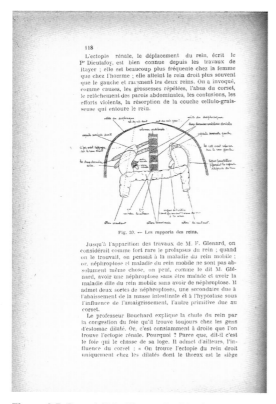

Figure 3.5 Page 118 in Chapter 7 of *Le Corset*.

Translation

Renal ectopia (the displacement of the kidney), writes Professor Dieulafoy,[30] has been well known since Rayer's work; it is much more common in women than in men, affects the right kidney more often than the left and rarely both kidneys. Repeated pregnancies, abuse of the corset, loosening of the abdominal walls, bruises, violent exertion, and resorption of the cellulo-fat layer surrounding the kidney have been cited as causes.[31]

[3.5]

Until the publication of the work of Mr. F. Glenard, kidney prolapse was considered very rare; when it *was* found, one thought of the disease of the mobile kidney; however, nephroptosis and mobile kidney disease[32] are not absolutely the same thing. One can, as Mr. Glénard[33] says, have nephroptosis without being sick and have so-called mobile kidney disease without having nephroptosis. He admits two kinds of nephroptosis, one secondary due to the lowering of the intestinal mass and hypostasis under the influence of weight loss, the other due initially to the corset.

Professor Bouchard[34] explains the fall of the kidney by the congestion of the liver that he always finds in people with dilated stomachs. However, it is constantly on the right that we find renal ectopia. Why? Because, he says, it is the liver that drives it out of where it is lodged. He also admits the influence of the corset: "Ectopia of the right kidney is found only in dilated people whose chest is the seat

30   Georges Dieulafoy, *Manuel de pathologie interne* (1898).
31   Of these listed possible causes, repeated pregnancies are more prevalent among women of this time period than any of the others—see footnote 88, among others, for discussion.
32   It is unclear to what this refers—it appears to be the same thing.
33   Inconsistent spelling is sic.
34   This source is not present in the bibliography, and without a first name or initial for Bouchard, I can find no further information.

119

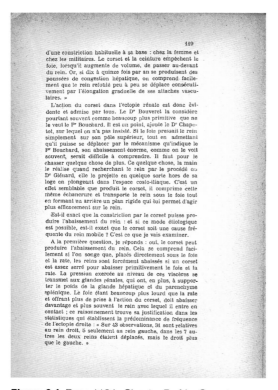

Figure 3.6 Page 119 in Chapter 7 of *Le Corset*.

Translation

of a habitual constriction at its base: in women and in the military. The corset and belt prevent the liver, as it increases in volume, from passing in front of the kidney. . . .

It is true that constriction by the corset can produce the lowering of the kidney: and if this etiological mode is possible, is it true that the corset is a frequent cause of the mobile kidney? That is what I will look at.[35]

To the first question, I can answer: yes, the corset can produce the lowering of the kidney. This is easily understandable if we consider that, placed directly under the liver and spleen, the kidneys are necessarily lowered if a corset is tight enough to lower the liver and spleen first of all. The pressure exerted on these viscera is then transmitted to the renal glands, which also have to bear the weight of the hepatic gland and the splenic parenchyma. The liver, being much heavier than the spleen and offering more grip to the action of the corset, must press down on the kidney with which it comes into contact more and more; this reasoning finds its justification in the statistics that establish the prevalent predominance of the right ectopia: "Out of 43 observations, 31 are related to the right kidney, 5 only to the left kidney, in the other 7 the two kidneys were displaced, but the right more than the left."

35 He has yet to state that the mobile kidney is harmful or causes illness, or indeed exactly what it is.

120

De ce que cet abaissement du rein par un corset serré est possible, s'ensuit-il que le corset soit la cause primitive très fréquente de l'ectopie rénale ? C'est ce que beaucoup d'auteurs ont soutenu, en s'appuyant surtout sur les statistiques que relèvent le déplacement du rein beaucoup plus souvent chez la femme que chez l'homme.

Sur 35 cas de rein déplacé, réunis par Fritz en 1859, on trouve 30 femmes et 5 hommes. Les statistiques plus récentes de Rosentein (1870) et de Ebstein (1875), parlent dans le même sens ; la fréquence de l'affection chez la femme est de 82% pour le premier et de 85% pour le second. Le professeur Tadenat, de Montpellier, a trouvé le rein mobile dans la proportion de 15 pour cent chez la femme, de 5 pour cent chez l'homme ; 120 fois à droite, et à gauche 4 fois.

Pour Mme Gaches-Sarraute : la fréquence des ectopies rénales est telle qu'une femme sur deux en est atteinte. (*Tribune Médicale*, 1895).

J'estime cette proportion exagérée, comme j'estime excessive l'opinion qui met à la charge du corset la grande majorité des cas de déplacement rénal.

Mme le Dr. Gaches-Sarraute qui ne ménage pas le corset—le type qu'elle a créé excepté, et cela se comprend—disait en mai 1895, à la *Société de Médecine publique et d'Hygiène professionnelle* : « Je ne voudrais pas exagérer et prétendre que le corset cause toujours des déplacements du rein et qu'il les cause seul ; je conviens que certains efforts violents, ceux qui se produisent pendant l'accouchement, en particulier, ainsi que le vide laissé par l'expulsion fœtale, peuvent avoir un influence réelle sur la production de ces déplacements, mais je ferai remarquer que les ectopies rénales se rencontrent aussi souvent chez les jeunes filles que les femmes qui ont eu des enfants, et que, d'autre part, ces ectopies s'accompagnent toujours de troubles gastriques, de dilatation et d'abaissement de l'estomac. Je puis donc, sans m'avancer trop, attribuer dans beaucoup de cas cette action néfaste au corset. »

Certes, je suis de l'avis de mon confrère quand elle dit que l'accouchement n'est pas la seule cause du rein mobile ; mais précisément parce qu'elle insiste en faisant remarquer que le rein flottant se rencontre chez les jeunes filles, je suis en droit de vouloir connaître comment, chez ces sujets, peut apparaître un déplacement rénal.

Translation

From the fact that this lowering of the kidney by a tight corset is possible, does it follow that the corset is the very common primary cause of renal ectopia?[36] This is what many authors have argued, relying mainly on statistics that the displacement of the kidney is seen much more often in women than in men.

Out of thirty-five cases of displaced kidney, collected by Fritz in 1859,[37] thirty are women and five men. The more recent statistics published by Rosenstein (1870) and Ebstein (1875)[38] are along the same lines the frequency of the condition in women is 82 percent for the first and 85 percent for the second. Professor Tadenat,[39] from Montpellier, found the kidney to be mobile in the proportion of 15 percent in women, 5 percent in men; 120 times on the right and on the left four times.

For Mrs. Dr. Gaches-Sarraute: the frequency of renal ectopia is such that one in two women is affected (*Tribune Médicale*, 1895).

I consider this proportion to be exaggerated, just as I consider excessive the opinion that charges the corset with the vast majority of cases of renal displacement.

Dr. Gaches-Sarraute, who does not spare the corset—apart from the type she created, and this is understandable—said in May 1895, to the Society of Public Medicine and Professional Hygiene: "I would not like to exaggerate and claim that the corset always causes displacements of the kidney and that it causes them alone; I agree that some violent efforts, those that occur during childbirth, in particular, as well as the emptiness left by the fetal expulsion, can have a real influence on the production of these displacements, but I will point out that renal ectopia is found as often in young girls as in women who have had children, and that, on the other hand, these ectopias are always accompanied by gastric disorders, dilation and lowering of the stomach.[40] I can therefore, without going too far, attribute in many cases these harmful effects to the corset."

Certainly, I agree with my colleague when she says that childbirth is not the only cause of the mobile kidney; but precisely because she insists by pointing out that the floating kidney is found in young girls, I have the right to ask how, in these subjects, a renal displacement can appear.

36   Renal ectopia is mostly congenital (Shortliffe 2019) and produces few (if any) symptoms, generally speaking. The prevalence in women rather than in men remains unexplained, but may have to do with cultural factors including pregnancy, the disavowal of women's pain by the medical community, etc. I wonder if the issue here is actually renal *torsion* which would be very painful, and more likely to occur with pressure from the corset? Regardless, O'Followell's next interjection has him once again disagreeing with his source material.

37   While I cannot find the text itself, nor anything about Fritz, the full reference is Fritz: Archives générales. 5. Sér. XIV. 1859.

38   German doctor Samuel Siegmund Rosenstein (1832–1906), *Die Pathologie und Therapie der Nieren-Krankheiten*.

      Ebstein probably refers to Wilhelm Ebstein (1836-1912), a German doctor most well known for a congenital heart defect which was named after him.

39   Tadenat is not listed in the bibliography, and I cannot find any further information.

40   It would be interesting to discover whether Dr. Gaches-Sarraute were talking about finding the ectopias during autopsy or if she were diagnosing them via palpitation. If it is the former, then it remains possible that the renal ectopia was congenital and merely correlated with the gastric disorders; if the latter, then it might merely signify a mobile kidney again in addition to the gastric disorders.

121

Les grossesses répétées donnent l'explication de certains cas d'ectopies rénales chez des multipares.

Quant à l'abus du corset, dont je reconnais le rôle étiologique, il explique certaines observations de déplacement du rein chez des sujets qui sont serré la taille. Mais comment expliquer la mobilité du rein chez des femmes nullipares ou chez des jeunes filles n'ayant, ni les unes ni les autres, porté de corset, comment l'expliquer chez les hommes ?

Translation

Repeated pregnancies can explain some cases of renal ectopia in the multiparous.

As for the abuse of the corset, whose etiological role I recognize, it accounts for some of the observations of kidney displacement in subjects who are tight waisted.[41] But how can one explain the mobility of the kidney in nulliparous women or in young girls who have neither worn a corset, or explain it in men?[42]

41 There remains a lack of definition about what O'Followell considers tight-waisting.

42 How indeed.

122

Les seules conclusions à tirer de ces différentes considérations, c'est qu'une constriction exagérée produite par le corset peut, s'exerçant indirectement sur les reins, les abaisser et abaisser particulièrement le rein droit en raison de son rapport avec le foie qui offre à l'action du corset plus de prise que la rate.

Cette action néfaste du corset peut s'exercer dans quelques cas exceptionnels, en dehors de toute autre influence, mais, le plus souvent, le corset n'agit que comme une cause adjuvante qui vient s'ajouter à d'autres facteurs étiologiques et pathogéniques, et son influence ne devient

Translation

The only conclusions to be drawn from these different considerations is that an exaggerated constriction produced by the corset can, when exerted indirectly on the kidneys, lower them and lower the right kidney in particular because of its relationship with the liver which offers the action of the corset more grip than the spleen.

This harmful[43] action of the corset can be exercised in some exceptional cases, apart from any other influence, but, more often than not, the corset acts only as an adjuvant cause that is added to other etiological and pathogenic factors, and its influence does not become

43 The lowering of the kidney has not been shown via evidence presented in *Le Corset* to produce harm.

In regard to the word "adjuvant" later in the sentence, a word now not often used outside of oncological medicine—it is a treatment that increases the immune response for the purpose of suppressing tumor growth. Here he is apparently suggesting that the corset is exhibiting the behavior of an enhancing agent—that it is creating a stronger inflammatory response than would otherwise be present.

123

néfaste que parce qu'elle s'ajoute à d'autres causes exerçant elles-mêmes une influence néfaste sur les viscères ; et ces autres causes sont multiples ; à celles que j'ai déjà citées, j'ajouterai les suivantes : une laxité anormale des tissus particulière aux neuro-arthritiques, la diminution de la courbure lombaire qui diminue la profondeur de la loge rénale, les affections utéro-ovariennes, etc.

Que l'action du corset sur le rein soit primitive ou secondaire, un sage éclectisme est de rigueur quand il s'agit de fixer les causes qui provoquent l'ectopie rénale, ce que je vais dire de l'influence du corset sur l'estomac et sur l'intestin le prouvera encore.

Il y a même des auteurs qui nient l'influence dangereuse pour le rein d'un bon corset bien fait et bien placé ; c'est ainsi que dans un article paru en 1905 dans la *Revue internationale de Médecine et de Chirurgie*, M. Legueu écrivait :

« Le corset qui a joué dans la pathologie féminie un grand rôle, auquel on a attribué une foule de misères, est-il responsable de la plus grande fréquence du rein mobile chez la femme ? Je ne crois pas. Trekaki (du Caire) a pu, il y a quelques années, faire des observations chez les femmes arabes qui ne portent point de corset, et il s'est rendu compte chez elles de la fréquence du rein mobile, dans la même proportion que chez les Européennes corsetées. Donc il ne faut pas incriminer le corset dans la genèse de cette maladie, réserve faite, bien entendu, pour l'influence fâcheuse que peut exercer un corset mal fait. Mais, ce qui est plus important à considérer, c'est la forme du buste, qui est très différente suivant les femmes. On peut distinguer les tailles basses des tailles hautes ; or, s'il y a des chances pour que le corset étrangle la taille au-dessus du rein chez les premières, chez les secondes, au contraire, le corset peut être un soutien, un élément de solidité pour le rein. »

[Fin.]

Translation

harmful only because it is added to other causes that themselves exert a harmful influence on the viscera. These other causes are multiple; to those I have already mentioned, I will add the following: an abnormal laxity of tissues peculiar to neuro-arthritics,[44] the decrease in lumbar curvature that decreases the depth of the renal lodge, utero-ovarian disease, etc.

Whether the action of the corset on the kidney is primary or secondary, a wise eclecticism is vital when it comes to fixing the causes that cause renal ectopia. What I will say about the influence of the corset on the stomach and on the intestine will prove it again.

There are even authors who deny the dangerous influence on the kidney of a good, well-made, and well-placed corset; thus, in an article published in 1905 in the *International Journal of Medicine and Surgery*, M. Legueu[45] wrote: "Is the corset that played a great role in feminine pathology, to which a host of miseries have been attributed, responsible for the greater frequency of the mobile kidney in women?" I don't think so. Several years ago Trekaki (from Cairo) was able to make observations on Arab women who did not wear a corset, and he realized they experienced the mobile kidney as frequently as corseted European women.[46] So we must not blame the corset for the genesis of this disease, with reservations, or course, for the unfortunate influence that can be exerted by a poorly made corset. But what is more important to consider is the shape of the bust, which varies greatly from between women. Smaller sizes can be distinguished from larger sizes; however, if there is a chance that the corset will strangle the waist above the kidney in the former, in the latter, on the contrary, the corset can be a support, an element of strength for the kidney."

[End.]

44   It is regrettable that there are many diseases and disorders that result in a laxity of tissue, and none of them is currently referred to as "neuro-arthriti[c]s." However, based on my own experience with tissue laxity and arthritis, O'Followell may have been referring to Ehlers-Danlos Syndrome, which is the category of genetic disorders that result from DNA variations in the genes that code for collagen production. (As noted above, I have this syndrome myself.) Commonly abbreviated as EDS, there are currently more than ten sub-classifications that are diagnosed either through symptoms or genetic testing. The most prevalent symptoms are soft, stretchy, excess skin; nervous system disorders, both localized to the extremities and generalized to the central and peripheral nervous systems; the tendency to sublux or partially dislocate joints throughout the body; and early onset osteoarthritis. Most people with EDS have most, if not all, of these symptoms. This may have been, previous to the naming of the syndrome in the early twentieth century, considered neuro-arthritis.

45   This source is not listed in the bibliography, and no more information is available.

46   See above, re.: correlation does not imply causation.

CHAPTER 8

130

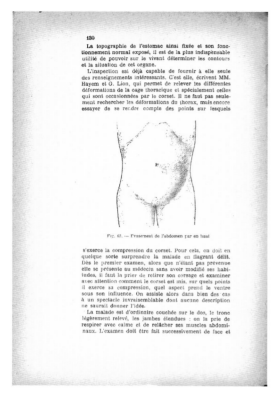

130

La topographie de l'estomac ainsi fixée et son fonctionnement normal exposé, il est de la plus indispensable
utilité de pouvoir sur le vivant déterminer les contours
et la situation de cet organe.

L'inspection est déjà capable de fournir à elle seule
des renseignements intéressants. C'est elle, écrivent MM.
Hayem et G. Lion, qui permet de relever les différentes
déformations de la cage thoracique et spécialement celles
qui sont occasionnées par le corset. Il ne faut pas seulement rechercher les déformations du thorax, mais encore
essayer de se rendre compte des points sur lesquels

Fig. 63. — Évasement de l'abdomen par en haut

s'exerce la compression du corset. Pour cela, on doit en
quelque sorte surprendre la malade en flagrant délit.
Dès le premier examen, alors qu'elle n'étant pas prévenue
elle se présente au médecin sans avoir modifié ses habitudes, il faut la prier de retirer son corsage et examiner
avec attention comment le corset est mis, sur quels points
il exerce sa compression, quel aspect prend le ventre
sous son influence. On assiste alors dans bien des cas
à un spectacle invraisemblable dont aucune description
ne saurait donner l'idée.

La malade est d'ordinaire couchée sur le dos, le tronc
légèrement relevé, les jambes étendues : on la prie de
respirer avec calme et de relâcher ses muscles abdominaux. L'examen doit être fait successivement de face et

Figure 3.7 Page 130 in Chapter 8 of *Le Corset*.

Translation

Observation alone is already capable of providing interesting information. It is this, write Messrs. Hayem and G. Lion,[47] that makes it possible to identify the various deformations of the rib cage and especially those caused by the corset. It is not only necessary to look for deformities of the chest, but also to try to realize the points on which

[3.7]

the compression of the corset is exerted. For this, we must somehow surprise the patient in flagrante delicto.[48] From the first examination, while not being warned, she presents herself to the doctor without having changed her habitual way of corseting, it is necessary to ask her to remove her bodice and carefully examine how the corset is put, on what points it exerts its compression, and what aspect the belly takes under its influence.

47 G. Hayem, "Chimisme stomacal," *Traité de médecine*. G. Lion, "Les signes objectifs des affections stomacales," in Archives générales de médecine (1895).

48 The only reason to do this is if you do not trust your patient to be honest with you.

136

> Que va deviner, sous l'influence du corset, cet estomac dont les diverses méthodes d'investigation que je viens d'esquisser brièvement ont permis de fixer la situation ? Il semble fort simple d'établir l'action de la compression du corset sur les organes abdominaux. Le problème est plus complexe qu'il ne le paraît.
>
> A côté de l'action pathogène de ce vêtement, viennent en effet se placer des causes adjuvantes, prédisposantes [sic.]

Translation

What can be divined, about being under the influence of the corset, from this stomach whose various methods of investigation that I have sketched briefly above and from the solutions which I have suggested? It seems very simple to establish the effect of the corset's compression on the abdominal organs. The problem is more complex than it seems, however.

Next to the pathogenic action of this garment, we must in effect place exacerbating, predisposing causes

137

> pour mieux parler : ce sont les causes de débilitation des parois abdominales et de la tonicité du tractus intestinal : les grossesses, la neurasthénie, la maladie de Glénard...

Translation

that speak more clearly to the issue: these are the causes of debilitation of the abdominal walls and the tone of the intestinal tract: pregnancies, neurasthenia, Glénard's disease...[49]

49 While both Glénard and O'Followell were attempting, with their discussions of various ptoses, to explain phenomenon they were seeing in the body, they also both were far too eager to make the leap from description to pathology. Twenty-first-century studies (Sarangapani et al. 2016; and Bestari et al. 2022) indicate that it is rare to see the stomach fallen far enough out of position to become pathological, and also that it is a symptom of an underlying disorder within the body, which symptom may also cause symptoms of its own. However, two things are stressed in the studies: the rarity, and the underlying disorder. In Sarangapani, the 21-year-old patient had a congenital elongation of the esophagus and laxity of the muscles supporting the stomach, allowing the stomach to descend into the pelvic cavity—something which would never occur ordinarily

without the exaggerated length of the esophagus. In Bestari, the 69-year-old patient had a duodenal tumor which pressed downward on the stomach, obstructing it and causing the ptosis. That patient was placed on palliative care, and soon died, but of the tumor not of the ptosis. Therefore, one must be careful even now to examine a "Glenard's Disease" (Glenard 1899) diagnosis for the underlying cause of the ptosis, which is then the cause of the other symptoms as well.

50   This is unproven/not demonstrated.

138

> Les résistances du thorax ne sont pas égales sur toute sa circonférence ; en arrière, il est absolument rigide, (colonne vertébrale), latéralement se trouve le maximum de sa souplesse, de sa flexibilité ; en avant, il n'y a qu'une échancrure : elle joue son rôle en permettant aux côtés de se rapprocher davantage de l'axe du corps ; c'est aussi une sorte d'issue offerte aux organes qui, chassés de leur loge, tendent à s'ouvrir un chemin en avant dans la partie de la paroi dépourvue de côtes.
>
> La compression va donc agir en déplaçant surtout les parties latérales du thorax. Elle peut se faire de deux manières différentes, suivant la nature des liens.

Translation

The resistance of the thorax varies over its entire circumference; behind it is absolutely rigid (spine), laterally is the maximum of its suppleness, flexibility; forward, there is only one indentation: it functions by allowing the sides to move closer to the axis of the body. It also offers a kind of exit to the organs which, driven from their proper location, tend to push forward into the part of the wall devoid of ribs.

The compression will affect most of all the lateral parts of the chest. It can be done in two different ways, depending on the nature of the closures on the corset.

139

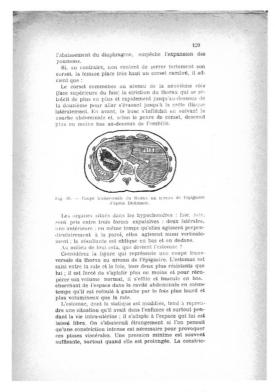

Figure 3.8 Page 139 in Chapter 8 of *Le Corset*.

Translation

If, rather than tightening her corset, the woman places an arched corset very high up on her chest, the following happens:

At the level of the ninth rib (upper face of the liver), the corset starts to constrict the thorax, which narrows increasingly and quickly to below the twelfth and pushes on the iliac crest laterally. Forward on the body, the busk bends following the abdominal curve and, depending on the type of corset, descends more or less below the umbilicus.

[3.8]

. . . .

The stomach, whose stasis is modified, tends to resume a situation it had in childhood and especially during the intrauterine life; it adapts to the space that is left to it freely. It would be wrong to assume, however, that intense constriction is necessary to cause these visceral ptoses. Minimal pressure is often sufficient, especially when prolonged.[50] Constriction

51   If the liver is "heading down and in," then how can it also be pushed upward into the ribs?

140

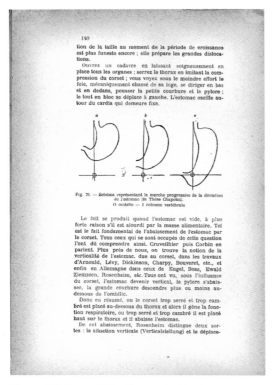

Figure 3.9 Page 140 in Chapter 8 of *Le Corset*.

Translation

while the girl is still growing is even more disastrous; it paves the way for future problems.

Open a corpse, carefully leaving all the organs in place. Tighten the chest, imitating the compression of the corset, and you see with even the slightest effort how the liver, mechanically driven from its lodge, heads down and in,[51] pushing the small curvature and the pylorus; the whole moves to the left in a block. The stomach oscillates around the cardia, which remains fixed.[52]

[3.9]

This occurs when the stomach is empty, but even more so if it is weighted down by the mass of food. This is the fundamental fact of the downward pressure of the corset on the stomach. Everyone who has dealt with this issue must have understood it that way. Cruveilhier and subsequently Corbin have talked about it. Closer to home, we find the notion of the verticality of the stomach due to the corset, in the works of Arnould, Lévy, Dickinson, Charpy, Bouveret, etc., and finally in Germany in those of Engel, Boas, Ewald Ziemssen, Rosenheim, etc. All saw how, under the influence of the corset, the stomach become vertical, the pylorus lower, and the great curvature descend more or less below the umbilicus.[53]

So, in summary, when corsets that are too tight and too arched are placed below the chest, they then interfere with respiratory function; if placed high on the chest, they lower the stomach. Rosenheim[54] has distinguished two kinds of lowering: the vertical situation (Verticalstellung) and the displacement

52 Having performed this particular experiment myself (Gibson 2020), the most one can do with one's hands is approximate a circular compression with no guarantee that one has gotten anything about it correct. Corsets on a living body would produce pressure from all sides. They would produce uniform pressure. The body within the corset would adjust, move within the corset, breathe, stretch the rib cage, and move the organs until discomfort was alleviated, and give signals of pain if the constriction were too tight, in the wrong place, or too prolonged. The donor corpse can merely tell the location of the various organs—which is the limit of what my own experiment set out to demonstrate—not the person's reaction to that location. It is possible to over-stress the ribs on a donor corpse, breaking them, whereas such compression on a living person would result in indications of patient pain well before fractures occurred. Rather than believing the living women who came to him and who did not attribute their discomfort to corseting, O'Followell turned to experiments with limited replicability and no measurable results in terms of health, life functionality, or comfort of the subjects.

    Here again we are subject to the paradox of attempting to determine quality of life from anything other than talking to living subjects. A living subject can tell a doctor whether their corset is comfortable and how taking the corset off changes their symptom profile, while a dead subject can only show that changes have occurred in organ position, not whether the changes were beneficial, neutral, or detrimental. I will also keep returning to this point as often as it is applicable: pregnancy and childbirth were far more impactful in terms of the movement and dislocation/prolapse/ptosis of the abdominal organs, yet women were expected to go through it multiple times and death was often recorded as childbirth/childbed without any other specificity in symptoms or the effects on the body.

53 Burdan et al. (2011) demonstrate the fact that the stomach can sit vertically in anatomically normal humans, dependent on body shape and size. While O'Followell and the people he cites here may not have had enough clinical experience to know this (as shown by the fact that this clarification is from 2011, and more than 100 years passed between O'Followell's work and the re-classification of the location of the stomach), he and the others are once again too quick to jump to pathology in regard to anatomical variation. Not every variation is an abnormality, not every abnormality is pathological or needs explanation, and not every pathology is symptomatic or, more to the point, painful, dangerous, or deadly. It is the difference between "I have observed this" and "I have observed this *problem*," which is a distinction that O'Followell and the other nineteenth-and early twentieth-century authors repeatedly do not make.

54 Theodor Rosenheim, *Uber die Verdauungskrankheiten* (Vienna: 1891).

141

ment par en bas et il ajoute, qu'à l'origine, ils se confondent et souvent se combinent.

Translation

that stems from below and he adds, that originally they meet and often combine.

142

Le corset peut donc produire de graves désordres dans le fonctionnement de l'estomac, mais le corset est-il coupable et la femme que l'emploie mal à propos et hors de propos n'est-elle pas la plus coupable ? Je veux pour l'établir, rapporter ici une observation de la thèse du

Translation

The corset can therefore produce serious stomach disorders, but is the garment at fault here, or the woman who uses it inappropriately and irrelevantly?[55] To establish this, I want to report here an observation of Dr. Chapotot's thesis,

55 Here again we have O'Followell's charge, repeated ad nauseum, that the woman is the cause of the harm by using the wrong corset, or using the corset incorrectly.

143

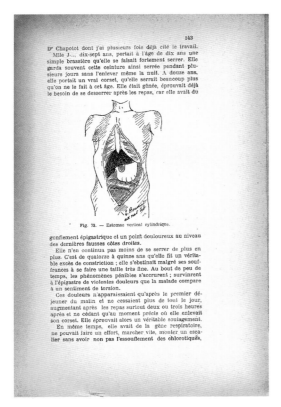

143

D' Chapotot dont j'ai plusieurs fois déjà cité le travail.
Mlle J..., dix-sept ans, portait à l'âge de dix ans une simple brassière qu'elle se faisait fortement serrer. Elle garda souvent cette ceinture ainsi serrée pendant plusieurs jours sans l'enlever même la nuit. A douze ans, elle portait un vrai corset, qu'elle serrait beaucoup plus qu'on ne le fait à cet âge. Elle était gênée, éprouvait déjà le besoin de se desserrer après les repas, car elle avait du

Fig. 73. — Estomac vertical cylindrique.

gonflement épigastrique et un point douloureux au niveau des dernières fausses côtes droites.
Elle n'en continua pas moins de se serrer de plus en plus. C'est de quatorze ans qu'elle fit un véritable excès de constriction ; elle s'obstinait malgré ses souffrances à se faire une taille très fine. Au bout de peu de temps, les phénomènes pénibles s'accrurent ; survinrent à l'épigastre de violentes douleurs que la malade compare à un sentiment de torsion.
Ces douleurs n'apparaissaient qu'après le premier déjeuner du matin et ne cessaient plus de tout le jour, augmentant après les repas surtout deux ou trois heures après et ne cédant qu'au moment précis où elle enlevait son corset. Elle éprouvait alors un véritable soulagement.
En même temps, elle avait de la gêne respiratoire, ne pouvait faire un effort, marcher vite, monter un escalier sans avoir non pas l'essoufflement des chlorotiques,

Figure 3.10 Page 143 in Chapter 8 of *Le Corset*.

Translation

whose work I have already cited several times.

Miss J. . ., seventeen years old, wore at the age of ten a simple bra that she was fastening very tight. She often kept this item tight for several days without removing it even at night. At twelve, she wore a real corset, which she laced much more tightly than one should at that age. She was uncomfortable and felt the need to loosen it after meals, because she had

[3.10]

epigastric swelling and a sore spot in the last false right ribs.[56]

Nevertheless, she continued to tighten it further still, particularly so when she was between the ages of fourteen to fifteen; despite her discomfort, she persisted in making her waist very narrow. After a while the pain increased; the patient experienced violent discomfort in the epigastrium, which she compared to a feeling of twisting.

These pains tended to appear after breakfast and lasted all day, increasing after meals, especially two or three hours after, and stopping only when she took off her corset. She then felt much better.

At the same time, she experienced respiratory problems, lacked energy to make an effort in her life, walk briskly, or climb a staircase without encountering the breathlessness ascribed to chlorosis,[57]

56 A sore spot in or under the right false ribs is most likely a gallbladder attack/gallstones (Mayo Clinic 2022). The presence of gallstones can account for all of this young lady's symptoms: pain, a twisting feeling, pain upon/after eating, relief with the removal of compressive clothing, trouble breathing, walking, and climbing, nausea, and jaundice/anemia. Gallstones were well known, and surgically treated, by 1908, with the first surgery occurring in the 1600s.

57 Iron deficiency (anemia), producing a green/yellow color to the skin.

144

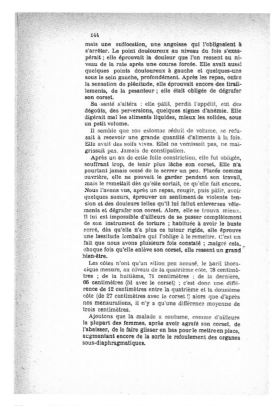

Figure 3.11 Page 144 in Chapter 8 of *Le Corset.*

Translation

which was so painful that she was forced to stop. The sore spot in the liver was exasperated [sic]; she was experiencing the pain in her spleen after forcing herself to run. She also had a few sore spots on the left torso and a few deep sores on her left breast.[58] After meals, in addition to the feeling of fullness, she still felt tightness, heaviness; she was forced to remove her corset.

Her health deteriorated: she turned pale, lost her appetite, was disgusted by meals, had deprivations, some signs of anemia. She digested liquid food poorly, but fared better with small amounts of solids.

It seems that her stomach reduced in volume, and was unable to receive a large amount of food at once. She was extremely thirsty. She did not vomit, nor lose weight nor experience constipation.

After a year of this tightlacing, she was forced to loosen her corset, although she still wore it. Being employed, she could not keep the corset on during her time at work, but put it back on as soon as she went out (and still does so). After a meal, we saw her flush, then turn pale, begin to sweat, and feel so tense and uncomfortable that she had to take off her clothes and unfasten her corset. Then she felt better. Moreover, it is impossible for her to do without her instrument of torture completely; accustomed to having a tightly supported bust, as soon as she is without this rigid brace, she experiences a lumbar weariness that forces her to put it back on. We have seen her do so several times, even though she feels much better every time she takes off her corset.[59]

The ribs have only been slightly damaged the thoracic barrel measures, at the level of the fourth rib, seventy-eight centimeters; the eighth, seventy-one centimeters: the last sixty-six centimeters (fifty-one with the corset); there is therefore a difference of twelve centimeters between the fourth and twelfth rib (twenty-seven centimeters with the corset!) while according to our measurements, there is only an average difference of three centimeters.

Let us add that the patient has a habit, like most women, after having fastened her corset, of lowering it, sliding down into place, thus further increasing the repression of the subdiaphragmatic organs.

58 Had the doctors looked past the corset, this young woman may have been evaluated for aggressive breast cancer.

59 As previously addressed, the corset is the primary undergarment of this time period. This very case study shows that pre-adolescent girls might wear a bra, but a young woman would wear a corset, and become acclimated to its wear based on how it fit her body. In the early 1900s, corsets might still be hand made at home, or they might be bespoke from a corsetier, or they might even be off the rack, with the fit and fashion of the garment depending on its construction—one made for a specific person would, by and large, fit better than one off the rack. However, as it is mentioned that at fifteen years old she was already in a work placement, and thus not independently wealthy/of a wealthy family, we can surmise that she may not have had a well-fitted corset. It is even possible that it was purchased second hand, more for the purpose of having a suitable garment for polite company rather than for a specific fit or style. Regardless of the construction or how it fit, the doctors certainly missed an underlying condition causing her issues.

145

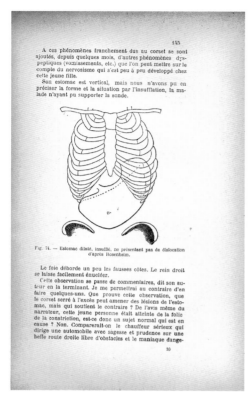

Figure 3.12 Page 145 in Chapter 8 of *Le Corset*.

Translation

To these phenomena frankly due to the corset have been added, in recent months, other dyspeptic phenomena (vomiting, etc.) that can be attributed to the anxiety that has gradually developed in this young girl.

Her stomach is vertical, but we could not specify the shape and the situation by the insufflation, the patient having not been able to tolerate the probe.

[3.12]

The liver pushes past the false ribs a little. The right kidney is easily enucleated.

This observation is self-explanatory, says its author as the study concludes. I will, however, allow myself to make a few more of them. It has been observed that, tightened to excess, the corset can damage the stomach, but who supports the opposite view? In the very opinion of the narrator, this young person suffered from the madness of obsessing about constriction; is she therefore a normal subject? No.[60] Would one compare the serious driver who steers a car judiciously and cautiously on a beautiful straight road free of obstacles with the dangerous maniac

---

60 At this sentence, one would hope that O'Followell is objecting on the basis of having suspected an underlying condition, however. . .

146

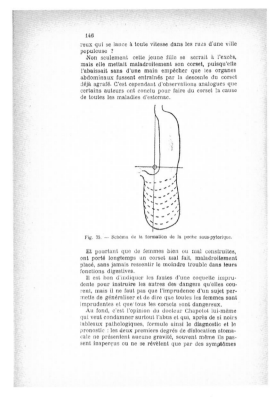

Figure 3.13 Page 146 in Chapter 8 of *Le Corset*.

Translation

who speeds through the streets of a populous city?

Not only did this girl lace her corset too tightly, but she put the garment on clumsily, given that she lowered it without one hand preventing the abdominal organs from being dragged down by the already fastened corset.[61] However, it is from similar observations that some authors have concluded that the corset is the cause of all stomach ailments.

[3.13]

And yet other women regardless of shape or size, have long worn badly made, awkwardly placed corsets without experiencing the least digestive discomfort.

It is good to point out the faults of a reckless coquette[62] in order to alert others to the dangers they run, but the recklessness of a subject should not be used to generalize and say that all women are reckless and that all corsets are dangerous.

Basically, it is the opinion of Dr. Chapotot himself who wants to condemn above all the abuse and who, after seeing such pathological examples, formulates the diagnosis and prognosis as follows: the first two degrees of stomach dislocation are not severe and often even go unnoticed or are revealed only by symptoms

61 . . . in this further sentence, he returns to blaming her for wearing the corset incorrectly.

62 As she was first seen at fifteen years old, of mid- to low-socioeconomic status (assumed due to her place in the working world), the potential to make a wealthy marriage (or at least an equitable one), would have most likely been a goal of this young woman. And a way to make a beneficial marriage was to be as fashionable as one could, which would have involved wearing a corset—the garment women wore in polite society—and having her clothing tailored to fit over. The use of the phrase "reckless coquette" denotes a person who cared nothing for her health so long as she could have her beauty, and its application to a juvenile patient is frankly shocking, even accounting for the time period and the prevalent attitude toward women then. Obviously the young woman *did* care for her health—she went to the doctor to find out why she was ill and in pain. Rather than trusting that she knew her clothing's effects better than they did and looking for an alternative cause for her illness, O'Followell and the other doctors used her as an example of reckless coquetry.

147

de peu d'importance qui disparaissent quand les femmes consentent à se serrer moins.

. . . .

Il est donc urgent, lorsqu'on assiste au début d'une dislocation de l'estomac par abus du corset, de prévenir la patiente et sans tarder de prendre toutes les précautions nécessaires pour écarter le danger et ne pas permettre à la poche sous-pylorique de se former.

« Les plus grands dangers viennent, en premier lieu, de ce que souvent on fait porter aux jeunes filles un corset

Translation

of little importance that disappear when women agree to lace more loosely.

. . . .

It is therefore urgent, when we witness the beginning of stomach issues caused by the abuse of the corset, to warn the patient and to take promptly all the necessary precautions to avoid further problems and not to allow the sub-pyloric pouch to form.

"The greatest dangers come, in the first place, from the fact that young girls are often made to wear a corset

148

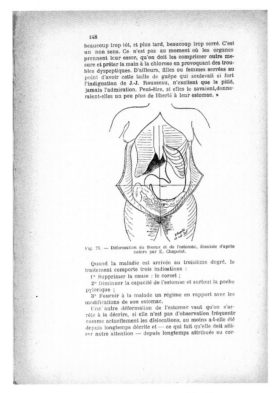

Figure 3.14 Page 148 in Chapter 8 of *Le Corset*.

Translation

far too early, and later, far too tight.[63] This is nonsense. It is not at the moment when the organs begin to grow that we must compress them excessively and lend a hand to chlorosis by causing dyspeptic disorders. Besides, those girls or women who tighten to the point of having that wasp waist that raised the indignation of J.-J. Rousseau so strongly, excite pity rather than admiration.[64] Perhaps if they knew that, they would give their stomachs a little more freedom."

[3.14]

. . . .

63 Who is doing the making, in this sentence? While society as a whole may be implicated, as in the next few sentences he uses "we," it is not society that he condemns. We see in the sentence beginning with "Besides" that he returns to condemning the women and girls for making themselves waspwaisted.

64 J.-J. Rousseau, *Émile ou de l'éducation* (1762).

No page number

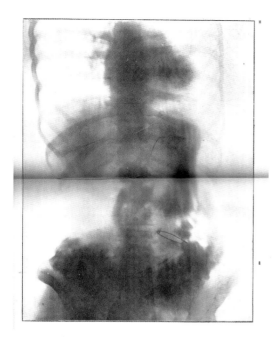

Figure 3.15 Two-page X-ray spread between Pages 152 and 153 of *Le Corset*, No Page Number.

Translation

Annotation page

154

> Je noterai encore ici un accident provoqué par le port du corset, il a été décrit par le Dr. Albert Mathieu qui le signale comme heureusement rare. Dans la dislocation de l'estomac il y a, dit cet auteur, tendance à l'abaissement du pylore et en conséquence coudure [sic.] du duodénum. Lorsque cette coudure [sic.] se fait au-delà de l'embouchure du cholédoque, la bile pourrait de son poids directement tomber dans l'estomac par la première portion du duodénum et le pylore dilaté. De là pénétration dans la poche gastrique d'une quantité considérable de bile (une malade de M. Weil en vomissait deux litres par jour) des troubles accentués de la digestion stomacale et des phénomènes d'épuisement.
>
> Je ne saurais examiner l'influence du corset sur l'estomac sans parler des savantes recherches faites sur ce sujet par le Professeur Hayem et par le Docteur G. Lion, médecin des hôpitaux. Je tiens à rapporter ici les lignes que ces auteurs ont consacrées à cette question car celle-ci mérite que l'on s'y arrête longuement et s'il est vrai que l'excès de constriction soit de l'avis de tous considéré comme très dangereux, il faut que les femmes soient bien pénétrées de cette vérité que la constriction même non exagérée mais habituelle surtout avec un corset mal fait ou mal placé peut être désastreuse particulièrement pour l'estomac.

Translation

I will also note here an accident caused by the wearing of the corset; it was described by Dr. Albert Mathieu,[65] who reports it as fortunately rare. In the dislocation of the stomach there is, according to this author, a tendency to lower the pylorus and consequently cause curvature[66] of the duodenum. When this curving occurs beyond the mouth of the bile duct, the weight of the bile could force it to fall directly into the stomach through the first portion of the duodenum and the dilated pylorus. From there, the penetration into the gastric pouch of a considerable amount of bile (a patient of Mr. Weil[67] vomited two liters a day) can accentuate digestion problems and feelings of exhaustion.

I cannot examine the corset's influence on the stomach without mentioning the scholarly research done on this subject by Professor Hayem and by Dr. G. Lion, a hospital doctor. I would like to discuss here these authors' work on this question because it deserves to be considered at length, and if it is true that the excess of constriction is, in the opinion of all, considered very dangerous, it is vital that women understood just how dangerous it is for their stomach, especially if they are wearing badly made or placed corsets.

65 Albert Mathieu (1855–1917), *Neurasthémie* (Paris: 1892). This source has been digitized, and is available through the Wellcome Collection: https://wellcomecollection.org/works/tjjzhxqe/items?canvas=161

66 Word in text is *coudure*, or sew, but is most likely a typo for *coubure*, or curve. However, "coudure" also means elbow-shaped, and so could indicate an elbow-like bend.

67 This is in the bibliography as Weill. Paul Weill, *Des neurasthénies locales* (Thesis, Nancy, 1892).

155

Parmi les déformations thoraciques et les déplacements viscéraux d'ordre mécanique, écrivent MM. Hayem et Lion étudiant la maladie du corset (*4e volume du Traité de Médecine*) ce sont ceux que l'on rencontre chez la femme comme conséquence du port du corset qui présentent la plus grande fréquence.

Les méfaits du corset doivent être recherchés avec d'autant plus de soin qu'ils ne s'accompagnent pas toujours de déformation manifeste de la cage thoracique et peuvent passer inaperçus.

D'une manière générale il faut considérer le corset comme un instrument désastreux. Il est la cause d'un nombre considérable de gastropathies [sic.] et on ne doit jamais négliger de déterminer avec la plus grande attention la part qui lui revient dans la création de l'état pathologique.

Il représente une sorte de gaine rigide inextensible qui tend à immobiliser tout le thorax inférieur et même une partie de la paroi abdominale, c'est-à-dire toute une région qui physiologiquement est soumise à des variations de forme et de volume en rapport, d'une part avec les mouvements respiratoires, d'autre part avec l'acte digestif. Dans certains cas, son action nocive dépend plutôt de l'immobilisation prolongée à laquelle il soumet ces parties que des déformations qu'il y détermine : c'est ainsi que ses effets peuvent être nuisibles avec une cage thoracique presque normale et que, inversement, le thorax peut être très déformé par suite d'une altération pathologique telle que le rachitisme sans troubles prononcés du côté des organes digestifs.

Cet instrument est généralement appliqué chez la femme à l'âge de douze à quatorze ans, à une époque où le développement corporel est loin d'être achevé. Il devient une habitude et ne gêne plus ou même paraît être un soutien quand il commence déjà à nuire. Les jeunes fil-

Translation

Among the thoracic deformities and mechanical visceral mechanical displacements, write Messrs. Hayem and Lion in their study of corset related ailments (fourth volume of the *Treatise on Medicine*),[68] those found most frequently occur in women as a result of corset-wearing.

The harms caused by the corset must be sought all the more carefully as they are not always accompanied by manifest deformation of the rib cage and might go unnoticed.

In general, the corset must be considered a disastrous instrument. It is the cause of a considerable number of gastropathies and one should always recognize the part it plays in the creation of the pathological conditions of the stomach.

It represents a kind of non-stretching rigid sheath that tends to immobilize the entire lower chest and even part of the abdominal wall—that is to say, a whole region that physiologically is subject to variations in shape and volume, related, on the one hand, to respiratory movements, and on the other to the digestive act.[69] In some cases, its harmful action depends more on the prolonged immobilization to which it subjects these parts than on the deformations it causes: this is how its effects can be harmful with an almost normal rib cage and, conversely, how the chest can be very deformed as a result of a pathological alteration such as rickets without pronounced disorders on the side of the digestive organs.[70]

This garment is usually worn by women from the age of twelve to fourteen years, at a time when body development is far from complete.[71] They become used to it, or even see it as a support, when in fact it has already begun to harm them. Young women

68   While a fourth volume of Hayem is listed in the bibliography, there is no co-written work with Lion, nor is there mention of the corset on page 415 of Hayem's *Leçons de thérapeutique* (*agents physiques et naturels*).

69   A very strongly boned corset prevents bending front to back and side to side, but does not immobilize the musculature, respiration, or gastric movement. One with less or weaker boning will not prevent bending (Bendall 2022).

70   This statement is reductive and unproven, while also contradicting previous statements in *Le Corset*. If deformation is possible without disorders, why flag deformation as a corset-related harm? If disorders can be present due to immobilization, without deformation, why immediately decide that the corset was responsible, despite corset wear patterns often not causing immobilization?

71   This is, of course, skeletally and in other ways, accurate, and would have been well known by 1908 through studies of comparative anatomy—the body is not fully formed until the early- to mid-twenties, and skeletal fusion does not end until approximately twenty-seven years of age. We also now know (although O'Followell would not have) that the frontal lobe does not finish development until approximately twenty-five years of age, and in the twenty-first century we are recognizing a prolonged period of adolescence. However, contrast this with two ideas—the age of "innocence" gone by fourteen (Müller 2006: 94), and O'Followell's own treatment of a fifteen-year-old girl in regard to her corset wear, calling her a "reckless coquette" for wearing her corset (see footnotes 58–62).

156

les perdent facilement conscience de la constriction qu'il exerce : elles sont de bonne foi quand elles affirment qu'elles ne sont jamais serrées, alors qu'elles portent sur le corps les stigmates d'une forte compression. L'action du corset sur le tronc est comparable à celle de cercles de tuteurs sur les arbres ; l'anneau rigide est débordé au-dessus et au-dessous par le développement du squelette et s'imprime sous forme d'un sillon plus ou moins complet. Ce sillon est surtout marqué en avant et latéralement au niveau des points les plus vulnérables, les plus tendres pourrait-on dire, de la cage thoracique.

. . . .

C'est aussi au corset qu'il faut rapporter de nombreux cas d'anorexie nerveuse. Incommodées par leur digestion

Translation

easily lose awareness of the constriction it exerts: they speak in good faith when they claim that the corset never feels tight, while they carry on the body the stigmata of a strong compression. The action of the corset on the trunk is comparable to that of circles of stakes on trees; the rigid ring is overflowed above and below by the development of the skeleton and is printed as a more or less complete groove.[72] This groove is especially marked forward and laterally at the most vulnerable points, the most tender one could say, of the rib cage.[73]

. . . .

It is to the corset that many cases of anorexia nervosa must be attributed. Inconvenienced by the extent to which eating

---

72 Not only is this inaccurate and would have been easily disproven at the time, it is also unsupported by any of the evidence given in *Le Corset.*

73 There is no evidence for this at all, either in *Le Corset* or in my own research.

157

qu'entrave le port d'un corset serré, les malades qui sont presque toujours dans ces cas des dégénérés héréditaires deviennent phobiques et réduisent leur alimentation à un degré extrême.

. . . .

Qu'il soit droit ou cambré, le corset quand il est serré comprime l'estomac et le disloque, et cette action funeste se traduit par toutes les lésions ou troubles fonctionnels que j'ai exposés plus haut. Et ces lésions et troubles fonctionnels se traduisent à leur tour sur le visage « sur la façade » comme dit M. Degrave par des rougeurs, de

Translation

hinders the wearing of a tight corset, the sick—who are almost always in these cases hereditary degenerates[74]—become phobic and reduce their diet to an extreme degree.[75]

. . . .

Whether straight or arched, when tight, the corset compresses the stomach and moves it out of its correct position; this fatal action results in all the functional lesions or disorders I have outlined above. And these lesions and functional disorders are in turn reflected on the face, "on the façade" as Mr. Degrave[76] says, by redness,

---

74 The phrase "hereditary degenerates" refers to the eugenicist idea that intelligence is a directly heritable trait, and that any mental illness, developmental disability, emotional instability, or physical deformity or impairment can be explained by bad breeding (López-Beltrán 2004; Thompson 2021). This, of course, is manifestly untrue and the causes of the above medical issues have been untangled from each other and clarified to be only partially genetically linked if at all, and considerably more likely linked to environment and circumstances. Eugenics, it should not need to be said, is a racist, sexist, classist, homophobic, and transphobic ideology. Yet during O'Followell's time period, even some of the most reasonable thinkers of the day embraced the idea of a certain type of human being as the "ideal" human and labeled it the natural order of the world. This was, after all, the way that the Western world was arranged—you can see my discussion of the idea of "civilization" in *The Corseted Skeleton* (Gibson 2020: 93–116). Being prevalent, however, did not excuse it from being racist, sexist, etc., particularly as it was used to justify the genocide perpetrated against Indigenous Americans and First Nations peoples, the practice of slavery, the subjugation of women (which was most famously decried well before O'Followell by none other than Mary Wollstonecraft in her 1793 book *A Vindication of the Rights of Women*), and, later in the twentieth century, the wholesale slaughter of Jews, Roma, disabled people, homosexuals and other so-called sexual deviants, and anyone determined sub-human by Germany's Nazi Party by way of the system of concentration camps.

75   The reduction of one's diet when eating makes one feel uncomfortable or sick, and is a very logical thing. While O'Followell considers this a case of anorexia nervosa, the concept of anorexia as a treatable medical condition was not very evolved in 1908 when he was writing. The disease, which is extremely complicated and must (currently) be managed with a team of doctors, including mental health professionals and dietitians, was seen as simply a willful deterioration of health done by the woman herself (Gull 1873; Lasègue 1873). It is still often seen, by doctors, patients, and onlookers alike, as a form of control exerted by the patient over their body (anorexia, despite its reputation, is not a disease that affects only women). Note, also, that O'Followell is stating contradictory things here—that the women who experience/express anorexia nervosa are hereditary degenerates, and also that they are purposefully harming themselves by tightening their corset to the degree that they no longer can or wish to eat.

76   Degrave, *La façade in La médication martiale*. This source is not extant, and I can find no biographical information about Degrave.

158

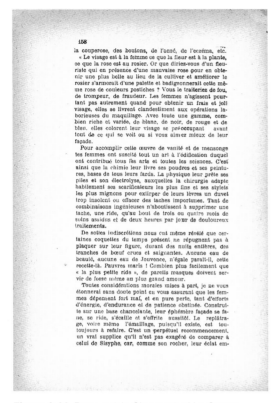

Figure 3.16 Page 158 in Chapter 8 of *Le Corset*.

Translation

rosacea, pimples, acne, eczema, etc.[77]

"The face is to the woman what the flower is to the plant, what the rose is to the rosebush. But how about a florist who, in the presence of a poor rose, wants to obtain a more beautiful one and instead of growing it and improving the rose bush, would arm himself with a palette and brush this same rose with counterfeit colors? You would call him crazy, deceptive, fraudulent. However, women do the same when, to obtain a fresh and pretty face, they exhaustively put on makeup. With a whole range, rich and varied, of white, black, red, and blue, they color their face, concerned above all with what is seen, or if you prefer, their façade.

To accomplish this work of vanity and lies, women have an artform of this edification, to which all the arts and sciences have contributed. This is how chemistry delivers them its powders and paints, bases all of their tints. Physics lends them its batteries and electrolysis, to which surgery skillfully adapts its finest scarifiers and cutest styluses to remove insolent down from their lips or to erase unwelcome stains. Yet so many of these ingenious combinations remove spots or wrinkles only after three or four months of diligent care and two hours a day of painful treatments.

Gossip has even told us that some of today's coquettes do not hesitate to put on their makeup, for entire nights at a time, their faces underneath the paint, raw and rare slices of beef. For those who had no beauty, any water of youth, it seems, would do. Poor husbands! How much easier than coping with "the smallest wrinkle," such masks must cause even the strongest love to founder.

   All moral considerations aside, I will probably not surprise you by assuring you that women spend their time very badly, and are wasting so much energy, on such stubborn pursuits. Built on a shaky base, their ephemeral façade faces, wrinkles, flakes, and crumbles immediately. The plastering, or even the enameling,[78] always has to be redone. It is a perpetual task, a real torment that one would not exaggerated if compared to that of Sisyphus, because, like his rock, their borrowed shine, their artificial beauty recedes and eludes them constantly.

77 While our overall health, including what we eat and how we absorb and process nutrients, can affect our complexion, it is not a one-to-one correlation as is implied here. In the next sentence and subsequent paragraphs, Degrave goes on to decry makeup, as well as cosmetic applications of chemical preparations, shaving, and washing one's face.

78 There is no evidence that anyone from this time period enameled their face.

160

Que le corset trop serré, et de forme défectueuse gêne considérablement la digestion, qu'il favorise la déformation de l'estomac, qu'il soit pour ce viscère un facteur important de dislocation, je l'accorde, et je crois ces faits exacts, je les ai plusieurs fois observés moi-même à des degrés divers, mais que faut-il en conclure, sinon que le port d'un mauvais corset est dangereux et que sa constriction exagérée est très dangereuse, pas plus. L'usage modéré ne doit pas être incriminé, et je ne saurais proscrire pour toutes les femmes l'emploi intelligent d'un vêtement utile, parce qu'il plaît à un certain nombre de jeunes filles ou de jeunes femmes d'en faire un emploi déraisonnable, car ne manquent-elles pas de raison ces pauvres jeunes filles qui, ainsi que le raconte le Dr. A. Mathieu, se retiennent de manger soit pour conserver cette finesse de taille qui fait l'envie de leurs amies, soit parce qu'étant trop serrées elles éprouvent après le repas un malaise plus ou moins considérable d'autant mieux qu'elles ont souvent, à un degré plus ou moins marqué, de la dyspepsie flatulente.

Rien d'étonnant dès lors à ce que les médecins de tous les temps se soient appliqués à signaler les dangers que fait courir l'abus du corset. Les femmes admettent sans discussion, qu'on souffre pour être belle ; avoir gagné quelques centimètres de pourtour de taille les console trop facilement des troubles dyspeptiques qui gâtent leur jeunesse et compromettent leur maturité.

Le médecin qui envisage la question du corset sans passion ne songe pas à supprimer le corset, mais il voudrait que ce vêtement ne fût pas nuisible.

« L'habitude du corset trop serré est le résultat et d'une mauvaise éducation et d'une coquetterie mal comprise. Les jeunes filles, même celles qui en ont le moins besoin, considèrent le corset comme un vêtement dont il est indécent de se passer ; elles prennent l'habitude d'être soutenues par lui, tout le haut du corps reposant sur les hanches par son intermédiaire.

Elles placent bien à tort leur orgueil dans une taille aussi fine que possible : elles ont tendance à croire qu'une taille filiforme est le trait le plus achevé de la beauté féminine. Il ne serait pas mauvais de leur faire savoir qu'il n'y a guère que les jeunes filles et les jeunes femmes qui soient de cet avis. » (*Gazette des Hôpitaux*, septembre 1893).

[Fin.]

Translation

That the corset is too tight, and of defective shape, that it considerably hinders digestion and promotes the deformation of the stomach, that it is an important factor of dislocation for this viscera, I grant, and I believe these facts to be accurate. I have observed them several times myself to varying degrees, but all we can conclude is that wearing a bad corset is dangerous—no more.[79] Moderate use should not be criminalized,[80] and I cannot forbid for all women the intelligent use of useful clothing, because it pleases a certain number of young girls or young women to make unreasonable use of it. Furthermore, they do not lack the reasoning as do these poor young girls who in full knowledge of their actions, as Dr. A. Mathieu recounts, refrain from eating either to preserve this finesse of size that is the envy of their friends, or because wearing corsets too tight they experience after the meal a more or less considerable discomfort all the better as they often have, to a more or less marked degree, flatulent dyspepsia.

The doctor who considers the question of the corset dispassionately does not think of removing the corset from the body, but he would like this garment not to be harmful.

"The habit of wearing the corset too tight is the result of bad education and misunderstood coquetry. Young girls, even those who need it the least, consider the corset as a garment that it is indecent to do without; they get into the habit of being supported by it, the whole upper body resting on the hips through it.

They mistakenly place their pride in [having] as slim a waist as possible: they tend to believe that a filiform waist is the most complete feature of female beauty. It would not be bad to let them know that only girls and young women are of this opinion."[81] (*Hospital Gazette*, Sept. 1893).

[End.]

79 The return of the concept of the "bad corset."

80 This idea of criminalization, even though here used in the negative ("moderate use should *not* be criminalized") echoes the twenty-first century discussion of abortion, birth control, and the right to control one's own body. He goes on to say that he "cannot forbid for all the women the intelligent use of useful clothing, because it pleases a certain number. . .to make unreasonable use of it. . . ." This distinction is one that O'Followell and those he quotes use repeatedly to toe the line when discussing proscriptions and prohibitions: if a woman is reasonable, she will do as they suggest; if she is not, then it is her fault for getting hurt by the corset. Again and again, the responsibility for corset related damage—which again, let us be clear, is unproven—is placed back upon the woman. For a much more in-depth discussion, see Chapter 4 of this book.

81 Here again we see this attributed to pride, vanity, and the very nature of being female, as opposed to a societal concept of the ideal female form, and a practice that at O'Followell's time of writing was in its fourth century.

The end quotation mark here is the concluding punctuation for the quote beginning on O'Followell's page 158.

CHAPTER 9

163

> J'ai montré comment la constriction de la taille agissait sur l'estomac, que résulte-t-il de cette constriction pour l'intestin ?
>
> L'influence de la constriction thoracique sur l'intestin écrivent les Drs. Dieulafé et Herpin, se manifeste surtout par la chute de l'un ou l'autre segment de cette portion du tube digestif en particulier par les déplacements du côlon transverse et des angles coliques. Les cas de sténose relevés par Buy dans son importante étude sur le tube intestinal (*thèse* Toulouse 1901) sont nombreux ; on peut en trouver en tous les points du côlon transverse. Buy explique un certain nombre de cas de sténose par la constriction thoracique ; ce sont ceux où le rétrécissement siège au point où le côlon transverse est en rapport avec le bord costal, il leur applique la théorie donnée par Charpy pour expliquer les cas de biloculation gastrique liée à la contracture musculaire.

Translation

I have discussed how constricting the waist affects the stomach, but what are the impacts on the intestine?

The influence of chest constriction on the intestine, write Drs. Diulafé [sic] and Herpin,[82] is manifested above all by the descent of one or the other segment of this portion of the digestive tract in particular by displacements of the transverse colon and colic angles. The cases of stenosis noted by Buy[83] in his important study on the intestinal tube (thesis, Toulouse 1901) are numerous; it can be found at all points of the transverse colon. Buy explains a number of cases of stenosis by chest constriction; these occur where the narrowing sits at the point where the transverse colon is in relation to the costal edge, and he applies to them the theory suggested by Charpy to explain the cases of gastric biloculation related to muscle contracture.

82 Herpin is not listed in the bibliography, and no biographical information is available.

83 Buy is not listed in the bibliography, and no biographical information is available.

164

Dans la première série de cas le rétrécissement siège nettement au point de la constriction et est provoqué dans un cas par le rebord costal ; dans un autre cas, par l'agent constricteur lui-même, puisque la sténose est-placée dans l'intervalle costo-iliaque. Le rétrécissement est nettement constitué par un refoulement des tuniques muqueuses et musculeuses formant une valvule à la manière de la valvule iloeo-coecale, mais, dans la constitution de laquelle entre aussi la couche musculeuse longitudinale. Ce plissement des tuniques est maintenu, fixé par les couches péritonéale et sous-péritonale [sic.] qui ne participent pas à l'invagination.

Dans la deuxième série d'observations ce sont les circonvolutions et flexuosités imposées à la masse intestinale par la compression qui provoquent l'apparition de points rétrécis au niveau des angles de coudure [sic.] et nous voyons, en outre, le refoulement à gauche de l'intestin grêle et de son meso [sic.], donner lieu aux sténoses les plus accentuées sur le segment du gros intestin qui est soumis à leur pression.

A l'aide de moules reproduisant la configuration de l'estomac chez des femmes de divers âges, Ziemssen a bien mis en évidence la situation de plus en plus vicieuse que donne à cet organe la constriction exagérée et prolongée de la taille par l'abus du corset : le grand axe tend à devenir vertical, l'estomac prend une forme cylindroïde qui rappelle celle du gros intestin dilaté et la région pylorique s'abaisse de plus en plus dans l'abdomen. De cet abaissement résulte un obstacle au passage de la masse alimentaire du pylore dans le duodénum ; de là l'exagération du péristaltisme stomacal, qui devient douloureux quelques heures après le repas, de là la dilatation de l'estomac et l'entéroptose [sic.] consécutive. Aussi, dans tous les cas d'atonie gastro-intestinale neurasthénique de la femme, faut-il conseiller à la malade d'éviter cette constriction de la taille et, dans les cas graves, lui faire comprendre la nécessité de supprimer le corset.

En paralysant la tonicité des muscles de l'abdomen, le corset a évidemment une grande importance pathogénique dans la production de l'entéroptose [sic.] et des autres ptoses consécutives et aussi de la neurasthénie qui les accompagne souvent (Dr. Butin).

Translation

In the first set of cases, the narrowing sits clearly at the point of constriction and is caused in one case by the costal rim; in another case, it is caused by the constrictor agent itself, since the stenosis is placed in the costoiliac interval.[84] The narrowing is clearly constituted by a discharge of the mucous and muscular tunics forming a valve in the manner of the iloeo-coecal valve, but in the constitution of which the longitudinal muscular layer is penetrated. This folding of the sheaths is maintained, fixed by the peritoneal and subparitoneal layers which do are not involved in intussusception.

In the second series of observations, it is the convolutions and flexuosities imposed on the intestinal mass by compression that cause the appearance of narrowed points in the angle of kinking and we see, in addition, the discharge to the left of the small intestine and its meso giving rise to the most accentuated stenosis on the segment of the large intestine that is subject to their pressure.

With the help of molds reproducing the configuration of the stomach in women of various ages, Ziemssen[85] has highlighted the increasingly vicious situation that gives this organ the exaggerated and prolonged constriction of the waist by the abuse of the corset: the main axis tends to become vertical, the stomach takes a cylindroid shape reminiscent of that of the dilated large intestine, and the pyloric region lowers itself more and more in the abdomen. This lowering results in an obstacle to the passage of the food mass into the duodenum; hence the exaggeration of stomach peristalsis, which becomes painful a few hours after the meal, which results in the dilation of the stomach and consequent enteroptosis. Also, in all cases of neurasthenic gastrointestinal atony in women, the patient should be advised to avoid constricting her waist in this way, and, in severe cases, to remove the corset.

By paralyzing the muscle tone of the abdomen, the corset obviously has a great pathogenic importance in the production of enteroptosis and other consecutive ptoses, as well as the neurasthenia that often accompanies them (Dr. Butin).

84 There is very little overlap between the rib cage and the location of the intestine. Now, if organs are moving around due to the constriction of the corset (as I have already granted that they must, though it remains not nearly as impactful as pregnancy), then they may be pressed upward underneath the rib cage, or downward into contact with the pelvic girdle. A recent MRI study shows complete intestinal motility while wearing a corset: https://www.youtube.com/watch?v=pf4s0O9B0NE.

85 Hugo William Ziemssen, *Über die physikalische Behandling chronischer Magen* (1888).

166

Le corset, imaginé tout d'abord pour dessiner la taille et maintenir dans une juste proportion les lignes ondoyantes du torse féminin, il lui est surtout demandé bientôt d'accentuer ces lignes et d'en affirmer la jeunesse.

Comme c'est un agent de constriction, on résistera difficilement à la tentation de pousser jusqu'à la limite où elle est supportable, au moins pendant quelques heures, cette constriction apparemment si peu nuisible.

Mais voilà le médecin qui intervient, il sait combien la compression est funeste aux organes, soit en diminuant leur volume, soit en modifiant leur forme, soit en les refoulant les uns contre les autres, soit en s'opposant au libre jeu que leur fonction nécessite ; il a observé quelles maladies provoque, quelles maladies entretient la constriction habituelle de ces organes et au nom de la conservation de la santé, il ne peut faire autrement que de proscrire le corset dont l'abus suit de si près l'usage.

Le foie et l'estomac sont déformés, allongés dans leur

Translation

The corset, first imagined to draw in the waist and maintain in a moderate proportion the undulating lines of the female torso, was soon seen as a way of accentuating these lines and to affirm the youth of the wearer.

As the corset is a constriction agent, it would be difficult to resist the temptation to push to the limit—where is bearable, at least for a few hours—how tightly it can be laced, which appears to be unharmful.

But here is the doctor who intervenes, knowing how fatal compression is to the organs, either by reducing their volume, or by modifying their shape, or by pushing them against each other, or by opposing the free play that their function requires. He has observed which diseases cause, and which diseases maintain, the usual constriction of these organs. In the name of the preservation of health, he can do nothing other than to proscribe the corset which when used, is then often abused.[86]

The liver and stomach are deformed, lying in the

86 The idea that women's abuse of the corset causes so many disorders masks other potential causes of those disorders, as we have already seen.

167

sens vertical, étranglés au niveau de la taille ; l'intestin est comprimé et ces organes sont entravés dans l'expansion ou les mouvements nécessaires à leur jeu physiologique. C'est une cause permanente de troubles circulatoires, respiratoires, digestifs. Les vapeurs dont se plaignent si souvent les femmes et dont on parlait tant sous Louis XV, à une époque où les femmes devaient avoir la taille fine, n'ont pas d'autre cause. La pauvre femme ne peut manger à sa faim ou bien elle étouffe. Il lui serait impossible de remettre son corset si elle le quittait après un repas. La constriction qu'elle supporte à la condition de rester bien droite parce que la moindre inclinaison du buste l'augmente encore, à condition de peu manger, de ne pas marcher, surtout de ne pas monter trop vite, serait intolérable si le repos de la nuit ne permettait à la femme de s'y soustraire. Les conséquences sur la forme et le jeu des organes deviennent à la longue, irréparables.

Translation

vertical direction, strangled at the waist; the intestine is compressed and these organs are cannot expand or move as they should do. It is a permanent cause of circulatory, respiratory, and digestive disorders. The vapors that women so often complain about and that were talked about so much under Louis XV, at a time when women had to have a thin waist, have no other cause. The poor woman cannot eat enough or else she suffocates from the pressure of the corset on her stomach. It would be impossible for her to put her corset back on if she took it off after a meal.[87] The constriction that she endures in order to sit straight—because the slightest inclination of the bust increases her discomfort even more, provided she eats little, does not walk, and in particular does not to rise too fast[88]—would be intolerable if resting at night did not allow the woman to escape it. The consequences for the shape and play of the organs are, in the long run, irreparable.

87 This assertion assumes a static nature to body, post-meal, but not pre-meal. Certainly a woman who removed her corset after a meal would eventually be able to fit back into it comfortably after digestion.

88 During this time period, it was considered unladylike to eat too much, walk vigorously, or climb anything other than stairs. The behaviors O'Followell believes demonstrate that the corset had harmed the woman were the very behaviors she was expected by society to adhere to if she wished to be thought gentile.

173

L'entéroptose [sic.] est donc une maladie d'allure névropathique ou dyspeptique, caractérisée par la chute, l'abaissement, la « ptose » de l'intestin et comme conséquence, par la ptose des autres organes abdominaux : rein, estomac, foie, rate ; comme la ptose de ces organes s'accompagne toujours de leur mobilité anormale, les maladies qu'on décrivait jadis comme autant de maladies différentes, telles que le rein mobile, le foie mobile, la rate mobile, rentrent donc aujourd'hui dans le cadre de l'entéroptose ; il en est de même pour un grand nombre de cas classés jadis sous le nom de dilatation de l'estomac et qui sont dûs [sic.] à ce que l'estomac est atonique et abaissé du fait de l'entéroptose [sic.].

Translation

Enteroptosis is therefore a neuropathic or dyspeptic disease, characterized by the fall, lowering, "ptosis" of the intestine and as a consequence, by ptosis of the other abdominal organs: kidney, stomach, liver, spleen; as the ptosis of these organs is always accompanied by their abnormal mobility, the diseases that were once described as so many different ailments, such as the mobile kidney, the mobile liver, the mobile spleen, are now part of enteroptosis; the same is true for a large number of cases formerly classified as stomach dilation and which are due to the fact that the stomach is atonic and lowered due to enteroptosis.

175

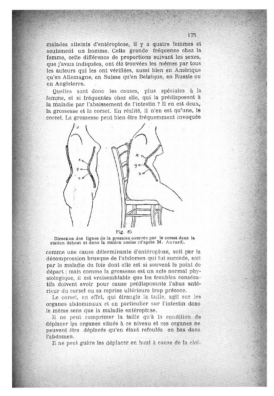

Figure 3.17 Page 175 in Chapter 9 of *Le Corset*.

Translation

What are the causes, more specific in women, and so frequent in them, that predispose them to the pathology that lowers the intestine? There are two: pregnancy and the corset.[89] Pregnancy may well be frequently invoked

[3.17]

as a determining cause of enteroptosis, either by the sudden decompression of the abdomen that follows it, or by the liver disease of which it is so often the starting point; but since pregnancy is a normal physiological act,[90] it is likely that the consequential disorders must have as a underlying cause the previous abuse of the corset or the subsequent premature resumption of it.

It is the corset, in fact, which strangles the waist, acts on the abdominal organs and in particular on the intestine in the same direction as enteroptosis disease.

89 Important to note here is the fact that while motherhood was idealized by the good majority of people during this time period (and still is), there were limited ways to prevent or contravene pregnancy, and most of those ways were, in 1908, either illegal or extremely dangerous. Condoms were often illegal to purchase, and the standard model of them was generally used more than once, leading to the spread of STIs/STDs. Contraceptive powders or douches were often made of corrosive chemicals or toxic substances (Chandrasekhar 1981). And there remained societal pressure to become a mother, and to do so often, so the fact that pregnancy was "so frequent in her" does not automatically indicate that it was also "special to the woman," unless O'Followell meant special in the manner of "peculiar to" or "exclusively experienced by."

90 During this time period, with the focus on hospitalizations for childbirth instead of midwifes and home births, maternal mortality rates soared (Louden 1986): https://pubmed.ncbi.nlm.nih.gov/3511335/ See also Fitzharris 2017.

REFERENCES

Bendall, S. (2022). *Shaping Femininity: Foundation Garments, the Body, and Women in Early Modern England*, London: Bloomsbury Visual Arts.

Bestari, M., et al. (2022). "Gastroptosis due to Gastric Outlet Obstruction Secondary to Duodenal Tumor: Glenard's Disease Revisited," in *Case Reports in Gastroenterology*, 16 (1): 89–93.

Burdan, F., et al. (2011). "Anatomical Classification of the Shape and Topography of the Stomach," in *Surgical Radiology Anatomy*, 34 (2): 171–8.

Chandrasekhar, S. (1981). *"A Dirty, Filthy Book": The Writings of Charles Knowlton and Annie Besant on Reproductive Physiology and Birth Control and an Account of the Bradlaugh-Besant Trial*, Berkeley, CA: University of California Press.

Collins, W. (1888). "The Effect of Tight Lacing upon the Secretion of Bile," in *The Lancet*, March 17, 1888, p. 518.

Cruveilhier, J. (1837). *Anatomie Descriptive*. Brussels: Meline, Cans, et Compagnie.

Dickinson, R. (1887). "The Corset: Questions of Pressure and Displacement," in *New York Medical Journal*, no further information given.

Fitzharris, L. (2017). *The Butchering Art: Joseph Lister's Quest to Transform the Grisly World of Victorian Medicine*. New York, NY: Macmillan.

Gibson, R. (2020). *The Corseted Skeleton: A Bioarchaeology of Binding*, Cham, Switzerland: Palgrave Macmillan.

Glenard, F. (1899). *Les Ptoses Viscérales, Diagnostic et Nosographie*.

Gull, W. (1873). "Anorexia Nervosa (Apepsia Hysterica, Anorexia Hysterica)," reprinted in *Obesity Research*, 5 (5): 498–502.

Lasègue, E.-C. (1873). "De l'Anorexie Hystérique," in the *Journal Française de Psychiatrie*, (32): 3–8.

López-Beltrán, C. (2004). "In the Cradle of Heredity; French Physicians and L'Hérédité Naturelle in the Early 19th Century," in *Journal of the History of Biology*, 37 (1): 39–72.

Loudon, I. (1986). "Deaths in Childbed from the Eighteenth Century to 1935," in *Medical History*, 30: 1–41.

Lucy's Corsetry. (2014). "MRI Scans in a Corset: Results," https://www.youtube.com/watch?v=pf4s0O9B0NE

Mayo Clinic. (2022). https://www.mayoclinic.org/diseases-conditions/gallstones/symptoms-causes/syc-20354214

Metropolitan Museum. (2022). https://www.metmuseum.org/art/collection/search/87018

Müller, A. (2006). *Fashioning Childhood in the Eighteenth Century: Age and Identity*, New York, NY: Routledge.

Murchison, C. (1877). "Clinical Lectures on Diseases of the Liver, Jaundice, and Abdominal Dropsy: Including the Croonian Lectures on Functional Derangements of the Liver," Delivered at the Royal College of Physicians in 1874, New York, NY: W. Wood.

Rousseau, J.-J. (1762). *Oeuvres de J.J. Rousseau de Genève, Volume 8*, "Émile ou de l'éducation," p. 23.

Sarangapani, A., et al. (2016). "Glenard's Disease," in the *Archives of Medicine and Health Sciences*, 4 (1): 153–4.

Shortliffe, L. (2019). "Ectopic Kidney," from the *NIH National Institute of Diabetes and Digestive and Kidney Diseases*: https://www.niddk.nih.gov/health-information/kidney-disease/children/

Thompson, M. (2021). "'The Offspring of Drunkards': Gender, Welfare, and the Eugenic Politics of Birth Control and Alcohol Reform in the United States," in the *Journal of Law, Medicine, and Ethics*, vol. 49: 357–64.

Trotman, B., and R. Soloway. (1975). "Pigment vs. Cholesterol Cholelithiasis: Clinical and Epidemiological Aspects," in *American Journal of Digestive Diseases*, 20 (8): 735–40.

Wollstonecraft, M. (1793). *A Vindication of the Rights of Women with Strictures on Political and Moral Subjects*, Dublin, IR: J. Stockdale.

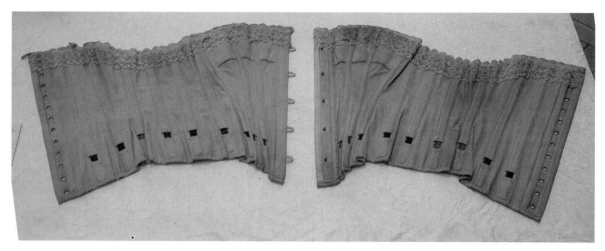

Figure 3.18 T.96&A-1984 from the Victoria and Albert Museum, exterior view. This corset was part of a lot donated by Mrs. S. Sinclair on behalf of the corsetier M. Yanovsky Ltd., which was closing down in 1984. Located at 41 Edgware Road, London, M. Yanovsky donated nine corsets, which create a representative sample of relatively standard or ordinary Victorian era corsets. Made in the year 1900 of plain white cotton, silk ribbon, and spring steel boning. Dimensions: bust 84cm; waist 77cm; hips 68cm; front 32.5cm; side 25cm; rear 31cm. Ratio of bust/waist/hips: 1:.92:.81. Photo © Rebecca Gibson, 2023.

Figure 3.19 T.96&A-1984 from the Victoria and Albert Museum, interior view. Photo © Rebecca Gibson, 2023.

4

POPULATION CONTROL, MISCARRIAGES, AND ABORTIONS
Covering Chapter 10 of *Le Corset*, on the Topic of the Genitals and Reproductive System

CHAPTER 10

183

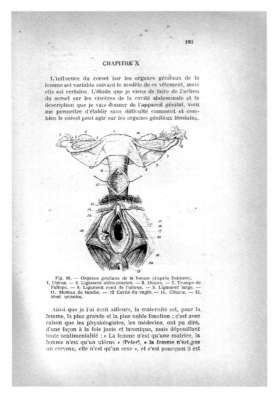

Figure 4.1 Page 183 in Chapter 10 of *Le Corset*.

Translation

[4.1]

[1]As I have written elsewhere, motherhood is, for women, the greatest and noblest function; it is with good reason that physiologists were able to say, in a way that was both fair and laconic, but free of sentimentality: "The woman is only a matrix, the woman is only a uterus" (Peter),[2] "the woman is not a brain, she is only a sex," and that is why Peter is

1 I began my conceptualization of these annotations well before the overturn of Roe v. Wade occurred and gave me such fodder for modern use of language regarding abortion. Let us begin.

In previous annotations, I have pointed out misogyny where I found it—subtle or overt—but to do so for this segment of the book which covers only one chapter, Chapter 10 of *Le Corset*, would be repetitive. I have had to come up with a new strategy.

Rather than delve into the history of gynecology too deeply, which I will come back to in the Afterword for this book, (for that, see Wilson 1993, *Women and Medicine in the French Enlightenment: The Debate over "Maladies des Femmes,"* as well as Owens 2018, among others), I will be pairing the misogyny, gynecological inaccuracies, disparagement of women's intelligence and potential, and other remarks by O'Followell and the doctors he quotes, with quotes from and articles about anti-abortion/pro-forced birth people from 2022, the year in which I am writing.

I regret that this will not be difficult.

It will not be a strain on my researching abilities to find ample quotes from politicians, pundits, clergy, and others, who, as O'Followell does in this very first sentence, reduce people with uteruses to mindless vessels, brood mares, milch cows, sub-human beings with no inner life, fit only to bear children. This hatred of non-breeding people, this loathing of people who control their own bodies, access to them, and what goes into or comes out of them, is being codified in US laws, preached in US churches, reified in US courts, hissed, screamed, growled, and cackled from newspaper and website headlines. It is being bantered at us on dates, screeched at us on the way to OB/GYN offices, repeated to us by people we thought we could trust. It is becoming foundational. This chapter will show you but a little of that. I hope it will anger you as much as it does me. I hope it will move you to action.

2   While this source is not listed in the bibliography, there is reason to believe that O'Followell did not have access to it either, merely lifting the passage in its entirety from another publication. Unable to find the Peter text, I put part of the quote, "**La femme n'est qu'une matrice, la femme n'est qu'un utérus**" into Google, to see if there might be a Google Books entry that I had missed. There was, but it was not Peter.

Published in 1902, *Hygiene de La Femme: Enfant—Jeune Fille—Femme—Mère et Aïule*, by Drs Platon and Sepet, contains this passage: ont **la maternité est la plus grande et la plus noble fonction** , à tel point **que Peter a pu dire**, dans une phrase précise **mais dénuée de toute sentimentalité** : "**La femme n'est pas un a cerveau, elle n'est qu'un sexe; la femme n'est qu'une matrice, la femme n'est qu'un utérus**."

Six years later, in 1908 in *Le Corset*, O'Followell writes: Ainsi que je l'ai écrit ailleurs, **la maternité est**, pour la femme, **la plus grande et la plus noble fonction** ; c'est avec raison que les physiologistes, les médicins, **ont pu dire**, d'une façon à la fois juste et laconique, **mais dépouillant toute sentimentalité** : " **La femme n'est qu'une matrice, la femme n'est qu'un utérus**" (Peter)," **la femme n'est pas un cerveau, elle n'est qu'un sexe**."

The passages are not identical, but I have highlighted in bold the way that they are close enough to show that O'Followell lifted not only the Peter quote, reversing the order of the text in the process, but the surrounding material. It does lead one to wonder how many other texts O'Followell plagiarized instead of quoting.

184

> particulièrement intéressant de rechercher si le corset gêne ou non le bon fonctionnement de l'utérus et de ses annexes.

Translation

particularly interested to investigate whether or not the corset interferes with the proper functioning of the uterus and its appendages.[3]

3 August 6, 2022: "The umbilical chord [sic] and placenta do not directly connect to the woman," –Salt Lake County Councilman Dave Alvord writes, a-factually (in Cruz 2022a).

189

> On peut définir la femme « un utérus servie par des organes ». La vie génitale joue, en effet, le principal rôle dans l'organisme de la femme. Aussi, est-ce bien dans l'utérus et autour de l'utérus qu'il faut chercher les causes habituelles de ses souffrances.

Translation

A woman can be defined as "a uterus served by organs."[4] Genital life plays the main role in the female body.[5] Also, it is in the womb and around the uterus that we must look for the usual causes of women's suffering.[6]

4 August 10, 2022: "My tweet was not a biology lesson but was intended to simply point out that a baby, the umbilical cord, and the placenta are part of a new and developing body, with its own unique DNA and gender, separate from the mother. Abortion involves the body of more than one human life. I stand by the tweet," –ibid.

The rejection of the idea of a woman being merely a womb, and that womb being unconnected to the rest of her body, can be seen throughout French medical history, which has included women and their perspectives since the 1600s (Broomhall 2004). Midwives, in particular, would be well aware of how the umbilical cord and placenta "worked" and were attached to the woman. What is so startling about the notion that the womb exists independently of the woman is also that during much of this time period in rural areas (and on the outskirts of urban ones), people would have had daily contact with farm (and wild) animals—watched bulls mount cows, watched deer in rut, watched dogs and cats in heat—and would have seen the act of procreation from conception to birth, as well as viewing the structures in question during butchering and cleaning animals for meat.

5   For repudiation of this idea, see the entirety of the Reddit page /r/NotHowGirlsWork where women speak about their experiences with men who do not understand female physiology.

6   July 11, 2022: "The womb is the only organ in a woman's body that serves no specific purpose to her life or well-being," Montana GOP State Rep. Brad Tschida, (in Cruz 2022a).

Was Representative Tschida calling us all hysterical? While he stopped short of using the word, hysteria is a specter that continues to haunt people with uteruses today. The original use of the term, from ancient Greece, was a diagnosis of "wandering womb," the idea being that the uterus could go walkabout through the body, causing mischief wherever it lodged.

For a modern takedown of this concept, see Rachel E. Gross' amazing book *Vagina Obscura* (2022), which deconstructs the historical and modern ways in which the gendered-female body has been obfuscated and negated. In it, she details how uterine tissue's regenerative ability can give us insight into longevity.

190

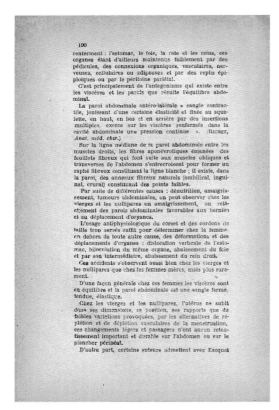

Figure 4.2 Page 190 in Chapter 10 of *Le Corset*.

Translation

Following different causes—undernutriton [sic], weight loss, abdominal tumors—we can observe in virgins and the nulliparous weight loss, a relaxation of the abdominal walls favorable to hernia, and the displacement of organs.

The antiphysiological [sic] use of the corset and too tightly tied waist bands is, apart from any other cause, sufficient to create in women organ deformities and displacements: vertical dislocation of the stomach, biloculation of the same organ, lowering of the liver and through it, the right kidney.

These issues have been observed in virgins and the nulliparous as well as mothers, but more rarely.

Generally speaking, in these women, the viscera are in balance and the abdominal wall is a firm, tight, elastic strap.

In virgins and the nulliparous, the uterus undergoes in its dimensions, position, and ratios only small variations caused by the alternating vascular repletion and depletion of menstruation. These slight and transient changes have no significant and lasting impact on the abdomen or perineal floor.

191

Chez la vierge et chez la nullipare, le canal vaginal est virtuel en ce sens que ses parois sont accolées. L'orifice vulvaire est fermé par l'hymen ou ses débris. Ventre sanglé, vulve fermée sont des caractéristiques de la vierge et de la nullipare. Chez elles, l'utérus et ses apparats sont solidement soutenus par le plancher périnéal.

On a bien observé le prolapsus de l'utérus chez des filles vierges, mais c'est là encore un fait exceptionnel.

Translation

In both virgins and the nulliparous, the vaginal canal is virtual in the sense that its walls are joined together.[7] The vulvar orifice is closed by the hymen or its debris.[8] A strapped abdomen or closed vulva are characteristics of these women. In them, the uterus and its apparatus are supported solidly by the perineal floor.

Uterine prolapse has been observed in virgins, but only very rarely.

7 This is false, simply based on common sense and on personal experience, but as that is not enough to make an ostensibly scientific counter claim, there is, in fact, a study to back that up: "... parity had little association with the overall surface contact and length of vagina" (Barnhart et al. 2006).

Whether this was common knowledge during the early 1900s is unclear, at least partially due to the fact that quite often doctors were squeamish about examining the vulva and vaginal canal (Owens 2018), yet a common examination for virginity was to look for a hymen, which, de facto, would indicate a 'sealed' vagina. However, see below ...

8 Hymens are not ubiquitous (Kimberley et al. 2012). Not only are not all people with a vagina born with a hymen, but if present a hymen can "break" in any number of ways that are unrelated to sex—heavy exercise, horseback riding, bicycle riding, etc. A vaginal examination may tell the doctor that one had been present (via the "debris" mentioned by O'Followell), but again, they are not ubiquitous, and thus an absence gives no

meaningful information. Nor, it should be said, does the presence of one—there are ways to have sex that will not result in a broken hymen. That is not to say that doctors at the time were cognizant of such, for a discussion of which see the charmingly (if exhaustingly) titled "The true history and adventures of Catharine Vizzani, a young gentlewoman a native of Rome, who for many years past [sic] in the habit of a man; was killed for an amour with a young lady; and found on dissection, a true virgin. With curious anatomical remarks on the Nature and Existence of the Hymen. By Giovanni Bianchi, Professor of Anatomy at Sienna, the Surgeon who dissected her" (1755).

199

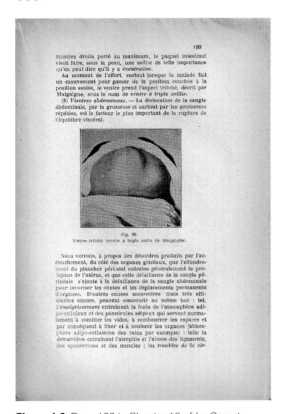

Figure 4.3 Page 199 in Chapter 10 of *Le Corset*.

Translation

[4.3]

We will see, with regard to the effect of childbirth disorders on the genitals, that the collapse of the perineal floor usually leads to uterine prolapse, and that this failure of the abdominal girdle leads to the fall and permanent displacement of organs.[9] Other ancillary (but still very efficiently damaging) causes can contribute to the same result. These might include weight loss leading to the melting of the adipo-cell atmosphere and the adipose pannicles that normally serve to fill voids—the spaces within the abdomen, and therefore to fix and support organs (adipo-cell atmosphere of the kidneys for example): as well as undernutrition leading to atrophy and atony of ligaments, aponeuroses, and muscles; circulation problems,

9 Uterine prolapse does correlate with multiparity, but it is currently understood that age and obesity are more closely correlated (Doshani et al. 2007).

200

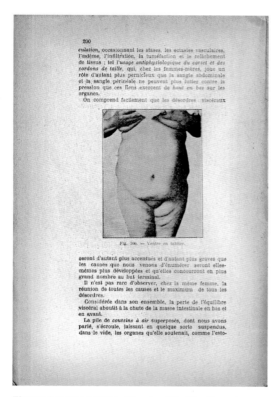

Figure 4.4 Page 200 in Chapter 10 of *Le Corset*.

Translation

causing stasis, vascular ectasia, edema, infiltration, swelling, and sagging of the tissues; other causes might include the antiphysiological use of the corset and waist bands, which, in women who have given birth, plays a role all the more pernicious as the abdominal and perineal girdles can no longer fight against the pressure that these links exert from top to bottom on the organs.[10]

[4.4]

10 The term "antiphysiological" here—literally against or contra the body—again indicates the control that O'Followell and the other doctors he quotes would like to exert over women, and the belief that they know better than the women what will make her comfortable during gestation. Such a take was not uncommon during much of medical history, with doctors and patients often disagreeing about courses of treatment, physicians doing outside consultations without their patients' knowledge, and the (occasionally necessary) inclusion of the patient's family in making decisions (Weston 2013).

This is mirrored in laws and beliefs at the time of writing which penalize people who might potentially bear a child for choosing to take medication they need for health conditions, when more than the patient's own health and needs are taken into account, often to their detriment. Headlines include: from July 2022, "Alabama Jailed Pregnant Woman for Months, Made Her Sleep on Floor Over Alleged Marijuana Use" (Cheung 2022); a follow-up article from November, "Alabama Woman Jailed for Using Drugs During Pregnancy Wasn't Pregnant" (Yurkanin 2022); and from September, "Teen Girl Denied Medication Refill Under AZ's New Abortion Law" (Foster 2022).

This also applies to seeking necessary abortions for fetal abnormalities or the health of the gestating parent: a headline from August 2022 ran "Mother Claims She Was Denied an Abortion Despite Baby's Condition" (Rosato 2022). The fetus had acrania and was non-viable; a quote from a news article from September stated "It was the kindness of strangers and the assistance of various nonprofit organizations and women's rights groups that helped Nancy Davis travel from Louisiana to New York City this week to terminate her pregnancy. Davis learned 10 weeks into her pregnancy that her fetus was developing without a skull" (Moon 2022). This does not even address child pregnancy due to rape, with or without incest.

206

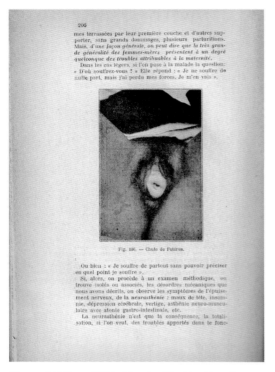

Figure 4.5 Page 206 in Chapter 10 of *Le Corset*.

Translation

In mild cases, if the patient is asked the question: "where does it hurt?," she replies, "It doesn't hurt anywhere, but I have no energy. I'm leaving."

[4.5]

Or: "I am in pain everywhere but am unable to explain how much."[11]

11 The accompanying photograph on this page shows an extremely prolapsed uterus, with the cervix protruding to the vaginal opening. While multiparity, age, obesity, and other factors contribute, as shown above, I would like to highlight O'Followell's quotation regarding a woman who suffers everywhere. A considerable number of systemic diseases (lupus, Ehlers-Danlos Syndrome which I have previously mentioned, rheumatoid arthritis, psoriatic arthritis, and chronic Lyme, to name only a few) involve multi-organ pain, inflammation, and degradation. The focus, again, on the corset, leads O'Followell to miss potential diagnoses, and this could have been prevented by way of a simple differential diagnosis.

208

Figure 4.6 Page 208 in Chapter 10 of *Le Corset*.

Translation

Aubeau's[12] interesting article not only proves the very important role that pregnancy plays in the etiology of enteroptosis (as I had argued by studying the influence of the corset on the intestine), but also makes it possible to understand how the corset can, by its constriction, act as an adjuvant cause of visceral ptoses, how it can have a harmful influence on the genitals, and how its constriction is all the more dangerous, that it is produced when the uterus contains a pregnancy.[13]

"In the very days when whalebone corsets were most abused, it was thought that they could hinder the regular process of pregnancy and cause the abortion of the fetus, so as early as the eighteenth century corsets were made that became useful only for pregnant women and others for newly delivered women."

Ambroise Paré had already spoken of "cases, things that compress the mother's womb as do buscs and similar things that prevent the child from taking natural growth so that mothers abort."[14]

Bouvier, who in many passages of his work has often defended the corset, condemns its use during gestation.[15] It is prudent, he says, during pregnancy, to remove the corset or at least simplify the garment as much as possible. Similar precautions should be taken after childbirth and during lactation.

Dr. Cazeaux also ranks among the causes of abortion the compression that some women exert on the lower abdomen by means of the corset.[16]

Dr. Penard, in his *Practical Guide to Childbirth*, says that a tight corset that encases the entire belly necessarily hinders the free development of the uterus and "at some point this organ revolts against this pressure, enters into premature contraction, peels off the egg, and expels it."[17]

12 Aubeau, *Clinique générale de chirurgie* (1902). While this source does not appear to be extant, that may be confounded by the fact that the name "Aubeau" as 'au beau' translates to "beautiful," and thus would be and still is a common phrase, rendering it nigh unsearchable.

13 According to O'Followell, the uterus, not the person, in this sentence, is pregnant. A recent news article shows what a pregnancy looks like before ten weeks (Noor 2022): a collection of nondescript cells on a petri dish. See also the discussion below about "the quickening."

14 From Paré (1634) translated by Thomas Johnson, from the Wellcome Collection [all spelling, punctuation, and capitalization are sic]: "Also whatsoever presseth or girdeth in the mothers belly, and therewith also the wombe that is within it, as are those Ivory or Whale-bone buskes, which women wear on their bodies, thereby to keepe downe their bellies; by these and such like things the childe is letted or hindered from growing to his full strength, so that by expression, or as it were by compulsion, hee is often forced to come forth before the legitimate and lawfull time." However, as previously mentioned, Paré's conception of what might cause harm, and his lack of distinction between proximal and secondary harms, complicates issues. He goes on to say "Thundering, the noyse of shooting of great Ordnance, the sound, and vehement noyse of the ringing of Bells constraine women to fall in travell before their time, especially women that are young, whose bodies are soft, slacke and tenderer than those that bee of riper years. Long and great fasting, a great fluxe of bloud, especially when the infant is growne somewhat great; but if it bee but two monneths old, the danger is not so great, because then hee needeth not so great quantity of nourishement, also a long disease of the mother, which consumeth the bloud, causeth the childe to come forth being destitute of store of nourishment before the fit time. Moreover, fulnesse, by reason of the eating great store of meates, often maketh or causeth untimely birth; because it depraveth the strength, and presseth down the child: as likewise the use of meats that are of an evill juice, which they lust or long for. But bathes, because they relaxe the ligaments of the woumbe, and hot houses, for that the fervent and choaking ayre is received into the body, provoke the infant to strive to goe forth to take the cold ayre, and to cause abortion."

So. We have corsets, thunder, gunfire, church bells, fasting, disease, eating meat, eating specific types of evil meat (possibly spoiled, or possibly forbidden, as meat was during Lent and other holy days), baths, and hot houses (we assume here he means warm domiciles, not greenhouses for forcing plants to grow out of season), all said to cause miscarriage or abortion. And this is merely the end of that particular paragraph from which O'Followell cherry-picked his information about corsets. The chapter in Paré, "The causes of Abortion or untimely birth," spans two full pages.

15 Bouvier does not seem to be extant, and without a first name or initial, or title, it is not possible to provide more information.

16 This source is not listed in the bibliography, but most likely refers to Pierre Cazeaux (1808–62), *Traité théorique et pratique de l'art des accouchements*. Three books are listed with the dates being 1841, 1845, and 1846, with no indication whether these refer to various volumes or to new/updated publications. While Cazeaux *does* attribute abortion to corseting (page 548), he also recommends it for difficult pregnancies (page 527), and in an 1885 publication writes "...the best means of relieving the patients is to support the abdomen, and at the same time raise it a little by means of a well-made corset; or of a large abdominal belt, the central portion of which embraces the sub-umbilical region, and whose two ends are attached to the back part of the corset..." (page 521), and "...At a more advanced stage, a body bandage, or a sort of corset; or belt for the abdomen, well adapted to the size and form of the belly, will afford much relief" (page 541).

17 This source is incorrectly listed in the bibliography as Pinard, not Penard. Penard, *Guide Pratique de l'accouchement*, listed in the BnF as *Guide pratique de l'accoucheur et de la sage-femme*, published in 1889 (https://gallica.bnf.fr/ark:/12148/bpt6k5802484m/f177.image.r=corset). The quote is: "L'usage d'un corset trop serré qui gêne le libre développement du ventre, l'abus du coït ou sa trop grande impétuosité sont des causes sérieuses d'avortement, dans les premiers mois du mariage surtout" (162)

Translated: "The use of a too tight corset which hinders the free development of the belly, the abuse of coitus or its too great impetuosity are serious causes of abortion, especially in the first months of marriage," another misquotation.

209

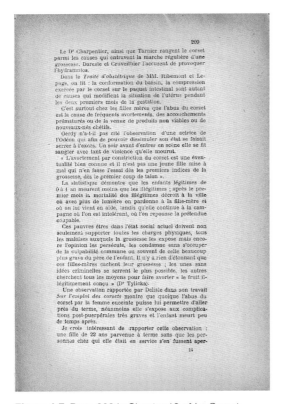

Figure 4.7 Page 209 in Chapter 10 of *Le Corset*.

Translation

Both Dr. Charpentier and Tarnier rank the corset among the causes that hinder the regular progress of a pregnancy.[18] Dareste and Cruveilhier claim it causes hydramnios.[19]

In the *Treatise on Obstetrics* by Messrs. Ribemont and Lepage, we read: the conformation of the pelvis and the compression exerted by the corset on the intestinal package are all causes that modify the situation of the uterus during the first two months of gestation.[20]

It is especially among unwed[21] mothers that the abuse of the corset is the cause of frequent abortions, premature deliveries, or the arrival of non-viable products or puny newborns.[22]

Didn't Gerdy cite the observation of an actress of the Odéon who, in order to conceal her condition, was tightened her corset to excess. One evening, before going on stage, she was strapped into the garment with so much violence that she died.[23]

"Abortion by constriction of the corset is a well-known possibility and there is not a young girl harmed who has not tried it from the first indications of the pregnancy, from the first stroke of the heel."[24]

Statistics show that from birth up to the age of on, legitimate children have a better survival rate than illegitimate children;[25] after the first month, the mortality of the illegitimates decreases in the city where, with more compassion, the unwed mother is forgiven and helped, while she fares worse in the countryside where there is more intolerance and the responsible party rejected.[26]

These poor beings in the state of today's society must not only bear all the physical burdens and discomfort to which pregnancy exposes them, but also be persecuted by public opinion, which condemns them without dealing with the dual or often much more serious guilt of the child's father.[27] It is no wonder that these unwed mothers hide their pregnancy; some lace as tightly as possible without any criminal intent, while others seek all means to abort "the illegitimately conceived fruit" (Dr. Tylicka).

An observation made by Delisle in his work *On the Use of Corsets*[28] shows that although the abuse of the corset by the pregnant woman may allow her to go close to term, nevertheless she exposes herself to very serious post-puerperal complications and the child could die shortly after.

I think it is interesting to report this observation: a twenty-two-year -old girl[29] had managed to disguise her pregnancy from her employers

18 Neither Charpentier nor Tarnier is in the bibliography, and these sources do not seem to be extant, although I can find a few tangential references to Tarnier.

19 Dareste is not in the bibliography, and although I have found one tangential reference to his work, that source is not extant either. Hydramnios (now called polyhydramnios; see Dashe et al. 2018) is a condition where there is too much amniotic fluid in the gestational sac. The Children's Hospital of Philadelphia lists maternal factors for this condition as diabetes, and fetal factors as malformation of the gastric tube, swallowing issues, "twin-to-twin transfusion syndrome," heart failure, and infection acquired during gestation (CHOP 2022). None of these is caused by constriction.

20 See above about the amount of fetal growth during the first ten weeks of gestation, which categorically cannot be impacted by constriction.

21 Let us pause briefly and think about why an unwed mother in the early 1900s would want to self-abort. We shall come back to this momentarily.

22 In 1883, Guy de Maupassant published a story called "Le Mère aux Monstres," about a young woman who would purposefully become pregnant out of wedlock, and tighten her corset against the pregnancies for the purpose of creating "monsters"—deformed children which she would subsequently sell to freakshows. The conception of the disabled as monstrous, and the mother as the producer of monsters, is one that persists (see Doyle 2019; Ussher 2005) This strikes the consciousness much like today's scaremongering and hatemongering around abortion, strikingly exemplified by such pundits as Tucker Carlson, who on October 24, 2022, opined: "Abortion politics is a total fixation of Democratic donors. It's the main thing they care about. Why is that, by the way? It's a religion. It's a child sacrifice cult" (in Media Matters 2022).

And yet, there were corsets that would support a pregnancy, such as corset number 48.363 from St. Fagans Museum in Cardiff, Wales. See Figures 4.11 and 4.12 below for discussion of this corset.

23 Pierre Nicolas Gerdy (1797–1856). Listed in the bibliography as "Gerdy, 1837, *Traité des bandages*, 2nd ed. Paris 1837," this source has been digitized on the internet archive, in limited form. I can find no story, verified or apocryphal, of an actress dying backstage at the Odeon, nor does Gerdy contain this anecdote (https:// ia801207.us.archive.org/12/items/b22009462_0003/b22009462_0003.pdf). This, of course, does not mean it did not happen, however, as usual we must take O'Followell's quoted sources with a grain of salt.

24 There is no citation for this quote, but two parts of this sentence need particular attention: first, the phrase "a young girl harmed," and second "from the first stroke of the heel." It is quite apparent that the first phrase is talking about rape, rape by deception, or abandonment. The euphemisms employed in *Le Corset* are, oddly, from a twenty-first-century point of view, not attached to abortion (our own sticky wicket of a subject) but to the concept of sexual activity of all types including rape/coerced sex/sexual assault.

Many laws in the US currently carve out exceptions for rape or incest, but those that do not are having profound effects on gestating parents, regardless of age. See: from July 1, 2022, "As Ohio Restricts Abortions, 10-year-old Girl Travels to Indiana for Procedure," (Rudavsky and Fradette). The rapist in question was a twenty-seven-year-old friend of the child's mother (Bruner et al. 2022); from September 26, 2022, "Affidavits: 2 More Pregnant Minors Who Were Raped Were Denied Ohio Abortions," (Schladen); and case number 1D22-2476 from the First District Court of Appeals in the State of Florida, an appeal for an abortion exception for a seventeen-year-old orphaned child (Florida's age of consent is eighteen, making this statutory rape), denied because ". . . the Appellant had not established by clear and convincing evidence that she was sufficiently mature to decide whether to terminate her pregnancy" (ruling by Judge Jennifer J. Frydrychowicz).

The second phrase refers to "the quickening," that period of time when a fetus can first be felt moving inside the womb, generally between three and four months of gestation (Broomhall 2004: 245). Without the quickening, women were reluctant to announce a pregnancy at all—there being dire consequences if they were wrong (a miscarriage being the least severe—if one was caught lying about a pregnancy, or proclaiming one where one did not exist, accusations of witchcraft could be leveled against her, particularly if a marriage were held (or postponed) due to the announcement, or if an inheritance rested on the presence of an heir (ibid; Wilson 1993)). In the 1800s, the harm of a pregnant woman resulting in miscarriage was made illegal by act of parliament in England (see Lord Ellenborough's Act of 1803) if it occurred *after* a woman felt the quickening. Yet according to a 1985 study, the average gestational date of the quickening is nineteen weeks (O'Dowd); a 1829 treatise by John Morley held that earlier symptoms of pregnancy were known. This, as previously seen, is an example of the medicalization of childbirth—prior to moving childbirth in-house to hospitals and doctor's surgeries, midwifery may not have "counted" a pregnancy lost before the quickening as a miscarriage or an abortion, nor, following Lord Ellenborough's Act, would the law.

However, this debate continues to rage on currently, as US courts debate the gestational age past which abortion should be illegal. See: from June 24, 2022, "Liberal Justices Deliver Blistering Dissent on *Roe*: Supreme Court Says 'a Woman Has No Rights to Speak Of'" (Cruz 2022b), sparked by a fifteen-week abortion ban in Mississippi; from November 2, 2022, "Nan Whaley: Gov. DeWine's Ohio Is 'a Place Where Women Won't Want to Be,'" (Heinrichs 2022), catalyzed by Ohio's so-called "heartbeat" bill; and the bill introduced to the second session of the 117th US congress by South Carolina senator Lindsey Graham titled "To amend title 18, United States Code, to protect pain-capable unborn children, and for other purposes," which would federally cap the fetal age for the performance of abortion at fifteen weeks. Of note: not only is this pre-quickening, it is also prior to what is currently considered the age of viability—the fetal age at which the fetus can survive outside of the womb, with medical intervention—often placed between twenty and twenty-four weeks of gestation (see Sekaleshfar 2009).

25 Without being able to access data on this, we might surmise that this is because of existing or newly acquired poverty; rejection by the other parent or by the gestating parent's family; lack of social and financial support both from relatives and from the community; the stigma of unwed motherhood causing a physical stress response; and other myriad ways unwed parents were disadvantaged, not the corset (Wilson 1993).

This circles back to the question of why an unwed woman might want to self-abort, or rid herself of a newborn child. The infant mortality rate for this period is so high that in order to perform statistical analysis on the average age at death, one has to specifically exclude that data. A live birth was no guarantee of a healthy child, and any child was an expense, a burden, more so if the parent had no support. Better to rid oneself of the products of conception as quickly as possible.

26 Again, O'Followell does not provide a source, data, or statistics for this claim that the city is more forgiving and supportive of unwed mothers than the country. However, there were more opportunities for unwed parents to claim charity in the cities due to the prevalence of churches, hospitals, poorhouses, and workhouses. Unfortunately, that support did not necessarily include forgiveness, and the stigma of unwed parenthood could continue to follow the parent throughout their life. Acceptance into a church parish might include being held up as an example of what one might become if one was not careful, or the prospect of being married off to whomever wanted a young and obviously fertile wife. Workhouses and poorhouses were places of malnutrition, abuse, and enough nominal piety that the inhabitants needed to express gratitude for their own suffering (McHugh 2007). And being given care in a hospital was likely to end with either permanent incarceration (as a precaution to keep the parent from bearing more illegitimate offspring) or an iatrogenic disease, which could result in sterility or death.

It is worth noting that French author Victor Hugo wrote an entire section of *Les Misérables* (1862)—the first section which comprises 216 pages—about Fantine, a woman who turns to prostitution to support her illegitimate child, Cosette.

27 This is the one time in this chapter during which men are held accountable for their role in pregnancy.

28 This work, in the bibliography as Delisle, *Sur l'emploi du corset* (1834), is not extant. This, again, may be falling prey to a common name, and no subtitle: "Delisle" translates to "of the island," and "of the use of the corset" is hardly a unique title.

29 The word used is *fille*, which translates to girl.

210

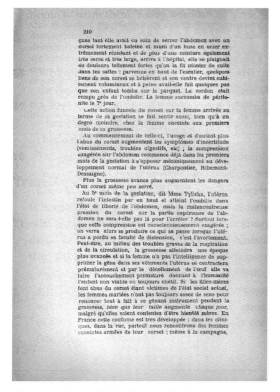

Figure 4.8 Page 210 in Chapter 10 of *Le Corset*.

Translation

as she had taken care to tighten her abdomen with a strongly baleinated corset equipped with an extremely rigid steel busk, as well as more than one tight and very wide belts. Arriving at the hospital, she complained of such severe pain that she was sent directly up to the ward: arriving at the top of the stairs, a few ties from her corset broke and her belly suddenly swelled. No sooner had she taken a few steps, than her child fell on the floor. The cord was broken near the umbilicus.[30] The woman succumbed to peritonitis on the seventh day.[31]

This fatal action of the corset on the woman in the last stages of gestation can also effect, although to a lesser degree, women in the first months of pregnancy.

In those early days, the use (and even more, the abuse) of the corset increase the symptoms of anxiety (vomiting, digestive disorders, etc.); exaggerated compression of the abdomens begins as soon as the first months of gestation and can physically inhibit the normal development of the uterus (Charpentier, Ribemont-Dessaigne).

The more the pregnancy progresses, the more the dangers of even a slightly tight corset increase.

. . . .

. . . . If unwed mothers abuse the corset, being victims of the current social state,[32] married women do not always have enough sense to completely renounce this annoying garment during pregnancy, even though their size increases every day and they are happy about becoming mothers.[33] In France, this custom is very common; both in clinics and in public, we meet pregnant women wearing corsets; even in the countryside,

30 A 2021 study (De Petris et al.) shows that umbilical cord ruptures are not uncommon, stating: "A review of stillbirths suggests that umbilical cord accident [sic] have at least an incidence of 1.5 stillbirths/1000 births." As the uterus sits behind the intestines, and the umbilical cord remains within the uterus, which itself is not/was not breached in the above anecdote, it seems very unlikely that the pressure of the corset could impact the umbilicus in any meaningful way.

31 An infection of the abdominal cavity, more likely brought on by a doctor's unwashed hands during delivery than the corset (for more information on puerperal fever and its connection to doctors' willful lack of sanitation, see Fitzharris 2017).

   In contrast, midwives, who had been licensed since 1560 in France (243 years before France would require certification for doctors (Crosland 2004; Pinell 2011)), were required to swear an oath to wash their hands before touching their patients (Broomhall 2004).

32 Refer back to footnotes 25 and 26 for a discussion on how the social state victimizes unwed parents.

33 Here O'Followell assumes several things not in evidence: that married women are corseting out of stupidity or lack of knowledge; that they are "happy to soon be mothers"; that they are annoyed by the corset during their pregnancy; that they, too, are not "victims of the current social state."

   In fact, we know that many people who use birth control or seek abortions are without the resources to raise children, be those resources social, mental, financial, or emotional. And those who *are* in the right space to bear and raise children may choose not to do so if there is a fetal anomaly, or may have no choice but to abort if the (much wanted) fetus miscarries. And yet: from November 18, 2022, a headline reads "Anti-Abortion Activists Sue the FDA to Reverse Approval of the Abortion Pill" (Rinkunas), the pill in question being one used to finalize incomplete miscarriages. Pregnant people are also often preyed upon by religious-based "women's health center" clinics which do not practice medicine and are not legally qualified to give medical advice. It is only since August 25, 2022 that Mike Isakowitz (letter from same), the Vice President of Google's department of Governement Affairs and Public Policy for the US and Canada, sent a letter to Congress promising to mark such deceptive clinics as not providing abortions.

211

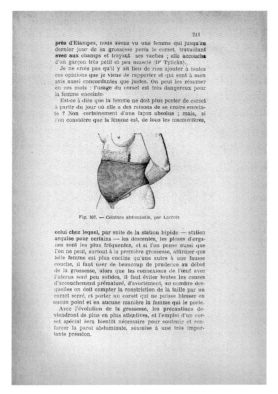

Figure 4.9 Page 211 in Chapter 10 of *Le Corset*.

Translation

near Etampes, we saw a woman who until the last day of her pregnancy wore a corset, even when working in the fields and milking her cows;[34] she gave birth to a very small and frail boy (Dr. Tylicka).

There is no need to add to all these opinions that I have just reported and which are, in my opinion, as consistent as they are right. We can summarize them in these words, however: the use of the corset is very dangerous for the pregnant woman.

Does this mean that the woman should no longer wear a corset from the day she has reason to believe she is pregnant? Not necessarily; but if we consider that the woman is, of all mammals

[4.9]

the one which, as a result of the bipedal station—a station acquired for some[35]—descents or organ ptosis, are more frequent, and if one also thinks that one cannot, especially in the first pregnancy, affirm that one woman is more prone than another to miscarriage, one must use great caution at the beginning of the pregnancy, while the connections of the egg with the uterus are not very strong. It is advisable to avoid all causes of premature delivery or abortion, among which one must count the constriction of size by a tight corset,[36] and instead wear a corset that cannot hurt at any point and in any way the woman who wears it.

With the evolution of pregnancy, precautions will become more and more available, and the use of a special corset will soon be necessary to support and strengthen the abdominal wall, which is under a great deal of pressure.

34   Listed in the bibliography as Tylicka (Me.), *Les Méfaits du Corset* (Thesis, Paris, 1899), this source is not extant though I sincerely wish it was. Dr. Justyna Budzińska-Tylicka was an extraordinary woman, who not only vocally advocated for birth control, but who also opened her own birth-control clinic. To be able to see what she wrote, beyond O'Followell's carefully chosen quotes and paraphrases, would truly open up a much fuller discourse on this topic.

   As we do not have that opportunity, we can only speculate that the milkmaid from Etampes did give birth to "a very small and frail boy," for reasons that may, or may not, have had to do with the corset. Dr. Tylicka was also an advocate for a robust and healthy diet; perhaps the milkmaid was lacking in nutrition.

35   This appears to imply that not all adult human women walk upright.

36   See above.

212

Il existe de nombreux modèles de ces corsets spéciaux, dits de grossesse, et j'en ai reproduit différents types dans le *Tome I* de cet ouvrage. Le corset de grossesse peut être disposé pour soutenir à la fois les seins et l'abdomen ; certains appareils, au contraire, sont divisés en deux parties : l'une, soutien thoracique ; l'autre, soutien abdominal

Translation

There are many models of these special corsets, called pregnancy corsets, and I reproduced different types in Volume I of this book.[37] The pregnancy corset can be arranged to support both the breasts and the abdomen; some devices, on the contrary, are divided into two parts: one supports the chest; the other, the abdomen.

37   This refers to the 1905 book discussed in depth in Chapter 1 of this book.

213

Quant à l'action du corset sur la matrice en dehors de

Translation

As for the action of the corset on the womb outside of

214

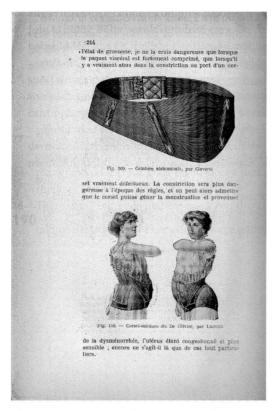

Figure 4.10 Page 214 in Chapter 10 of *Le Corset*.

Translation

the state of pregnancy, I believe it is dangerous only when the visceral package is compressed strongly. Only when there is real abuse in the constriction or wearing of a truly defective[38] corset

[4.10]

will constriction be more dangerous during menstruation, and it can then be admitted that the corset can interfere with menstruation and cause

[4.10]

dysmenorrhea, the uterus being congested and more sensitive; yet these are only very special cases.[39]

[End.]

38 Here we return to O'Followell's main theme—the woman abuses the corset, or the corset is defective and it is the woman's fault for wearing it.

39 The modern news article sources for this chapter span an incredibly brief five months, from June 24, 2022, when the Supreme Court of the United States handed down the Dobbs decision (SCOTUS 2022), overturning

Roe v. Wade, to November 22, 2022, when I sit in Indiana, a Republican-dominated state with strict abortion laws, writing this book. Gathering enough articles to populate this chapter took less than twenty minutes of work. Women, trans men, and non-binary and intersex people with uteruses are being denied their personhood on an hourly basis, the courts having granted us less right over our bodies than if we were dead, and we are repeatedly facing the bodily and health-related consequences of the malicious cruelty and indifference of the courts and lawmakers of this country.

I am furious that in the 114 years since O'Followell's publication of *Le Corset*, much of the legal and public opinion on bodily autonomy has remained the same; and that enough people believe that half the population does not deserve full bodily rights to ensure that such is codified in our laws. O'Followell put forth two laws that would punish women for corseting and tight lacing because he believed that women given control of their bodies would use that control to abort, and that such control should be taken away from them, by men, and should reside only in the hands of (male) doctors and (male) lawmakers. In 2022, in the US, we no longer have the absolute right to bodily autonomy; to self-abort, to induce miscarriage, to access all forms of birth control depending on who employs or insures us. We no longer (if we ever did) have the right to the impenetrable boundaries of our bodies. The dialogue has moved beyond corseting, of course, but the argument remains the same: people with the potential to bear children are not considered fully human in the eyes of people who cannot, and the latter control the courts and the law and access to medical treatment. In the five months since the Dobbs ruling, it has become perfectly clear: a sub-set of the American population would see us die rather than allow us to control our own bodies. Lest you think this is about protecting children or the life of the fetus, you may refer back to earlier referenced news items in which the fetus was already dead. This is about control. This is about terrorizing people who have the audacity to insist on our own equality. This is about disciplining the body, punishing the mind, enforcing birth and breeding in replication of a patriarchal mindset that requires compliance. To quote Adam Serwer, who was writing in 2018 about right-wing politics: "the cruelty is the point."

When we are reduced to our uterus and its contents—a practice that goes back to antiquity, when we are denied our humanity, when our rights are aborted (pun intended) in favor of the potential of a fetus, this is not an accident. While Title IX of the Education Amendments of 1972 states "[N]o person in the United States shall, on the basis of sex, be excluded from participation in, be denied the benefits of, or be subjected to discrimination under any education program or activity receiving Federal financial assistance," and the equal protection clause of the fourteenth amendment of the US constitution states "[N]o State shall make or enforce any law which shall abridge . . . nor deny to any person within its jurisdiction the equal protection of the laws," the enforcement of these laws is limited, leaving the adjudication of state laws up to the individual states until appealed. A federal law making abortion legal and protected would supersede any state laws, but no such law is in place. Another law that would help is the Equal Rights Amendment, which remains unratified, and thus even more toothless than the oft-quoted but rarely enforced equal protection clause. The ERA states "Equality of rights under the law shall not be denied or abridged by the United States or by any state on account of sex." Yet on October 7, 2022, Representative John Curtis of Utah said, regarding the law in his state, one of the most restrictive in the nation, "If you're a woman, it stinks that most of these legislators are men. Most of these decisions are made by men. I wish it were other than that. I wish as a man, I didn't have to make this decision" (Rinkunas 2022a). He appears to have forgotten that a) he does not have to make that decision (indeed, he could make a different one); and b) he could step down from his position, opening it up to, potentially, be held by a woman. One wonders why twelve states, Utah among them, do not feel that the ERA is important enough to add to the US constitution.

While we are here, however, let us return to birth control. Abortion is, at its most fundamental, a form of birth control. A way of controlling one's fertility. Of removing an unwanted pregnancy. Of controlling birth.

But it is not the only way to do so, nor is it even close to being the most efficient, accessible, convenient, cost-effective, or hassle-free method.

Of the entire gamut of birth-control methods (chemical, barrier, and surgical, comprising dozens of options between the three types), only two are meant to be used exclusively by people who ejaculate instead of people who ovulate. The majority of ways to prevent unwanted pregnancy create monetary and access burdens on women, trans men, and non-binary and intersex people. People who ejaculate can insist on wearing condoms, or can get a (potentially reversable) vasectomy, whereas people who ovulate must endure hormone imbalances (pills, patches, rings, implants, intrauterine devices); place unpleasant substances in their bodies (gels, foams, films); or undergo invasive procedures (non-hormonal intrauterine device implantation) or inpatient surgeries (hysterectomy, tubal ligations, oophorectomy) to assure there are no unwanted pregnancies. Why is there no hormonal birth control available for people who ejaculate? In clinical trials, the male subjects reported side effects. "The most common side effect was acne, and sometimes that acne was pretty severe. Some men also developed mood swings and in some cases those mood swings got pretty bad" (https://www.npr.org/sections/health-shots/2016/11/03/500549503/male-birth-control-study-killed-after-men-complain-about-side-effects). Imagine having "pretty severe" acne, a condition which occurs naturally in approximately 15 percent of female adults. The sacrifices one must make . . .

Side effects of hormonal birth control for people who ovulate include, but are not limited to: weight gain, blood clots, increased risk of breast cancer, increased risk of stroke, liver disease, blurred vision, high blood pressure, migraines, breakthrough bleeding, unexplained uterine bleeding, and yes, acne. These symptoms, considerably more numerous and severe than those of the pill for people who ejaculate, are caused by birth control currently on the market. There has been no move to take these methods off the shelf in order to unburden people who ovulate. The unequal burden, like the cruelty, is the point—if you want to have sex, but not have children, if you want to have control over your body and your sexuality, you must pay.

If you take away nothing else from this chapter, I hope this will remain in your mind: there are two realities in the US, the reality for people seen as whole human beings with full rights, and the reality for those of us who are denied some of those rights based on our anatomy and our potential to bear children. And a lot of the ideas which populate that second reality remain in circulation because of medical malfeasance from O'Followell and doctors like him.

REFERENCES

14th Amendment to the United States Constitution. (1868).

Barnhart, K., et al. (2006). "Baseline Dimensions of the Human Vagina," in *Human Reproduction*, 21 (6): 1618–22.

Bianchi, G. (1755). *The True History and Adventures of Catharine Vizzani, a Young Gentlewoman a Native of Rome, Who for Many Years Past in the Habit of a Man; Was Killed for an Amour with a Young Lady; And Found on Dissection, a True Virgin. With Curious Anatomical Remarks on The Nature and Existence of the Hymen. By Giovanni Bianchi, Professor of Anatomy at Sienna, the Surgeon Who Dissected Her.*

Broomhall, S. (2004). *Women's Medical Work in Early Modern France*, Manchester: Manchester University Press.

Bruner, B., et al. (2022). "Arrest Made In Rape of Ohio Girl That Led to Indiana Abortion Drawing International Attention," in *The Columbus Dispatch*. https://www.dispatch.com/story/news/2022/07/13/columbus-man-charged-rape-10-year-old-led-abortion-in-indiana/10046625002/

Cazeaux, P. (1841). *Traité Théorique et Pratique de l'Art des Accouchements.*

Cazeaux, P. (1885). *Traité Théorique et Pratique de l'Art des Accouchements* (possibly a second edition—no other information given.)

Cheung, K. (2022). "Alabama Jailed Pregnant Woman for Months, Made Her Sleep On Floor Over Alleged Marijuana Use," in *Jezebel*. https://jezebel.com/alabama-jailed-pregnant-woman-for-months-made-her-slee-1849507595

CHOP. (2022). https://www.chop.edu/conditions-diseases/amniotic-fluid-problemshydramniosoligohydramnios

Crosland, M. (2004). "The *Officiers de Santé* of the French Revolution: A Case Study in the Changing Language of Medicine," in *Medical History*, 48: 229–44.

Cruz, C. (2022a). "A Non-Exhaustive List of the Weirdest Shit Politicians Have Said About Women's Bodies," in *Jezebel*. https://jezebel.com/a-non-exhaustive-list-of-the-weirdest-shit-politicians-1849401421

Cruz, C. (2022b). "Liberal Justices Deliver Blistering Dissent on Roe: Supreme Court Says 'A Woman Has No Rights to Speak Of,'" in *Jezebel*. https://jezebel.com/liberal-justices-deliver-blistering-dissent-on-roe-sup-1849104981

Dashe, J., et al. (2018). "SMFM Consult Series #46: Evaluation and Management of Polyhydramnios," in *Society for Maternal-Fetal Medicine*, (46): B2–B8.

de Maupassant, G. (1883) "La Mère aux Monstres."

De Petris, et al. (2018). "Rupture of Umbilical Cord at Birth: An Unusual Case of Acute Neonatal Haemorrhage," in *Clinical Case Reports and Reviews*, 4 (8): 1–2.

Doshani, A., et al. (2007). "Uterine Prolapse," in the *British Medical Journal*, 335 (7624): 819–23.

Doyle, J. (2019). *Dead Blondes and Bad Mothers: Monstrosity, Patriarchy, and the Fear of Female Power*, New York, NY: Melville House.

Equal Rights Amendment. (1923).

Fitzharris, L. (2017). *The Butchering Art: Joseph Lister's Quest to Transform the Grisly World of Victorian Medicine*, New York, NY: Scientific American/Farrar, Straus, and Giroux.

Florida Appellate Court. (2022). *Case No. 1D22-2476, In Re: Jane Doe 22-B.*

Foster, B. (2022). "Teen Girl Denied Medication Refill Under AZ's New Abortion Law," in KOLD News. https://www.kold.com/2022/10/01/teen-girl-denied-medication-refill-under-azs-new-abortion-law/

Gerdy, P. (1837). *Traité des bandages*, 2nd edn, Paris

Gross, R. (2022). *Vagina Obscura: An Anatomical Voyage*, New York, NY: W. W. Norton and Co.

Heinrichs, A. (2022). "Nan Whaley: Gov. DeWine's Ohio is 'A Place Where Woman Won't Want to Be,'" in *Jezebel*. https://jezebel.com/pro-choice-ohio-voters-are-probably-going-to-reelect-an-1849728361

Hugo, V. (1862). *Les Misérables*. Brussels, Belgium: Librairie internationale A. Lacroix, Verboeckhoven et Cie.

Isakowitz, M. (2022). Letter from Google to the US House of Representatives regarding Crisis Pregnancy Centers.

Kimberley, N, et al. (2012). "Vaginal Agenesis, the Hymen, and Associated Anomalies," in *Pediatric and Adolescent Gynecology*, 25: 54–8.

McHugh, T. (2007) *Hospital Politics in Seventeenth-Century France: The Crown, Urban Elites, and the Poor*, New York, NY: Ashgate Publishing.

Media Matters. (2022). "Tucker Carlson Calls the Democratic Party 'A Child Sacrifice Cult,'" in *Media Matters For America*. https://www.mediamatters.org/fox-news/tucker-carlson-calls-democratic-party-child-sacrifice-cult

Moon, J. (2022). "Alabama AG: State May Prosecute Those Who Assist in Out-Of-State Abortions," in *Alabama Reporter*. https://www.alreporter.com/2022/09/15/alabama-ag-state-may-prosecute-those-who-assist-in-out-of-state-abortions/

Morley, J. (1829). *An Essay of the Symptoms of Pregnancy, from the Earliest Stage to the Period of Quickening, with a Physiological Explanation of the Physical and Mental Changes Produced by the Impregnated Uterus upon the System of the Mother*.

Noor, P. (2022). "What a Pregnancy Actually Looks Like Before 10 Weeks—In Pictures," in *The Guardian*. https://www.theguardian.com/world/2022/oct/18/pregnancy-weeks-abortion-tissue

NPR Staff. (2016). "Male Birth Control Study Killed After Men Complain About Side Effects," on *National Public Radio*. https://www.npr.org/sections/health-shots/2016/11/03/500549503/male-birth-control-study-killed-after-men-complain-about-side-effects

O'Dowd, M. (1985). 'Quickening—A Re-Evaluation,' in the *British Journal of Obstetrics and Gynaecology*, 92: 1037–9.

Owens, D. (2018). *Medical Bondage: Race, Gender, and the Origins of American Gynecology*, Athens, GA: University of Georgia Press.

Pinell, P. (2011). "The Genesis of the Medical Field: France, 1795–1870," in *Revue Française de Sociologie*, 52(5), 117–51.

Platon and Sepet. (1902). *Hygiene de La Femme: Enfant—Jeune Fille—Femme—Mère et Aïule*.

Rinkunas, S. (2022). "Anti-Abortion Activists Sue the FDA to Reverse Approval of the Abortion Pill," in *Jezebel*. https://jezebel.com/anti-abortion-activists-sue-the-fda-to-reverse-approval-1849802704

Rinkunas, S. (2022a). "GOP Lawmaker on Abortion Bans: 'I Wish, As a Man, I Didn't Have to Make This Decision,'" in *Jezebel*. https://jezebel.com/gop-lawmaker-on-abortion-bans-i-wish-as-a-man-i-didn-1849630520

Rosato, C. (2022). "Mother Claims She Was Denied an Abortion Despite Baby's Condition," in *WAFB*. https://www.wafb.com/2022/08/15/mother-claims-she-was-denied-an-abortion-despite-babys-condition/

Rudavsky, S., and R. Fradette. (2022). "As Ohio Restricts Abortions, 10-Year-Old Girl Travels to Indiana for Procedure," in the *Indianapolis Star*. https://www.dispatch.com/story/news/2022/07/01/ohio-girl-10-among-patients-going-indiana-abortion/7788415001/

Schladen, M. (2022). "Affidavits: 2 More Pregnant Minors Who Were Raped Were Denied Ohio Abortions," in the *Ohio Capital Journal*. https://www.cincinnati.com/story/news/2022/09/27/affidavits-2-more-raped-minors-were-denied-ohio-abortions/69520380007/

SCOTUS. (2022). *Dobbs, State Health Officer of the Mississippi Department of Health, et al., v. Jackson Women's Health Organization, et al.*

Sekaleshfar, F. (2009). "Reinterpreting the 'Quickening' perspective in the Abortion Debate," in *Theoretic Medical Bioethics*, 30: 161–71.

Serwer, A. (2018). "The Cruelty is the Point," in *The Atlantic*. https://www.theatlantic.com/ideas/archive/2018/10/the-cruelty-is-the-point/572104/

Title IX of the Education Amendments of 1972. (1972). *Public Law No. 92-318, 86 Stat. 235*.

Ussher, J. (2005). *Managing the Monstrous Feminine*, London: Taylor and Francis Group.

Weston, R. (2013). *Medical Consulting by Letter in France, 1665–1789*, Burlington, VT: Ashgate Publishing Company.

Wilson, L. (1993). *Women and Medicine in the French Enlightenment: The Debate over* Maladies des Femmes, Baltimore, MD: Johns Hopkins University Press.

Yurkanin, A. (2022). "Alabama Woman Jailed For Using Drugs During Pregnancy Wasn't Pregnant," in the *Alabama News*. https://www.al.com/news/2022/11/alabama-woman-jailed-for-using-drugs-during-pregnancy-wasnt-pregnant-lawsuit-says.html

Figure 4.11 Item number 48.363 from St. Fagans Museum in Cardiff, Wales, exterior view. Made between 1900 and 1907, this white cotton corset is trimmed with light blue/green ribbon and lace at the top. There are two suspenders and clasps for stockings built into the front. The corset is an underbust fitting that extends down over the abdomen, with gussets and width enough to cradle a pregnant torso. Dimensions: bust 69cm; waist 52cm; hips 93cm; front 36cm; back 38cm; sides 36cm. Ratio: .74:.56:1. Photo © Rebecca Gibson, 2023.

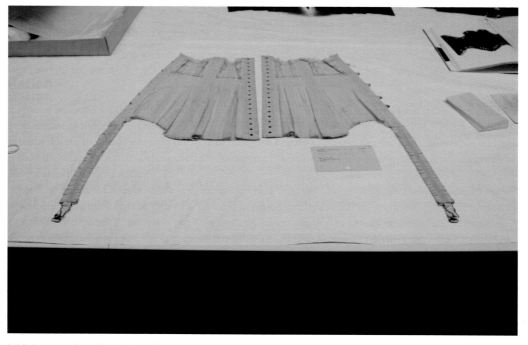

Figure 4.12 Item number 48.363 from St. Fagans Museum in Cardiff, Wales, interior view. Photo © Rebecca Gibson, 2023.

5

THE WOMAN WANTS TO LOOK BEAUTIFUL TO PLEASE HER MAN
Covering Chapters 11–15 of *Le Corset*, on the Topics of Which Corsets Women Should Wear, If They Should Wear Them at All, and Why Women Choose to Wear the Corset

CHAPTER 11

215

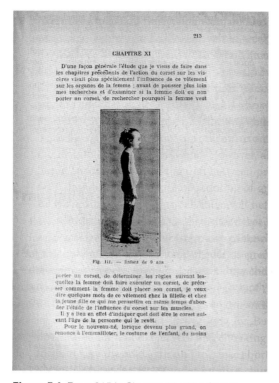

Figure 5.1 Page 215 in Chapter 11 of *Le Corset*.

Translation

. . . . before pushing my research further and examining whether or not the woman should wear a corset, to find out why the woman wants

[5.1]

to wear a corset, to determine the rules according to which the woman must perform corseting,[1] or to specify how the woman must place her corset, I want to say a few words about this garment as used by the little girl and on the young woman which allow me at the same time to approach the study of the corset's influence on the muscles.

1 This *is* an interesting question, because he is acknowledging the performativity of fashion/costuming/dress (for theories behind this, see Barthes 1967; Entwistle 2000), and the fact that society demands women wear the corset, and punishes them if they do not. None of the work-arounds discussed in this chapter or elsewhere will create the same silhouette as the corset the women are already wearing, thus all his suggestions will bring down that punishment on them.

217

Figure 5.2 Page 217 in Chapter 11 of *Le Corset*.

Translation

[5.2]

"It does not seem that this opinion has prevailed to this day, and many girls having bad posture, with protruding shoulder blades and curved bust, lacking, in a word, energy and strength, are equipped with so-called support corsets. These corsets, which cover the entire dorsal region, are complemented by straps that surround the scapulohumeral joint in order to pull it back. At the front, they are formed by a panel placed on the top of the chest. The whole system tends to immobilize the bust to straighten it. This method seems illogical to me, at least in all cases where there are no anatomical lesions . . . ."

220

Dans ce cas, et quand je m'adresse à une maman qui est de bonne foi et veut bien accepter un conseil—car combien souvent un malade vient demander au médecin un avis avec l'intention bien ferme de ne suivre cet avis que s'il lui est agréable—quand donc, dis-je, j'ai à faire à une cliente qui ne demande qu'à être convaincue, je fais avec un crayon un trait sur la partie supérieure du corset, indiquant que tout ce qui est au-dessus de ce trait doit être supprimé, je fais en outre délacer le corset et porter à deux ou trois œillets plus bas le niveau des points où les cordons se tirent pour rapprocher les deux pièces du corset ; puis celui-ci étant descendu sur le bassin, j'indique qu'il faut ajouter à la partie inférieure du corset, une bande qui le rallonge, et à cette bande alors seront fixées les jarretelles.

Quand je revois me jeune patiente avec son corset ainsi modifié, avec son corset mal fait antérieurement et ultérieurement retouché à peu près, soit par la corsetière soit par la mère elle-même, bien qu'il s'agisse alors d'un corset qui n'ait pas été fait sur mesure et d'après des données fixées à l'avance, et qui par conséquent ne saurait

Translation

In this case, and when I speak to a mother who has come to see me in good faith and willing to accept advice—because how often does a patient come to ask the doctor for an opinion with the firm intention of following this advice only if it is pleasing to her[2]—when, say, I have to deal with a client who only asks to be convinced, I draw a pencil line on the upper part of the corset, indicating that everything above this line must be removed. I also have her unlace the corset and lower it to two or three eyelets below the level where she uses the cords to pull the two pieces closer together; then the corset being lowered on the pelvic basin, I indicate that it is necessary to add a strip of fabric that lengthens it to the lower part of the corset. The garters will then be fixed to that strip.

When I see that she has made these changes . . . regardless it cannot

[2] This entirely discounts the possibilities that women and girls were comfortable in their corsets, that they were seeing him for complaints unrelated to corseting, or that they were unable for various reasons to do as he asked. "Medically noncompliant" is a phrase that, in the twenty-first century, often is added to the charts of people who cannot afford their medications, or who have conflicting medical needs and thus cannot fulfil them all, or who know their own tolerances and abilities and refuse to do activities or take medication that they know will make things worse. "Complex history" or "bad historian" will be added to the charts of people who disagree with their doctors' diagnoses or treatment plans, or whose medical past is filled with multiple attempts to solve a medically difficult problem.

Le Corset has already shown multiple instances where O'Followell missed diseases and disorders that needed differential diagnoses, and this clearly indicates his fixation on the corset over the wellbeing of his patients. This tendency is mirrored in modern medical misogyny, where women's pain, and particularly the pain of women of color, is routinely dismissed.

221

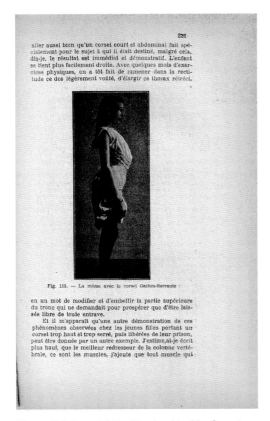

Figure 5.3 Page 221 in Chapter 11 of *Le Corset*.

Translation

fit as well as a short abdominal corset made especially for the subject for whom it was intended. Despite this, I say, the result is immediate and demonstrative. The child stands upright more easily.[3] A few months of physical exercise will correct this slightly hunched back, and widen this narrowed chest.

[5.3]

In short, it will modify and beautify the upper part of the trunk which only required to be left free of any hindrance in order to prosper.

3   The "problem" of children slouching is an ever-present one, not limited to the late 1800s/early 1900s, and it is unsurprising that some strapping in the form of a child's corset would force them to stand up straight. Yet, until the 1700s, children were dressed much like or identical to adults (Perrot 1994; Bendall 2022), making the issue of the corset a modern one. For discussion of a child's corset, see Bath Fashion Museum's I.27.86 in Figures 5.16 and 5.17 at the end of this chapter.

222

....De même chez les fillettes et chez les jeunes filles, provoquez par l'exercice modéré et bien compris le travail de leurs membres, n'apportez en outre aucune entrave à la contraction musculaire et vous verrez le buste de vos enfants se développer d'une façon rationnelle qui sera bien autrement l'expression du beau qu'une poitrine étriquée, qu'un thorax rétréci.

Les plus grands dangers viennent en premier lieu de ce que souvent on fait porter aux jeunes filles un corset beaucoup trop tôt et plus tard beaucoup trop serré.

Translation

.... Similarly in girls and young women, moderate exercise including, it goes without saying, moving their limbs, will not inhibit muscular contraction and you will see the bust of your children develop in a reasonable way that will be much different from the expression of beauty than a narrow breast or shrunken chest.

The greatest dangers come in the first place from the fact that young girls are often made to wear a corset much too early, and later, much too tight.[4]

4   While he does go on to define "much too early, and ... much too tight," these are still illogical arguments, based on the idea that corsets are inherently harmful and that women are set on abusing their bodies and passing that abuse down to their daughters.

225

Le corset, dès qu'il est appliqué, produit donc la déformation de cette région ; de plus en substituant à la ligne droite une ligne brisée, en vertu du théorème géométrique qui veut que la ligne droite pour se rendre d'un point à un autre soit le plus court chemin, il détermine l'incurvation du buste en avant. Il se passe là le même fait que celui de l'arc qu'on viendrait à tendre et dont les extrémités se rapprocheraient. L'action du corset à ce niveau est complexe d'ailleurs, car il a également pour effet de gêner le redressement du corps.

Translation

As soon as it is put on, the corset deforms this part of the body; moreover, by substituting a broken line for a straight one, by virtue of the geometric theorem that the straight line to get from one point to another is the shortest path, it pushes the curve of the bust forward.[5] The action here is similar to that which occurs when a long-bow stretches and its ends get closer together. The action of the corset at this level is complex, because it also has the effect of hindering the straightening of the body.

5 This makes no sense at all—the body is full of curves, and later he rails against the straight corset/corset ligne.

226

...effectué par l'extension de l'articulation coxo-fémorale. La colonne vertébrale reste rigide, elle n'y participe pas.

Donc le seul fait de changer la forme de la paroi antérieure du corps a pour résultat apparent d'incurver le buste, d'en gêner le redressement, de l'immobiliser et de favoriser la propulsion en avant de la masse intestinale ;

Translation

. . . carried out by the extension of the coxofemoral joint. The spine remains rigid; it does not participate in it.

So the mere fact of changing the shape of the anterior wall of the body has the apparent result of curving the bust, hindering its straightening, immobilizing it, and promoting the forward propulsion of the intestinal mass;

229

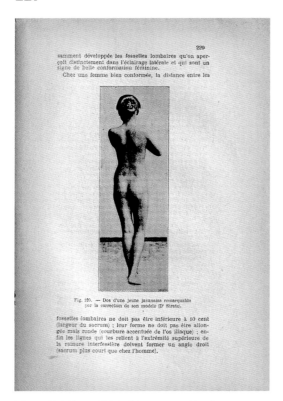

Figure 5.4 Page 229 in Chapter 11 of *Le Corset*.

Translation

In a well-conformed woman, the distance between
[5.4]
lumbar dimples must not be less than ten per cent (width of the sacrum); their shape should not be elongated but round (accentuated curvature of the iliac bone); finally, the lines that connect them to the upper end of the inter-gluteal groove must form a right angle (sacrum shorter than in men).[6]

6   This is just phrenology for the butt. Phrenology, the pseudo-science of reading personality traits from the contours of the skull, was practiced during O'Followell's time. One can still purchase mock-ups of phrenology diagrams/ceramic heads at certain novelty shops. Here, O'Followell again ignores individual variation in favor of pathology.

230

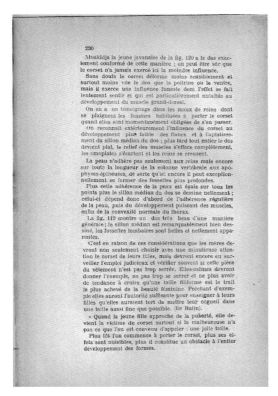

Figure 5.5 Page 230 in Chapter 11 of *Le Corset*.

Translation

Muakidja, the young Javanese shown in Figure 120, has her back conformed in exactly this way; we can be sure that the corset has never exerted the slightest influence here.[7]

No doubt the corset deforms the back less noticeably and especially less quickly than the chest or belly, but it still exerts a fatal influence the effect of which if felt slowly and which is particularly harmful to the development of the large dorsal muscle.

This is corroborated by the kidney ailments complained of by women accustomed to wearing the corset when they are momentarily forced to do without it.[8]

The influence of the corset is recognized externally by the weaker development of the flanks and the flattening of the median groove of the back: later the entire back becomes flat, the muscle tone disappears completely, the shoulder blades move apart, and the kidneys widen.[9]

. . . .

"When the girl approaches puberty, she becomes the victim of the corset especially if the unfortunate one does not have what we have agreed to call "a pretty size."[10]

The sooner one begins to wear the corset, the more harmful its effects are, and the more it constitutes an obstacle to the full development of forms.

[7] While no doubt correct that the Javanese did not corset, this is really quite racist, contributing to the othering and exoticization of non-white, non-European races. Despite the fact that this was a widely accepted idea during this time, so was anti-racism. We will return to this below. However, I have previously mentioned that this is couched in a discussion of "civilized" vs. "savage," an argument of which O'Followell was no doubt aware (Balch 1904; Ribeiro 1986).

Many fashion scholars make note of the fact that fashion and morality were closely linked, and that the corset in particular was used to show civilized, moral, and appropriate behavior (Berlanstein 1984; Newton 1974; Perrot 1994; Ribeiro 1986; Shrimpton 2016; Styles 2007).

[8] He does not specify which kidney ailments, and occasionally uses kidney (the organ) interchangeably with kidney (the medial curvature of the abdominal cavity, giving the female form its characteristic shape). It is unclear to which he is referring here.

[9] This is accurate, as shown by my own research (Gibson 2020). There was considerable spinous process atrophy, and distortion of the spinous processes downward and away from the center line, creating extreme angles from the norm and weakened muscle attachment points. But is it harm? Were the women O'Followell examined complaining of weak back muscles? Almost certainly we will never know for sure—his work is so filtered through his own biases, and much of the work done by other doctors of the time (as shown through my annotations here) is unavailable either in print or digitally.

[10] "A pretty size" in this case could refer to any number of things, but because the corset is said to help with that we can assume that it means full busted, small waisted, and broad hipped, but also slender.

231

Pas plus qu'on ne peut fixer d'une manière générale le moment du plein épanouissement, pas plus on ne peut dire d'une manière générale quel est l'âge où il faut adopter le corset.

Le corset est nuisible avant ce moment, il est recommandable au contraire pendant et après. Mais comme le plein épanouissement survient tantôt dès la quinzième année, tantôt seulement à la trentième ou plus tard encore, il n'est possible de donner une réponse sûre que dans chaque cas particulier.

En tout cas, on peut affirmer qu'il ne faut pas adopter le corset avant que les hanches aient atteint une largeur suffisante pour offrir un appui, sans qu'il soit nécessaire de serrer.

Aussi, Mesdames, ayez pitié de vos filles, je vous en prie, et empêchez-les de déformer leur corps de trop bonne heure. Elles auront le temps de la faire plus tard, mais vous n'aurez alors aucun reproche à vous adresser ». (Dr. Stratz).

« Quand les jeunes filles connaîtront bien les méfaits du corset mal compris et trop serré, elles n'en abuseront plus ou tout au moins en abuseront moins. Elles n'en seront plus les premières victimes, elles cesseront d'être les martyres d'une coquetterie néfaste. Elles élèveront leurs enfants dans les mêmes idées. Mais, pour cela il importe que l'éducation et l'instruction hygiéniques soient faites et que les éducatrices comprennent et mettent en pratique la parole de Fonssagrives : Elever une jeune fille, c'est former une mère. »

En laissant ces organes des jeunes filles se développer sans entraves on leur prépare d'heureuses maternités, n'oublions donc pas que les vierges sont des mères futures : *Virgines futurae virorum matres.*
[Fin.]

Translation

Nor can we fix in a general way the moment of full development; nor can we say in a general way what is the age at which one must adopt the corset.

The corset is harmful before this time; it is, on the contrary, recommended on the during and after. But since full development[11] occurs sometimes as early as the fifteenth year, yet sometimes only in the thirtieth or even later, it is impossible to give a definitive answer in each case.

In any case, it can be said that the corset should not be adopted until the hips have reached a sufficient width to offer support, without the need to tighten.

Also, ladies, please have mercy on your daughters and prevent them from distorting their bodies too early. They will have time to do it later, but then you will have no reason to reproach yourself." (Dr. Stratz).[12]

"When young girls are well acquainted with the ill effect of the poorly understood and tight corset, they will no longer abuse it—or at least abuse it less. They will no longer be the first victims and will cease to be the martyrs of a harmful coquetry.[13] They will raise their children with the same ideas. But for this it is important that the health education and instruction be done and that educators understand and put into practice the word of Fonssagrives:[14] To raise a young girl is to train a mother."[15]

By allowing these organs of young girls to develop unhindered, they are prepared for happy motherhood, so let us not forget that virgins are future mothers: Virgines futurae virorum matres.

[End.]

11   I am unsure what "full development" means here, despite the fact that it is repeated several times—possibly he means when someone has stopped growing, anatomically speaking, but that occurs much before the age of thirty.

12   This refers to Carl Heinrich Startz (1858–1924), German-Russian gynecologist. No title is listed, however.

13   The tight, restrictive, highly contoured corset was already on the way out in 1908 (Edwards 2017/18), and within the next decade would be gone entirely due to several factors including the war. The replacements, often made of newer/modern materials, such as rubber and elastic, were more flexible and produced a sleeker, more up and down silhouette, lending their influence to the age of the flappers. Although we are seeing this in hindsight, a benefit which O'Followell did not have, we must recall that he is not opposed to the corset itself, but to what he considers "bad" corsets and vain women. Yet here, again, O'Followell's actual target is not the wellbeing of the woman, it is her vanity. He places this under the guise of concern about her health, but the main point of the sentence is not harm, it is coquetry.

14   This source is not listed in the bibliography, but refers to Jean-Baptiste Fonssagrives (1823–84), a maritime doctor who later taught medicine in Paris.

15   This returns us to the ideas found in Chapter 10 of *Le Corset*, where the woman's only purpose in life is seen to be a mother. See Chapter 4 of this book for further discussion.

CHAPTER 12

232

J'en ai dit assez pour qu'il me soit permis de poser cette question : La femme doit-elle [sic.] porter un corset ? A ceci j'ai répondu par avance quand au cours de mon étude historique (1) j'écrivais : L'usage du corset est utile, l'abus du corset est dangereux et quand j'ai dans les chapitres précédents expliqué cette réponse par l'examen de l'influence du corset sur les viscères thoraciques et abdominaux de la femme. Cette étude toutefois ne suffit pas, il me faut développer encore cette réponse.

Translation

I have said enough for me to ask this question: Should women wear corsets? I answered in advance when during my historical study (1) I wrote that while the use of the corset is useful but the abuse of it is dangerous,[16] and when I explained this answer in previous chapters by examining the influence of the corset on women's thoracic and abdominal viscera. This study, however, is not enough, and I must develop this answer further.

16 While the flagging of this particular ideology feels repetitive, it serves to emphasize how O'Followell himself is being repetitive.

233

Comme on le voit il ne s'agit dans ces conclusions que du danger qui peut résulter du port d'un corset ou serré ou mal fait. Chacun comprendra après ce que j'ai exposé précédemment, ce qu'il faut entendre par constriction abusive ; je n'insisterai donc pas, quant aux mots : « corset mal fait », il faut entendre par là un corset mal fait pour la personne qui le porte, un corset non fait pour la femme qui le revêt. En d'autres termes si le corset confectionné peut être employé pour protéger les chairs contre la constriction par les cordons ou par les ceintures des vêtements il sera toujours plus dangereux, à conditions égales, que le corset sur mesure lequel outre qu'il fera toujours la femme plus élégante, pourra causer moins de préjudice à sa santé.

Translation

As we see, these conclusions are only about the danger that can result from wearing an overly tight or poorly made corset. Everyone will understand, given what I have outlined above, what I mean by "abusive constriction"; I will not insist, therefore, that for the phrase "badly made corset," we mean a corset made badly for the person who wears it, but rather one not made specifically for the woman wearing it.[17] In other words, if the made corset can be used to protect the flesh against constriction by the laces or belts on the clothes, it will always be more dangerous, under equal conditions, than the custom corset which, besides always making the woman look more elegant, will cause less harm to her health.

17 This sentence and the next seem reasonable at first glance, and hold up in terms of fashion fitting better when it is made for a person. However, it is during this time that we see off-the-rack or ready-to-wear clothing (Perrot 1994) begin to increase (it is cheaper, easier to access, more convenient, and matches the buying power of the women of this time): in 1908, there were hundreds of thousands more women in the workforce than even in the decade before, (Hooks 1947), earning their own money and doing jobs that may have impinged on the time needed to either make their own clothing or get it bespoke. Women were balancing elegance and form with practicality, economy, and function. It remains considerably cheaper today to buy off the rack, even if one tailors the clothing oneself, than to have bespoke clothing made.

236

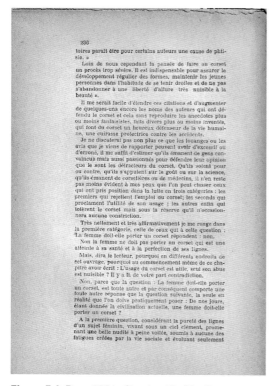

Figure 5.6 Page 236 in Chapter 12 of *Le Corset*.

Translation

Very clearly and very affirmatively I fall into the first category, that of those who respond to the question of whether women should wear corsets with "no."[18]

No, the woman should not wear a corset that impairs her health and the natural perfection of her lines.

But, the reader will say, why in different places of this book, why at the very beginning of this chapter, to have written: The use of the corset is useful, only its abuse is harmful? You are contradicting yourself.

No, because the question of whether women should wear corsets is quite different and therefore has a completely different answer than the following question, the only one in reality that must practically be asked: Nowadays, given today's societal norms, should a woman wear a corset?

To the first question, considering the ideal of the purity of the lines of a female subject; we see her living under a mild sky, walking with her beautiful nakedness barely veiled, subjected to none of the fatigues created by social life and evolving only

---

18   Apart from those being advertised in the front and back matter of *Le Corset*, developed by and licensed to O'Followell's medical cronies; see Chapter 1 and the afterword of this book.

237

dans l'existence pour y promener sa beauté et y procréer dans les meilleures conditions possibles et avec les fatigues les moins grandes possibles ; à cette première question je réponds sans hésiter : Pas de corset, pas de corset !

Mais il s'agit dans la seconde question d'une toute autre femme ; celle que nous devons considérer maintenant est obligée par les mœurs actuelles à se vêtir de vêtements plus ou moins nombreux, plus ou moins compliqués, plus ou moins lourds ; elle évolue sous un ciel plus ou moins clément, sujet à des variations de température parfois brusques ; elle se livre quotidiennement sans considération de son état physiologique au surmenage d'une vie de plaisir ou de travail, et malgré tout cela cette femme reste femme et veut le rester le plus longtemps possible et pour cela elle veut garder sa beauté ou les apparences de sa jeunesse ; alors la question change et aussi la réponse et c'est pourquoi je dis : Pour une telle femme, oui l'usage du corset est utile, l'abus du corset est nuisible.

. . . .
[Fin.]

Translation

to spend her existence walking in its beauty and bringing a family into the best possible conditions and with the fewest possible stresses; to this question I answer without hesitation: No corset, no corset![19]

But the second question is about a completely different woman; the one we must consider now is obliged by current mores to dress in more or less numerous clothes, more or less complicated, more or less heavy; she evolves under a more or less mild sky, subject to sometimes sudden variations in temperature; she indulges daily without consideration of her physiological state in doing too much for work or pleasure, and despite all this, this woman remains a woman and wants to remain so as long as possible and for this she wants to keep her beauty or the appearances of her youth. Here the question changes, as does the answer, and that is why I say: for such a woman, yes, the use of the corset is useful, but the abuse of it is harmful.[20]

. . . .
[End.]

19 There is a discussion here about civilization that O'Followell leaves out, obfuscated by the phrase "none of the fatigues created by social life." See Chapter 2 of this book, footnote 7 above and footnote 20 below for references to that discussion.

20 Here we return to that discussion of "civilization" and the idea that the corset civilizes the woman—moving her away from nature and toward culture (Gibson 2020). She must use the corset, says O'Followell, to maintain her womanly figure and keep her beauty, but she must not abuse it. And the phrase "this woman remains a woman and wants to remain so as long as possible" is fascinating to examine in the hierarchy of races set forth by both early anthropologists, and doctors, with the white European man at the top, and the white European woman just slightly below him, but still above everyone "uncivilized" and "unclothed," as seen above.

CHAPTER 13

238

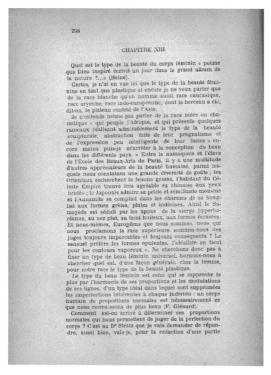

Figure 5.7 Page 238 in Chapter 13 of *Le Corset*.

Translation

What type of beauty does the female body have that becomes a "poem that inspired God [which he] once wrote in the great album of nature? . . ." (Heine).[21]

Certainly, I have in mind here only the type of feminine beauty as plastic, flexible and changeable, and again I mean only the white race that is also called Caucasian race, Aryan race, Indo-European race, whose cradle was, it is said, the central plateau of Asia.[22]

I never hear about the beauty of black or chamitic[23] race "that populates Africa, and which presents some branches admirably realizing the type of sculptural beauty, apart from their prognathism[24] and the unintelligent expressions of their faces;"[25] even less can I understand the conception of beauty in the different countries. "Between the Namaquois[26] and the student of the École des Beaux-Arts de Paris, there are a multitude of other appreciators of human beauty, among whom we see a great diversity of tastes; the Orientals are looking for the plumper woman, the inhabitant of the Celestial Empire finds very pleasant his Chinese with bridled eyes; the Japanese admires his small and semillant mousmé,[27] and the Annamite[28] was pleased by the charms of his kong-hai with her slender forms, flat and indecisive. Thus the Samoyed[29] is seduced by the appas[30] of the hyperborean virgin, with a flat nose, oily complexion, crushed features. And we, Europeans that we are, we who proclaim ourselves the superior race, are we always impeccable and always consistent judges? The sensual prefers opulent forms, the idealist holds for vaporous contours." Let us therefore not seek to determine a type of universal feminine beauty; let us limit ourselves to seeking what is, in a general way, in women, for our race the type of plastic beauty.

The type of the beautiful feminine is the one that comes closest by the harmony of its proportions and the modulations of its lines, of an ideal type in which the imperfections inherent in each individual are removed: a human body of normal proportions is necessarily the most beautiful thing we know (F. Glénard).

21 This source is not listed in the bibliography, but is "Le Cantique des Cantiques" (1850), by Christian Johann Heinrich (Henri) Heine (http://www.larecherchedubonheur.com/article-6201450.html)

22 And here we move into the part where O'Followell is overtly racist toward non-white women. While many of these attitudes are context dependent, meaning they were widely accepted at the time and based on the so-called "science" of racial hierarchies, this remains white supremacism, and we cannot ignore the consequences of O'Followell's (and others') writings.

23 Dictionaries seem to think he means Hamitic, a now outdated way of referring to the peoples and languages of the Horn of Africa.

24 Prognathism is a misalignment of the jaws (either mandibular or maxillary), causing an overbite or underbite, and a protrusion of one jaw past the other. This particular facial shape occurs in all populations in the world to various degrees, but was once thought to be indicative of African ancestry. Biological anthropology no longer uses facial shape to determine race, ethnicity, or ancestry, due to the fact that the difference within populations is greater than the difference between populations. However, during O'Followell's time, the so-called "hierarchy of races" was still very much believed accurate, stemming from early biological anthropology and the measure of skull size and other anthropometrics done by Samuel George Morton (1799–1851), Francis Galton (1822–1911), and Alphonse Bertillon (1853–1914), among others.

25 The phrase ". . . the unintelligent expressions of their faces" used to dismiss an entire race of people is unspeakably racist. It is cruel. Also, in possibly the mildest charge one could make against this phrase which deserves complete and utter condemnation, it goes against the spirit of scientific and medical inquiry. How can we trust anything O'Followell has written, when he categorizes people by the color of their skin and the shape of their face? The worth of patients as case studies is that one individual is a curiosity, and enough exemplars of a certain disease or disorder can add up to a syndrome which can be diagnosed, yet within that syndrome the patients are still individuals. He completely fails to do this for corseting "damage" and ignores the practice of science for base and racist generalizations.

26 Namibians/Hottentots. This term, and the term Hottentots, are both obviously antiquated, and no longer used.

27 This translates literally to "sparkling moss."

28 This refers to the Vietnamese.

29 The Samoyedic people of northern Russia.

30 Charms.

239

> .... Nous trouvons la Vénus de Milo belle comme elle est, mais, habillée à la mode actuelle, elle nous semblerait affreuse, car les vêtements qu'on porte aujourd'hui lui épaissiraient encore la taille. Vous admirez la Vénus de Milo et vous admirez une taille fine, mais une fois la femme mince déshabillée, vous serez obligés de conclure qu'elle doit être laide puisqu'elle ne ressemblera pas à la Vénus.
>
> Et pourtant l'expérience vous donnera tort. Vous serez donc obligé de conclure autrement, et dans ce sens qu'on a beau connaître par cœur la Vénus de Milo, cela ne donne aucunement le droit de porte un jugement sur le corps d'une femme habillée.

Translation

.... We find the Venus de Milo beautiful as it is, but, dressed in current fashion, it would look awful to us, because modern clothes would make its waist appear thicker.[31] You admire the Venus de Milo and you admire a slim waist, but once the slim woman is undressed, you will be forced to conclude that she must be ugly since she will not look like the Venus.

And yet experience will prove you wrong. You will therefore be forced to conclude otherwise, and in this sense that we may know by heart the Venus de Milo, it does not give us any right to make a judgement on the body of a clothed woman.

31   Here again we see O'Followell's willingness to compare living women to artwork—one that he expressed to its fullest in the 1905 book, following Lord (1868). See Chapter 1 of this book, footnote 63, for a discussion of O'Followell's use of Lord's work.

240

> La statue de Vénus remplit les conditions que nous exigeons d'une figure féminine normale. Chez la danseuse voici ce que nous constatons : l'usage du corset a déterminé un rétrécissement artificiel de la taille, les seins sont mal placés, la position des genoux est défectueuse ; enfin l'articulation du pied est trop forte.
>
> La conception de la beauté chez les modernes est donc

Translation

The statue of Venus fulfills the conditions we demand of a normal female figure. In the dancer here is what we find: the use of the corset has determined an artificial narrowing of the waist, the breasts are poorly placed, the position of the knees is defective; finally the joint of the foot is too strong.[32]

The conception of beauty among modern people is therefore

32 It is unclear if he is referring to the statue as badly formed, or a living dancer.

241

> basée sur une connaissance de la tête, des mains et des bras, acquise par l'expérience quotidienne, et en ce qui concerne les autres parties du corps sur l'impression d'ensemble qu'a laissée la vue de reproductions artistiques.
>
> Le public en général, n'est donc pas compétent pour juger la beauté féminine ; d'une part il est trompé par des reproductions infidèles, et d'autre part le corset, la chaussure, tous les vêtements en somme contribuent à lui créer des illusions ; l'idéal qu'il conçoit n'est donc nullement en rapport avec la réalité.

Translation

based on a knowledge of the head, hands, and arms, acquired through daily experience, and with regard to other parts of the body on the overall impression left by the sight of artistic reproductions.

The general public, therefore, is not competent to judge female beauty; on the one hand it is deceived by unfaithful reproductions, and on the other hand the corset, the shoe—all clothes, in short—contribute to create illusions for it; the ideal it gives rise to is therefore in no way related to reality.[33]

33 Ideals are never related to reality, but the idea that the comparison between artwork, the living clothed body, and the living naked body creates some sort of lack of ability to know what attracts oneself is not born out by experience, and discounts the tastes, knowledge, and experiences of the "general public." One can see this in a fashion scholar contemporary to O'Followell—Auguste Racinet—who compiled a magnificent and comprehensive tome of *Costume History* (1888). Originally in six volumes, it begins in the "Ancient World" and ends in the ninenteenth century, detailing the fashion of everything from the military to the court across the entire globe. It also spans socio-economic class, showing not only courtly fashions, but that of the least well paid too.

242

> Un exemple suffira pour montrer comment des connaisseurs eux-mêmes peuvent se laisser entraîner par le courant de l'opinion à des conceptions erronées.
>
> Je choisis à cet effet la Vénus florentine d'Alexandre Botticelli, à laquelle les préraphaélistes ont donné l'éclatant témoignage d'une admiration sans bornes.
>
> Voici cependant, continue le docteur Stratz, ce que je voudrais répondre à leurs tirades : « la figure de la Vénus de Botticelli est pleine d'un charme délicat et mélancolique qui produit une profonde impression ; mais si l'on examine la figure de plus près, on découvre dans le cou long et mince, dans les épaules tombantes, dans le thorax étroit et affaissé, dans les seins qui se trouvent par suit trop bas et trop rapprochés, le type bien caractérisé de la phtisique dont la beauté si triste inspire ici comme dans la réalité un vif sentiment de pitié. Et si nous réfléchissons que Simonetta Catanea est née en 1453 et qu'après s'être mariée en 1468 avec Marco Vespucci elle est morte de la phtisie dès 1476 à peine âgée de vingt-trois ans, il nous paraît bien vraisemblable qu'elle a servi de modèle pour la Vénus de Botticelli et que l'artiste, pour des raisons faciles à imaginer, n'a légèrement changé que les traits du visage : Botticelli a donc, sans le savoir, fait d'un type de belle phtisique son idéal. Ses héritiers et ses imitateurs ne s'en sont pas rendu compte et, séduits par son idéal, ils ont imprimé à des modèles parfaitement sains une partie des symptômes de la phtisie, créant ainsi des êtres hybrides, impossibles dans la réalité.

Translation

An example will suffice to show how connoisseurs themselves can be led by current opinion to wrong conclusions.

To this end, I choose the Florentine Venus of Alexander Botticelli, for which the Pre-Raphaelites had boundless admiration.

Here, however, continues Dr. Stratz, is what I would like to respond to their effusiveness: "Botticelli's figure of Venus is full of a delicate and melancholic charm that leaves a deep impression; but if one examines the figure more closely, one discovers in the long and thin neck, in the drooping shoulders, in the narrow and sagging chest, in the breasts which are then too low and too close, the well-characterized type of the phtisic[34] [sic] whose beauty so sad inspires here as in reality a strong feeling of pity. And if we think that Simonetta Catanea[35] [sic] was born in 1453 and that, after marrying Marco Vespucci in 1468, she died of phthisis in 1476 at just twenty-three years old, it seems very likely to us that she served as a model for Botticelli's Venus and that the artist, for reasons easy to imagine, changed the facial features only slightly: Botticelli therefore, without knowing it, made a type of beautiful phtisic his ideal. His heirs and imitators did not realize it and, seduced by his ideal, they imprinted on perfectly healthy models part of the symptoms of phthisis, thus creating hybrid beings, impossible in reality.[36]

34 Now spelled phthisic, this is a person with chronically inflamed lungs or another lung illness, like tuberculosis, which is, of course, not caused by corseting (Klebs 1909).

35 Cattaneo.

36 It appears that history was wrong about the reason behind Simonetta's death (Pozzilli et al. 2019), but O'Followell could not have known that. However, he still gives artistic styles and trends more weight and influence than they were at all capable of. Whether or not the phthisic form became desirable or fashionable, it would not have easily been imitated, nor does it have anything to do with corseting, despite the conflation of corseting with bad lung health.

251

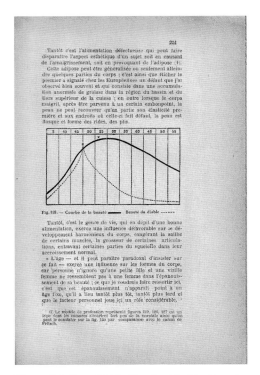

Figure 5.8 Page 251 in Chapter 13 of *Le Corset*.

Translation

Sometimes a poor diet can make the aesthetic appearance of a subject disappear either by causing weight loss or by causing adiposis (1).

This adiposis can be generalized or only affect a few parts of the body; this is how Richer first reported in European women a defect that I have observed very often and which consists of an abnormal accumulation of fat in the region of the pelvis and the upper third of the thigh; in addition, when the body loses weight, the skin can only partially recover its primary elasticity and in places where that is lacking, the skin is flaccid and forms wrinkles or folds.

[5.8][37]

Sometimes, it is the kind of life, which despite a good diet, exerts an unfavorable influence on the harmonious development of the body, exaggerating the protrusion of certain muscles, the size of certain joints, and hindering certain parts of the skeleton in their normal growth.

Age—and it may seem paradoxical to insist on this fact—exerts an influence on the body's physical appearance, for no one is unaware that a little girl and an old woman do not resemble a woman in the full bloom of beauty; what I would like to point out here is that this development does not appear at a fixed age, that varies from person to person.

(1) The occupational model shown in Figures 119, 126, and 127 is a type whose measurements deviate very little from normal, as can be seen in Figure 130 by comparison with the Fritsch canon.

37   Regrettably, the text on this page does not discuss the image, because the image of the beauty curve is what really requires discussion here. In the next footnote, I will ask you to return to this graph.

252

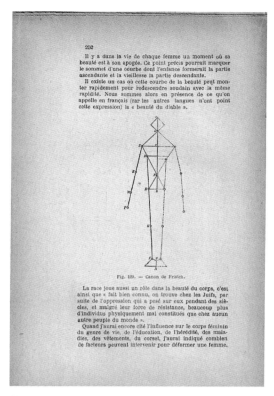

Figure 5.9 Page 252 in Chapter 13 of *Le Corset*.

Translation

There is a moment in every woman's life when her beauty is at its peak. This precise point could mark the top of a curve of which childhood would form the ascending part and old age the descending part.

There is a case where this curve of beauty can rise quickly and then descend with the same speed. We are then in the presence of what is called in French (because other languages do not have this expression) the "beauty of the devil."[38]

[5.9]

Race also plays a role in the beauty of the body, as "a well-known fact is that one finds among the Jews, as a result of the oppression that has weight on them for centuries, and despite their strength of resistance, many more physically ill-constituted individuals than in any other people in the world."[39]

38 See graph on page 213. The "beauté du diable" or beauty of the devil, according to the graph that O'Followell just completely made out of whole cloth, peaks at 17.5 years old, and by the time a woman is 32.5 years old, she holds the same sexual appeal as . . . a five year old girl. Among the many confusing things about this graph, perhaps the most confusing is why it begins at a non-sexual/non-marriageable age. Also worth noting is that the sudden rise of the "beauté du diable" is matched by its sudden descent, indicating that women not so blessed (cursed?) have a slower fade into non-beauty.

39 As an ethnically Jewish woman who has heard everything from opinions on my nose, to opinions on my hair, to opinions on my body type, I am personally offended and made weary by this ignorant, racist commentary on Jewish beauty, which was ignorant and racist during O'Followell's time. The dangerous stereotypes of Jews as ugly, and that ugliness as a moral failing, continue to this day, with such things as fictional goblin caricatures that emphasize beaked noses and wavy dark hair, to political cartoons that include the idea of Shylock-based characters.

That O'Followell is writing shortly before the rise of Nazi Germany is of note in regard to the existence and perpetuation of anti-Jew stereotypes in casual usage at the time. *Le Corset* is a book explicitly meant to train a new generation of doctors about the potential for corset damage. As such, it is ostensibly a professional medical textbook, yet the author has veered off into antisemitism. To repeat: antisemitism is being set up to be taught to doctors in 1908 as a factual determiner of beauty.

One aspect O'Followell did get right, however, although he could not have known it in 1908, is the generational effects of trauma—not on beauty, but on the epigenetics of a population. A 2018 study shows that the trauma of experiencing the horrors of concentration camps lives on in the expression of genes that code for how a person deals with stress (https://www.research.va.gov/currents/1016-3.cfm).

253

> Quant aux femmes dont le corps n'a pas les lignes de la beauté celles-là sont légion. Eh bien ! toutes femmes ayant été belles et femmes ne l'ayant jamais été, toutes veulent le paraître aussi longtemps qu'un artifice de toilette pourra les y aider, voilà pourquoi la femme gardera son corset.
>
> Etre une beauté, ce n'est pas là le souci de la femme. Si peu y pourraient prétendre ! Ce que veut la femme c'est *paraître* belle ; c'est plaire. Reste à savoir comment la femme peut plaire, pourquoi la femme veut plaire.
> [Fin.]

Translation

As for women whose bodies do not possess the lines of beauty, these are legion. Well! All women, beautiful or not, want to look as attractive as possible for as long as beauty aids can help them do so, and that is why the woman will keep wearing her corset.

Being a beauty is not the concern of the woman. So few could lay claim it! What the woman wants is to *look* beautiful; it's pleasing. It remains to be seen how the woman can please, why the woman wants to please.

[End.]

CHAPTER 14

254

> Chercher comment la femme s'y prend pour plaire à l'homme, c'est répondre à cette question : quelles femmes plaisent aux hommes.

Translation

To work out how women go pleasing men is to answer this question: *which* women please men.[40]

40   One cannot look at women or men as a monolith, nor list out desirable properties which make women pleasing to men. Not every man who has relationships with women who do not fit the mold is "settling," and not every woman who does not fit the mold is "undesirable."

255

> 1° La femme qui plaît aux hommes, n'est pas la femme belle. La beauté n'a plus d'influence sur les hommes. La femme belle est admirée ; elle n'est pas aimée. Je serais assez de l'avis de M. Rafford Pyke sur ce point. Seulement je ferai remarquer que la statistique est excessivement difficile sur cette affaire, parce que le nombre des femmes belles est excessivement restreint. Les femmes jolies sont, Dieu merci, très nombreuses ; les femmes que l'on peut appeler belles sont des exceptions infiniment rares. Dès lors quelle statistique établir ? Voit-on beaucoup de femmes belles rester sans preneur ou sans adorateur ? On ne le peut pas, puisqu'il n'y a presque pas de femmes belles. Si l'on en rencontre une qui soit demeuré délaissée, ce peut être un pur hasard et l'on n'en peut rien conclure.
> 2° La femme qui plaît aux hommes, toujours d'après M. Rafford Pyke, est la femme gracieuse plutôt que la femme jolie.

Translation

1. Women who please men are not necessarily beautiful. Beauty no longer has any influence on men. The beautiful woman is admired; but she is not loved.[41] I would agree with Mr. Rafford Pyke[42] on this point. Only I would point out that the statistics are excessively difficult on this matter, because the number of beautiful women is extremely small. Pretty women are, thank God, very numerous; women who can be called beautiful, however, are infinitely

rare exceptions. So what statistics should be established? Do we see many beautiful women remaining without a suitor? We can't, since there are almost no beautiful women. If we meet one who has been overlooked, it may be pure coincidence and we cannot draw any conclusions from that.

    2. The woman who pleases men, always according to Mr. Rafford Pyke, is graceful rather than pretty.

41   I am not certain here if he is using "admired" to mean gazed upon, though it would fit with the feel of the sentence.

42   Rafford Pyke, an alias used by Harry Thurston Peck, is for some reason always called "Mr. Rafford Pyke" by O'Followell, which is odd—O'Followell often truncates authors' names to the point where they are difficult to search out. The extent to which this is a divergence from O'Followell's usual style makes me wonder if he is doing it to be rude, despite the fact that he appears to agree with Pyke's (or Peck's) assessments. However, true to form, Pyke is not in the bibliography, and while much of his work is extant I am unable to determine which would relate to women's beauty.

256

3° La femme qui plaît, c'est la femme élégante, c'est-à-dire : la femme qui plaît, c'est la femme qui sait s'encadrer. C'est la femme qui s'habille bien, premier cadre, et pour bien s'habiller je n'ai pas besoin de dire qu'il faut savoir choisir les couleurs et les dessins d'ajustement conformes à sa personnalité et s'y adaptant naturellement.

Translation

3. The woman who pleases is the elegant woman, that is to say: the woman who pleases, it is the woman who knows how to frame herself. It is the woman who dresses well, top of the line, and to dress well it goes without saying that it is important to choose the colors and styles that suit one's personality.

257

Il y a, en effet, bien peu de femmes qui peuvent montrer nues des formes impeccables, presque toutes ont besoin de mentir à l'homme par l'arrangement du costume et, en cette façon de mentir, elles sont expertes plus que dans toutes les autres.

Le corset est là qui lui apporte son aide trompeuse et quand, grâce à lui, grâce à ses dessous, grâce à sa robe, la femme est arrivée à plaire ; à son tour, prise à son mensonge, elle s'estime non seulement élégante mais belle estimant certificats de beauté ses succès auprès des hommes.

Translation

There are, in fact, very few women who look wonderful naked; almost all of them need to lie to the man by the way they dress and, in this way of lying, they are the undisputed experts.

The corset is used to help women in this deception given that, thanks to it, thanks to her underwear, thanks to her dress, the woman has managed to please; in turn, she is caught up in her lie, considering herself not only elegant but beautiful, and seeing her successes with men as certificates of beauty.[43]

43 There are three instances of the verb "to lie" and one of "to deceive" in the previous two sentences. O'Followell apparently not only thinks women are out to trick men, but that men are stupid enough to not understand the concept of a corset.

258

> Et elles plaisent et elles représentent du plaisir parce que peu d'hommes malheureusement songent à faire de la femme une compagne et que presque tous poussés par l'instinct ne voient dans l'être féminin qu'un instrument de jouissance.
>
> C'est ainsi que la femme coquette et élégante l'a compris, inconsciemment peut-être, mais non moins certainement et c'est pourquoi elle a compris aussi comment dans notre civilisation, elle peut par la constriction du corset, par l'art du costume, augmenter la mise en valeur ou produire l'illusion des lignes ondoyantes qui sont celles de la beauté féminine ; lignes ondoyantes, apparentes ou réelles, auxquelles elle doit d'être désirée par eux.

Translation

And they please and they represent pleasure because few men unfortunately think of making the woman a companion; almost all, driven by instinct, see in the feminine being only an instrument of enjoyment.[44]

This is how the coquettish and elegant woman understood it, unconsciously perhaps, but no less certainly and that is why she also understood how in our civilization, she can—by wearing a corset, by the ways she dresses—the costume, increase the enhancement or produce the illusion of the undulating lines that embody female beauty; undulating lines, apparent or real, to which they must be aspire.

44 And yet somehow this becomes the responsibility and fault of the woman, again.

259

> Mais pourquoi la femme veut-elle [sic.] dissimuler ces défauts et ces pauvretés, pourquoi veut-elle [sic.] par des artifices divers

Translation

But why does the woman want to hide these defects and these shortcomings? Why does she want by various artifices,

260

> par ce contraste que produit une taille fine augmenter ou simuler l'opulence de la croupe et des seins ? C'est que les régions mammaires et fessières constituent encore dans notre civilisation actuelle des régions d'attirance du regard et du désir masculin. De tout temps, des femmes dépourvues de charmes mammaires ont eu recours à des artifices de toilette.

Translation

by this contrast that produces a slim waist increase or simulate the opulence of the derriere and breasts? It is that, even today, the mammary and gluteal regions still constitute the parts of the body to which the male gaze and desire is most attracted? Historically, flat-chested women have resorted to artificial aids.[45]

45 Let us contrast this with O'Followell's discussion of the Botticelli Venus/Simonetta Cattaneo. Depictions of *la bella Simonetta* show her small breasted and thick waisted, yet he acknowledges her as the standard of beauty of her time, a model for all models.

262

Rien n'est changé maintenant : la femme est aujourd'hui pour l'homme avant tout un objet de jouissance ; subordonnée au point de vue économique, il lui faut considérer dans le mariage sa sécurité ; elle dépend donc de l'homme, elle devient une parcelle de sa propriété. Sa situation est rendue plus défavorable encore par ce fait que, en règle générale, le nombre des femmes est supérieur à celui des hommes. Cette disproportion numérique, excite la concurrence rendue plus âpre encore par suite de ce que nombre d'hommes pour toutes sortes de raisons ne se marient pas. C'est ainsi que la femme est obligée, en donnant à son extérieur l'allure la plus avantageuse possible, d'entamer, avec toutes celles de ses congénères du même rang qu'elle la lutte pour l'homme (*La Femme*, Bebel).

L'amour n'est en effet qu'un piège tendu à l'individu. La nature ne songe qu'au maintien de l'espèce et pour la perpétuer, elle n'a que faire de notre sottise. A ne consulter que la raison quel est l'homme qui voudrait être père et se préparer tant de soucis pour l'avenir ; quelle femme pour une épilepsie de quelques minutes se donnerait une maladie d'une année entière (Chamfort).

Translation

Nothing has changed: today, the woman is above all an object of enjoyment for the man; given that she plays a subordinate role economically, he must consider his security in marriage; she therefore depends on the man, she becomes his property.[46] Her situation is made even more unfavorable by the fact that, as a rule, there are more women than men. This numerical disparity makes the competition even more bitter given that, for all kinds of reasons, many men do not marry. This is how the woman is obliged, by making her appearance as attractive as possible, to give herself an advantage among her peers in the struggle for a partner man (*The Woman*, Bebel).[47]

Love is indeed only a trap set for the individual.[48] Nature thinks only of the maintenance of the species and to perpetuate it; it does not care about our foolishness. To consult only one's reason, what explains a man who would like to be a father, but who must prepare for so many worries for the future; what woman for an convulsion of a few minutes would give herself an illness of a whole year (Chamfort).[49]

46 While customarily O'Followell is correct about this, legally he is incorrect. Women in France at in 1908 had the right to own property and open bank accounts independent of their husbands. However, in custom and in practicality, most likely not many women did so. A woman would be subordinate from the economic point of view because of her lesser earning power, and because of the economic domination of her husband. Were he to give her an allowance, and not object to her holding her own bank account, she need not be "a parcel of his property."

Use of that phrase requires some unpacking. To be "a parcel of his property" does not just imply but outright states ownership. That she is his to do with as he wants. That he finds no value in her beyond her beauty, his ability to enjoy her. It is a dismal view of not only women's other features (see again Chapter 4 of this book for a longer discussion on misogyny and its continual harms to women's rights and social standing), but also of men's drives, intelligence, desires, fidelity, and emotional maturity. Though, he is using this to discuss the entrapment of men by female corseting, and therefore, of course, it is not the man's fault for being entrapped.

47 Bebel is not listed in the bibliography, but refers to *Woman and Socialism* (1879) by August Bebel (1840–1913), in which he is arguing against women's dependence on men, directly contra to the chosen paraphrase by O'Followell.

48 Again, an extremely miserly view of humanity, implying that women, who entice men to love them through their use of corsets, are setting the trap.

49 "... for a convulsion of a few minutes ...," here referring to orgasm, and "... give herself an illness of a whole year ..." to pregnancy. Even ignoring the misunderstood nature of the female orgasm (Gross 2022), a process that even today is under-researched and not taken seriously by most of the medical community, we can imagine it was even less understood or valued at the time. O'Followell implies here that the female orgasm is trivial, and that motherhood is the only reason to entrap men into sex, and therefore into marriage and parenthood. Yet if a woman did want sex for pleasure, if she found enjoyment in it, if she had explored her own body and learned about her desires and pleasures, and if she did experience orgasm, she too had no options other than divest herself of the respect of society and her social status to enjoy sex as an unmarried woman, or to marry and hope that her partner would be attentive to her, match her sex drive, and work with her to have as many or as few children as she wished to bear.

To fully appreciate the speciousness of O'Followell's argument, let us return to the state of birth control at the turn of the twentieth century. The Pill was still several decades away, and birth control was dubiously/variously legal depending on where one lived (Chandrasekhar 1981). The diaphragm was available, having been created in the mid-1800s, but came with its own problems in terms of needing to have a prescription for it, needing to care for and clean it between uses, needing to insert it hours before sex (which assumes one knows when sex will happen and consents to sexual acts at that time), and associated rubber and latex allergies. Various caustic douches and other substances could be used after sex, but might be painful or harmful. In 1908, there were few legal and practical options. The rhythm method or natural planning might work, but because of the variability of people's menstrual cycles it has never been the most reliable way of preventing pregnancy. Often, during O'Followell's time, the result of sex was pregnancy, wanted or not. Having spent an entire chapter on the wickedness of women tightening their corset to abort, one thinks he might have made the connection that not all pregnancies are wanted, and not all women are trying to entrap men into fatherhood.

265

> « Le vêtement développe un sentiment qui souvent s'associe à l'amour, la curiosité ; il exalte aussi ce désir au pa-

Translation

"The garment develops a feeling that is often associated with love—curiosity; it also exalts this desire at the paroxysm;

266

roxysme ; souvent l'excitation sexuelle tombe en même temps que les vêtements de la femme qui s'offre à nous sans combat » (Joanny Roux).

.... Habillez chez le grand couturier la Vénus de Milo, voire la Joconde, elle aura l'air d'une chienlit. Le mannequin rêvé par tous les artistes de l'aiguille est la femme sans contours, le schéma de femme, sur lequel on peut draper et suspendre indéfiniment des étoffes, des dentelles, des broderies. La beauté de la femme contemporaine est essentiellement une beauté de habillée, où le visage même et la chevelure sont œuvres d'art . . .

Translation

often sexual arousal falls at the same time as the clothes of the woman who offers herself to us without a fight" (Joanny Roux).[50]

.... Dressed at the great couturier even the Venus de Milo, or even the Mona Lisa, would look like shit in a bed.[51] The model dreamed of by all the artists of the needle is the woman without contours, a blank canvas on which one can drape and hang countless fabrics, lace, and embroidery. The beauty of the contemporary woman is essentially a beauty of dress, where the face itself and the hair are works of art . . .

50 This is in the bibliography as *Psychologie de l'instinct sexuel* 1899 by Joanny Roux (1866–1909), and is an accurate quote, but fails to adequately demonstrate or explain why men would detumesce when faced with a naked woman.

51 Chienlit, literally translates to dog's bed, but colloquially means shit/shit the bed/shit in the bed, chie-en-lit. Its origin stems from a Parisian Carnival/Masquerade character, dressed in bedroom attire, who has made a mess of the bed itself—whether though mere chaos, or through decorative use of stains to indicate fecal matter. Prior to the most famous use of the term by Charles de Gaulle in 1968, though scatological it was not always attached to a female character. So while O'Followell was being uncharacteristically vulgar and deliberately offensive, he was not necessarily employing his usual misogyny.

268

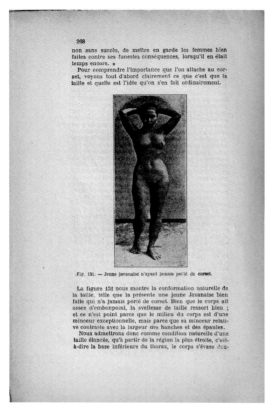

268

non sans succès, de mettre en garde les femmes bien
faites contre ses funestes conséquences, lorsqu'il en était
temps encore. »
Pour comprendre l'importance que l'on attache au corset, voyons tout d'abord clairement ce que c'est que la
taille et quelle est l'idée qu'on s'en fait ordinairement.

Fig. 131. — Jeune Javanaise n'ayant jamais porté de corset.

La figure 131 nous montre la conformation naturelle de
la taille, telle que la présente une jeune Javanaise bien
faite qui n'a jamais porté de corset. Bien que le corps ait
assez d'embonpoint, la sveltesse de taille ressort bien ;
et ce n'est point parce que le milieu du corps est d'une
minceur exceptionnelle, mais parce que sa minceur relative contraste avec la largeur des hanches et des épaules.
Nous admettrons donc comme condition naturelle d'une
taille élancée, qu'à partir de la région la plus étroite, c'est-
à-dire la base inférieure du thorax, le corps s'évase dou-

Figure 5.10 Page 268 in Chapter 14 of *Le Corset*.

Translation

To understand the importance we attach to the corset, let's first clearly see what size is and how we normally understand it.

[5.10]

Figure 131 shows us the natural confirmation of the waist, as presented by a well-made young Javanese woman who has never worn a corset. Although the body is quite overweight, her slender size is evident; and this is not because the middle of the body is exceptionally slim, but because its relative slimness contrasts with the width of the hips and shoulders.[52]

We will therefore admit as a natural condition of a slender waist, that from the narrowest region, that is to say the lower base of the thorax, the body flares up gently

52 See previous discussion of racism.

269

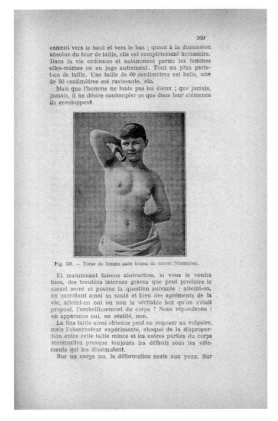

Figure 5.11 Page 269 in Chapter 14 of *Le Corset*.

Translation

upwards and downwards; as for the absolute dimension of the waist circumference, it is completely incidental.[53] In ordinary life, and especially among women themselves, we judge differently. At most, we are talking about size. A size of 60 centimeters is beautiful, a size of 50 centimeters is delightful, etc.

But let man not tempt the gods; because never, ever, does he desire to contemplate what they encompass in their idea of clemency.

[5.11]

And now let us disregard, if you will, the serious internal disorders that the tight corset can produce and ask the following question: do we achieve, by sacrificing our health and many of the pleasures of life, do we achieve, yes or no, the true goal that we had proposed, the beautification of the body? We will answer: in appearance or, in reality, no.[54]

53 Ratio vs. waist size; see Gibson 2020.
54 This is, of course, incredibly subjective.

271

L'importance du rôle du corset dans la toilette féminine est donc capitale. Sans corset « lui faisant une jolie taille » pas de robe qui « habille bien » sans vêtement qui la pare et la répare, nul moyen pour la femme d'attirer le regard et d'attiser le désir.

Translation

The importance of the role of the corset in the female toilette is therefore crucial. Without a corset "making her a pretty size," no dress that "drapes well," without clothing that adorns and repairs her, there can be no way for the woman to attract the eye and stir up desire.

272

Que si quelqu'un n'était point convaincu de ces vérités, je lui citerai une vieille loi anglaise promulguée sous Charles II ; loi dont le texte, chose peu banale, n'a jamais été abrogé.

Cette loi édictait « que les femmes de tout âge, de tout rang, de tout métier ou grade qui par le port du corset, trompent les sujets masculins de Sa Majesté et les induisent par ce moyen en mariage soient atteintes par les peines applicables à la sorcellerie, à la magie noire et autres crimes de ce genre, en vertu des lois existantes, et que leur mariage soit déclaré nul par suite de la condamnation. »

. . . .

De tout ce qui précède, il m'apparaît bien résulter que je puis poser et résoudre ces deux questions—toutes conditions de costumes et de mœurs égales d'ailleurs— ; la femme doit-elle [sic] porter un corset ? non. La femme portera-t-elle un corset ? oui.

. . . .

En résumé, le costume agit sur celui qui le porte et c'est pourquoi la tradition clairvoyante a établi un habit spécial à chaque sexe, à chaque âge, à chaque profession. Le costume développe et renforce les idées que sa forme suggère et parfois impose. Aussi n'est-ce pas sans logique que les féministes avisées et hardies ont souvent protesté contre la tyrannie de leurs vêtements et surtout contre celle des armatures si gracieuses qui les doublent et les soutiennent.

Translation

Were anyone were not convinced of these truths, I would quote to him an old English law promulgated under Charles II, the text of which, unusually, has never been repealed.

This law provided that "women of any age, rank, profession or class who, by wearing the corset, deceive his Majesty's male subjects and induce them by this means into marriage shall be attained by the penalties applicable to witchcraft, black magic, and other such crimes, under existing laws, and that their marriage be declared null and void as a result of the conviction."[55]

. . . .

From all the above, it seems to me that I can ask and resolve these two questions—all conditions of equal costumes and morals by the way—does the woman have to wear a corset? No. Will the woman wear a corset? Yes.

. . . .

In short, the costume has an effect on the wearer and that is why the clairvoyant tradition has established a special dress for each sex, for each age, for each profession. The costume develops and reinforces the ideas that its shape suggests and sometimes imposes. So it is not without logic that wise and bold feminists have often protested against the tyranny of their clothes and especially that of the graceful armatures that doubles the shape of their body and supports them.

55 The annulment of the marriage is the least concerning thing about this law, which straight out and without equivocation declares that women who wear corsets are deceiving men by supernatural means. Charles II reigned over Scotland between 1649 and 1651, and over England, Scotland, and Ireland from 1660 to 1685, which means he would have assisted the clergy in presiding over the Great Scottish Witch Hunt of 1649–50, as well as the enactment of the Scottish Witchcraft Act of 1649, making anything considered witchcraft both a felony (state criminalization) and heresy (religious criminalization) punishable by death.

I am unable to confirm the text of this law, and in fact a blog called "The Statutes Project" says that it is a "fake law" (Levin 2018) meant to stir fears about women and femininity, but not created as an actual proposed law. However, its inclusion, accurate or not—and to be clear, O'Followell thought it was accurate—gives you a firm understanding of O'Followell's take on whether or not women seek to entrap men with their corset wear.

273

> Et c'est pourquoi ne pouvant faire disparaître le corset, le médecin doit s'efforcer de faire disparaître ses dangers dans la plus grande mesure possible.
> Donc je ne perdrai pas mon temps en d'inutiles anathèmes contre le corset, je vais m'efforcer de trouver avec cet ennemi de la santé de bien des femmes un *modus vivendi* qui satisfasse le monde médical sans mécontenter le public féminin. La tâche est délicate, aussi ai-je droit à quelque indulgence si je ne la remplis pas au gré de tous.
> Je fais d'abord examiner quel corset la femme doit porter puis j'étudierai comment elle doit lacer son corset.
> [Fin.]

Translation

And that is why, not being able to make the corset disappear, the doctor must strive to make its dangers disappear to the greatest extent possible.

So I will not waste my time in useless railing against the corset; instead, I will strive to find a way to combat this enemy of the health of many women with a modus vivendi that satisfies the medical world without dissatisfying the female public. The task is delicate, so I am entitled to some indulgence if I do not pleas everyone in the process.

I first examine which corset the woman should wear and then I will study how she should lace it.

[End.]

CHAPTER 15

274

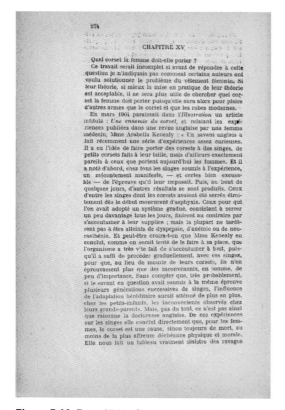

Figure 5.12 Page 274 in Chapter 15 of *Le Corset*.

Translation

What corset should the woman wear?

This work would be incomplete if, before answering this question, I did not indicate how some authors wanted to solve the problem of women's clothing. If their theory is better, the implementation of their theory acceptable, there is no point looking for which corset the woman must wear, since she will then have other ways of pleasing than the corset and modern fashions.

In March 1904 an article appeared in *L'Illustration* entitled "Une Ennemie du Corset," which recounted the experiments published in an English journal by a woman doctor, Mrs. Arabella Keneally:[56] "An English scientist has recently made a series of curious experiments. He had the idea of making monkeys wear corsets, small corsets made to their size, but moreover exactly the same as those worn today by women. And he first noted, in all the monkeys subjected to the experiment, a manifest misunderstanding—and certainly excusable—of the test he imposed on them. Then, after a few days, other results occurred. Those of the monkeys whose corsets had been tightly laced from the beginning died of asphyxiation.[57] Those for whom a graduated system had been adopted, consisting of tightening a little more every day, ended up instead getting used to their torment; but most soon developed dyspepsia, anemia, or neurasthenia.[58] And perhaps we will believe that as Mrs. Keneally [sic] concludes, and as one would be tempted to do in her place, that the organism very quickly became accustomed to everything, since it was enough to proceed gradually, with these monkeys, so that, instead of dying as a result of wearing corsets, they simply experience some inconvenience: in short, nothing that important. Not to mention that, most likely, if the scientist in question had subjected several successive generations of monkeys to the same test, the influence of hereditary adaptation would have increasingly mitigated, in grandchildren, the disadvantages observed in their grandparents. But, this is not at all how the English doctor reasoned. From these experiments on monkeys she directly concludes that, for women, the corset is a cause, if not always of death, then at least of the most awful physical and moral decay.[59]

56 Dr. Arabella Kenealy, spelled Keneally by O'Followell, (1859–1938), anti-feminist, is not listed in the bibliography, but the short article is available as "The Curse of Corsets" by Arabella Kenealy (1904).

57 This is grotesque. Animal abuses in the name of science are still carried out to this day, and I can find little more to say about this than the fact that even if they had the purest motives, which they did not—there was no need for this experiment to "prove" something not in evidence in the human population—the experiment itself was not set up correctly. They tortured monkeys to death for zero results.

58 I am relatively certain this is where a missing quotation mark would go.

59 This conclusion is illogical—did she witness "moral decay" in the monkeys? How was their baseline "morality" measured? Also, examining O'Followell line by line and quote by quote as I have done here, and paying close attention to his liberal use of paraphrasing and cherry-picking quotations, I have demonstrated that he does not have a single example of a woman conclusively dying because of the corset.

278

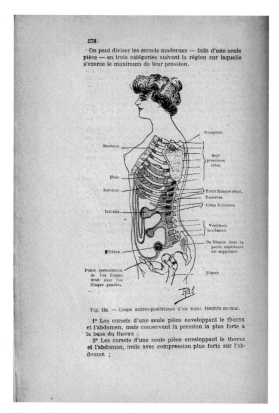

Figure 5.13 Page 278 in Chapter 15 of *Le Corset*.

Translation

Modern corsets—made from a single piece with no back lacing—can be divided into three categories according to the region on which the maximum pressure is exerted.

[5.13]

1. Corsets of a single piece that envelop the chest and abdomen, but retain the strongest pressure at the base of the chest;

2. Corsets of a single piece that envelop the chest and abdomen, but exert stronger compression on the abdomen;

279

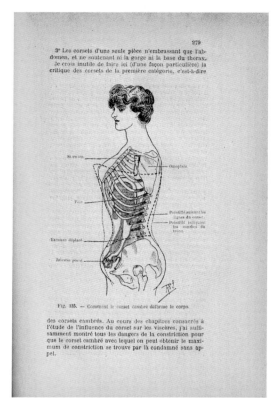

Figure 5.14 Page 279 in Chapter 15 of *Le Corset*.

Translation

3. The corsets of a single piece that cover only the abdomen, and support neither the throat nor the base of the chest.

I think it is useless to criticize here (in a particular way) the corsets of the first category, that is to say

[5.14]

arched corsets. During the chapters devoted to the study of the influence of the corset on the viscera, I have sufficiently shown all the dangers of constriction that the arched corset poses given that it can be used to maximum constriction. It is thus condemned without appeal.

280

...j'aborde l'étude critique des corsets de la deuxième catégorie, c'est-à-dire des corsets droits.

....

Vous dormez mal, n'est-ce-pas, Madame ? A minuit, une heure, deux heures du matin, vous êtes en proie à un malaise quelquefois tellement angoissant que vous croyez que c'est la fin. Torturée par des pincements, déchirements, dans la région du cœur, qui palpite et s'affole, me-

Translation

...and here I address the critical study of the second category of corsets, that is to say straight corsets.

....

You sleep badly, don't you, Madam? At midnight, one o'clock, two o'clock in the morning, you are in the grip of a malaise sometimes so distressing that you believe the end is nigh. Tortured by pinching and tearing around the heart, which pulsates and panics, threatens

281

nace d'éclater, vous ressentez des aigreurs, des brûlures à l'estomac et à la gorge, vous vous asseyez, vous vous levez, vous vous recouchez, tournez et retournez dans votre lit comme jadis sur son gril devait faire le martyr saint Laurent rôti par des charbons ardents. Vous vous endormez enfin, peut-être après avoir, à plusieurs reprises, largement imploré un alcool de menthe ou de mélisse, votre arme de chevet qui ne sert, par surcroit, qu'à vous acheminer vers l'alcoolisme insidieux. Le génie du mal vous nargue encore en votre sommeil qu'il surcharge et assombrit de noirs cauchemars, de rêves pénibles.

Véritable bourreau, ce sommeil se prolonge bien avant dans la matinée, et au réveil vous constatez amèrement que ce sommeil de plomb ne vous a procuré aucun repos. Et vous vous levez fatiguée, affaissée, exténuée.

Cette lassitude, cet effondrement de votre personne ne feront trêve que lorsque vous aurez mis votre corset. Vous en concluez que le corset est bienfaisant pour vous. Et cependant n'en croyez rien, car le corset, ce faux ami, et cause de tout le mal. Le port habituel du corset a rompu, en effet, l'équilibre de vos organes abdominaux.

Translation

to burst, you taste bitterness in your mouth, burning in the stomach and throat, you sit, you get up, you go back to bed, tossing and turning like St Lawrence being roasted on a grill by burning coals.[60] You finally fall asleep, perhaps after having repeatedly begged for mint or lemon balm liqueur, your bedside weapon that only serves, moreover, to lead you to insidious alcoholism. The evil genius still taunts you in your sleep that it overloads and darkens with dark nightmares, painful dreams.

A true executioner, this sleep continues well until the morning, and when you wake up you bitterly note that this leaden slumber has not given you any rest. And so you get up tired, sagging, exhausted.

This weariness, this collapse of your person, will not stop until you have put on your corset. You conclude that the corset is beneficial for you. And yet do not believe anything, because the corset, this false friend, causes all evil. The usual wearing of the corset has, in fact, disrupted the balance of your abdominal organs.

60 These symptoms do not describe corset-less sleep, but they do describe either Gastroesophageal Reflux Disease (GERD) which is severe heartburn caused by various structural or mechanical issues in the digestive tract, or a panic attack. While GERD would not be considered a distinct condition until much later, dyspepsia was the term for severe reflux and other indigestive issues in the early 1900s and was often diagnosed at the time.

282

> Dans le principe, toutes ces manifestations morbides s'effacent et disparaissent à mesure que la journée s'avance. Vous en êtes quitte pour quelques éblouissements, quelques vertiges, quelques bouffées de chaleur, quelques vapeurs.

Translation

In principle, all these morbid manifestations fade away and disappear as the day progresses. You are left with sore eyes, some dizziness, a few hot flashes, some vapors.

283

> Par ce temps de revendications féminines, à une époque où se fait sentir le besoin impérieux, la soif insatiable de liberté et d'indépendance, où la raison proteste et aspire, à briser toute entrave, où l'être naturel se rebiffe contre les conventions sociales ou mondaines qui l'ont déformé, ces considérations sont ici à leur place et ne sent pas à dédaigner : stigmate d'esclavage, *carcere duro,* le corset ajoute à l'infériorité naturelle de la femme et d'autant plus regrettable que celle-ci est consentie, voulue. Apôtres due féminisme, démolissez donc avant tout cette nouvelle Bastille, ou bien transformez-la !!! Que ce soit un confortable et secourable palais, non plus une prison !
>
> Il serait injuste, il est vrai, de ne pas reconnaître les importants progrès qui se sont réalisés dans l'industrie du corset. On ne peut que louer les efforts admirables de ces ardentes réformistes qui se doublent d'incomparables fées du chiffon. Nous ne voyons plus guère aujourd'hui, sur les dames soucieuses de leur santé et de leur beauté, ces affreux instruments de torture qui gonflant le ventre comme une outre, séparent nettement le corps en deux, le faisaient ressembler à un grotesque et ridicule sablier.

Translation

In this time of women's demands for suffrage, at a time when there is an urgent need, an insatiable thirst, for freedom and independence, when reason protests and aspires to overcome any obstacle, when the natural being rebels against the social or worldly conventions that have distorted it, these considerations remain and should be ignored: stigma of slavery, carcere duro, the corset adds to the natural inferiority of women, all the more regrettably given that it is consented to, wanted.[61] Apostles of feminism, demolish first and foremost this new Bastille, or transform it!!! Let it be a comfortable and helpful palace, rather than a prison!

It would be unfair, it is true, not to acknowledge the significant progress that has been made in the corset industry. One can only praise the admirable efforts of these ardent reformists who are coupled with the incomparable fairies of the rag.[62] We hardly see today, on ladies concerned about their health and beauty, those awful instruments of torture that inflate the belly, clearly separate the body in two, and make it look like a grotesque and ridiculous hourglass.

61 If one sees the corset as a prison, and oneself as being shackled inside it, the comparison to slavery might be apt, however, O'Followell fails to demonstrate that most, or even many, women felt this way (see also Bendall 2022 for a discussion of comfort and the corset). The end of the sentence, ". . . consented, wanted," indicates that they do not—that it is he, and his specifically picked authors, who feel that way. Not, of course, to gloss over the statement that it ". . . adds to the natural inferiority of women . . .," a statement inconsistent with his earlier claims that women are entrapping men. One might look at this contradiction in a theory-driven, subaltern-based way, insisting that the only power granted to women is their appearance, and so they are making men do their bidding with this control, and yet he also says that the corset fails to produce a beautiful, attractive, compelling woman. Then there is his reference to feminism, which is particularly ironic coming so soon after the reference to women's inferiority.

62 Slang meaning something akin to the modern "clothes horse," someone who enjoys or is even devoted to the newest fashions, and who thus carries with them an air of frivolity.

286

> On trouve cette harmonie chez la Vénus de Milo et chez la Vénus de Médicis, qui cependant n'ont pas la taille fine. C'est que le nombre de centimètres à la ceinture importe peu pour la beauté. Ce qui importe, c'est la silhouette, c'est l'ensemble, c'est l'harmonie.
>
> Vous pêchez donc contre l'esthétique, Mesdames, quand, sans considération pour l'ampleur du reste du corps, vous serrez exagérément votre taille au point de faire déborder des hanches luxuriantes qui pourraient parfois rivaliser avec celles de la Vénus hottentote ou Vénus Callipyge.
>
> N'oubliez pas que la coquetterie est l'art de se faire belle et qu'une des principales conditions de l'esthétique est l'harmonie des proportions. Si donc vous voulez être belles, ne cherchez pas la taille fine, méfiez-vous du corset droit.

Translation

This harmony is found in the Venus de Milo and the Venus de Medici, which however do not have slim waists. Belt measurements do not matter when it comes to beauty. What *does* matters is the silhouette—the whole, the harmony.

So you are sinning against aesthetics, ladies, when, regardless of the size of the rest of the body, you over-tighten your waist to the point of overflowing lush hips that could sometimes compete with those of the Hottentot Venus[63] or Venus Callipyge.[64]

Do not forget that coquetry is the art of making oneself beautiful and that one of the main conditions of aesthetics is the harmony of proportions. So if you want to be beautiful, do not look for the slim waist and beware the straight corset.

63 Saartjie Baartman, a Khoikhoi woman taken from her native South Africa by Black Dutch slave owners, was brought to Europe and exhibited in freakshow attractions where Europeans could pay to examine her nearly naked body (Gould 1982). Her captor eventually sold her to a French man, and she died, impoverished, in Paris, in December 1815. Her body was dissected by George Cuvier, curator of the Muséum national d'Histoire naturelle (MNHN). Cuvier took a death cast of her entire body, removed and made wet preparations of her brain, buttocks, and genitals, and skeletonized her. The wet preps were subsequently lost, but her skeleton remained on display until 1974, and was returned to South Africa only in August 2002.

64 A marble statue of a Venus/Aphrodite figure with large hips and buttocks. The word "callipyge" means nicely or well-shaped buttocks.

299

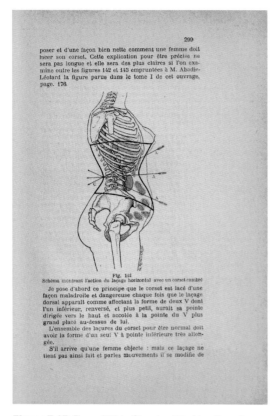

poser et d'une façon bien nette comment une femme doit
lacer son corset. Cette explication pour être précise ne
sera pas longue et elle sera des plus claires si l'on examine outre les figures 142 et 143 empruntées à M. Abadie-
Léotard la figure parue dans le tome I de cet ouvrage,
page. 176.

Fig. 143
Schéma montrant l'action du laçage horizontal avec un corset cambré

Je pose d'abord ce principe que le corset est lacé d'une
façon maladroite et dangereuse chaque fois que le laçage
dorsal apparaît comme affectant la forme de deux V dont
l'un inférieur, renversé, et plus petit, aurait sa pointe
dirigée vers le haut et accolée à la pointe du V plus
grand placé au-dessus de lui.

L'ensemble des laçures du corset pour être normal doit
avoir la forme d'un seul V à pointe inférieure très allon-
gée.

S'il arrive qu'une femme objecte : mais ce laçage ne
tient pas ainsi fait et par les mouvements il se modifie de

Figure 5.15 Page 299 in Chapter 15 of *Le Corset*.

Translation

[5.15]

I first pose this principle that the corset is laced in an awkward and dangerous way whenever the dorsal lacing appears to affect the shape of two Vs, one of which is lower, inverted, and smaller, and would have its point directed upward and attached to the tip of the larger V placed above it.

The set of corset laces to be normal must have the shape of a single V with a very elongated lower tip.

If it so happens that a woman objects: saying but this lacing does not hold so that by and by the movements change it in such a way

300

telle sorte que la partie supérieure du laçage ne reste pas la plus large comme vous le voulez pour laisser bien libre l'expansion de la partie inférieure de la cage thoracique, je lui réponds : fixez votre lacet par quelques points, tant d'un côté que de l'autre, au niveau des œillets supérieurs.

Un corset est pour moi serré quand le lacet dénoué à la taille, les parties supérieures du corset s'écartent l'une de l'autre sous l'influence d'une inspiration aussi profonde que possible.

Pour réaliser le laçage normal et sans danger, il faut que ce soit au niveau des œillets inférieurs et non au niveau des œillets de la partie moyenne que s'opère la traction ; il en résulte qu'instinctivement, dans le second cas, la femme tire sur les lacets en écartant les bras du corps, en les allongeant, et en les élevant.

Translation

that the upper part of the lacing does not remain as wide as you might like so that the lower part of the rib cage can freely expand, I suggest to her: change where you set your laces by a few holes, both on one side and on the other, at the level of the upper eyelets.

In my view, a corset is tight when the lace is untied at the waist and the upper parts of the corset move apart from each other when you take as deep an breath as possible.[65]

To carry out normal and safe lacing, traction should happen at the level of the lower eyelets and not at the level of the eyelets of the corset's middle section: it follows that instinctively, in the second case, the woman pulls on the laces by spreading the wings of the corset, lengthening them, and raising them.

65   Here, at last, we get a definition for tight-lacing. And what a disappointing definition it is. In my experiences wearing a corset, this effect can be had with any experience where the laces have been correctly aligned (think a well-laced shoe vs. one that has been sloppily laced), so that when one breathes in, the garment breathes with you.

302

C'est pourquoi je recommande toujours de mettre son corset de la façon suivante : le délacer très largement, le placer à volonté sur le corps par une ou deux agrafes, puis fixer les jarretelles ; dégrafer ensuite le corset ; appliquer alors soigneusement de bas en haut le corset sur les régions qu'il devra occuper définitivement, une fois la femme habillée, puis procéder au laçage comme je l'ai expliqué plus haut.

Jamais, et je le répète, jamais une femme ne doit appliquer sur son corps un corset à peine délacé, qui après avoir été agrafé sera descendu sur l'abdomen en tirant sur les parties latérales inférieures du corset. En agissant ainsi, la femme tiraille tous ses viscères, les déplace en les attirant par en bas et augmente les dangers de la constriction en faisant agir celle-ci sur des organes primitivement tiraillés et descendus par cette dangereuse manœuvre.

Translation

That's why I always recommend putting on your corset as follows: loosen it very widely, place it at will on the body and securing it with one or two hooks, then fix the garters; then unhook the corset; then carefully put it back on from bottom to top on the parts of the body it will spend most on once the woman is dressed. Then proceed to lacing, as outlined above.

Never, and I repeat, should a woman don an only slightly loosened corset, which after being hooked will be lowered on the abdomen by pulling on the lower lateral parts of the garment. By doing so, the woman pulls all her viscera, moves them by dragging them up from below, and increases the dangers of constriction by forcing the garment on organs originally pulled and lowered by this dangerous maneuver.

303

Je voudrais que les femmes soient bien pénétrées des principes et des explications que je viens de donner, elles sont le résultat non pas de ma seule expérience personnelle, mais mieux encore de celle de médecins distingués et de corsetières intelligentes.

Malheureusement je n'ai pas seulement à lutter et avec moi ceux qui ont déjà combattu ce bon combat contre l'ignorance de la femme en la matière, mais contre la routine de certaines corsetières et il faut bien le dire contre la sottise masculine.

Translation

I would like women to truly grasp the principles and explanations I have just given: they are the result not only of my personal experience, but (even better) that of distinguished doctors and expert corset-makers.

Unfortunately I must still struggle, alongside allies who have fought this good fight, not only against the ignorance of women in this matter, but also against the methods of some corset-makers and if must be said against male foolishness.[66]

66 Note the difference in how he speaks about women vs. how he speaks about men. Women abuse the corset. Men are foolish for enjoying the corseted waist. This is mirrored in today's discussions of sexual assault and rape, where people wonder what women were wearing, where they were walking, what they were doing, and why they didn't do more to prevent sexual assault and rape, why they didn't fight back more or say no louder. But men? Boys will be boys! See the full confirmation hearing of Supreme Court Justice Brett Kavanaugh, particularly the testimony and cross examination of Dr. Cristine Blasey Ford (Senate of the United States 2018). Dr. Blasey Ford had to leave her residence to evade death threats to herself and her family, and has had to move several times since the 2018 confirmation hearing, paying for her own security ever since. Brett Kavanaugh got to have a seat on the highest court in the land.

304

Quant à la sottise masculine, parlons-en maintenant car il faut lutter contre elle ; et pour que la femme puisse réaliser le maximum de commodité avec le maximum d'élégance, il faut, —l'accord du médecin et de la corsetière étant complet,—il faut que l'homme se mette de la partie.

La femme, je l'ai prouvé et je me suis appuyé sur de suffisantes compétonces [sic.], pour que je puisse dire que je l'ai bien prouvé, la femme ne veut qu'une chose, plaire. Les hommes s'étant extasiés sur les femmes à taille fine, les femmes se sont dit : faisons-nous des tailles fines. Or, au fond cela est absolument égal à l'homme que sa compagne ait une taille plus ou moins fine. A quelques centimètres près, l'homme n'y regarde pas, ce qu'il veut c'est avoir une femme élégante et désirable, rien ne lui étant plus sensible pour son amour-propre que de sortir avec une femme dont on remarque la grâce ou la beauté.

Translation

As for male foolishness, let us talk about it now because we must fight against it; and for the woman to be able to combine maximum convenience with maximum of elegance—the agreement of the doctor and the corset-maker being complete—it is necessary for the man gets involved.

As I have proved, the woman wants only one thing: to please. Men were ecstatic about slim-waisted women, so the women said to themselves: let's make our waists slim. However, basically it is all to a man whether his companion has a more or less slim waist. Within a few centimeters, the man does not pay much attention to it: what he wants is to have an elegant and desirable woman, nothing being more boosting for his self-esteem than to go out with a woman whose grace or beauty we notice.

305

....Je ne demande pas à la femme la suppression de son corset, il lui est utile pour soutenir le poids des vêtements, que lui imposent les coutumes de nos régions, il lui est nécessaire pour se défendre contre les années qui apportent avec elles les maladies, et emportent avec elles la fraîcheur de la jeunesse ; il lui est indispensable dans sa lutte sexuelle.

Par contre, je demande à la femme de ne plus être une « snobinette de minceur » de serrer moins son corset et d'écouter plus les bons conseils ; qu'elle ait en résumé un peu moins de folie et un peu plus de docilité.

....

Enfin, vous maris ou amants, en ne répétant pas à tout propos et surtout hors de propos à vos compagnes lorsque passe près de vous une femme à la taille mince : Oh ! la jolie taille ! Vous parlez ainsi sans raison, car vous qui venez de vous exclamer sur l'exiguïté d'un tour de taille, vous seriez désolé de contempler nu le corps de votre femme ou de votre amie bâtie comme vient de vous apparaître vêtue la passante dont vous avez admiré la forme.

Il est vrai que dans l'immense majorité des cas une femme est moins belle de lignes que son corset ne la fait paraître : mais il n'en résulte pas qu'elle serait bien faite

Translation

..... I do not ask the woman to reject her corset completely: it is useful for her as a way of supporting the weight of the clothes, which are imposed on her by modern fashion; it is necessary for her to defend herself against the years that bring with them ill health but take away the freshness of youth; and it is indispensable to her in her sexual struggle.

On the other hand, I ask the woman to no longer be a "snobinette [sic] of thinness," to tighten her corset less, and to listen more to the good advice; that she is, in short, a little less crazy and a little more docile.[67]

....

Finally, you husbands or lovers, do not make irrelevant comments to your companions when a woman with a slim waist passes by: Oh! How dainty! You speak like this for no reason, because you who have just exclaimed about a tight waistline, would be sorry to contemplate the naked body of your wife or attractive girlfriend as you have just appeared to dress the passerby whose shape you have admired.

It is true that in the vast majority of cases a woman is less beautiful in her natural form than her corset makes her appear: but it does not mean that she would be as well done

67 We can return here to the discussion of hysteria—the idea that a woman in control of her body and her sexuality, whose womb wanders and is outside of the social norms, is mad, and a docile woman is what men desire and what women should desire to be. In the case of women, we can turn this argument around and say that women who wish to not be thought mad must perform docility.

306

si son corps était tel que le moule son corset. « Devenez donc artistes et déclarez hautement que les tailles de guêpes sont laides puisque la nature ne les a pas faites ainsi ».

Lors donc que entre le médecin, la corsetière et l'homme, l'entente sera parfaite sur la nécessité qu'il y a de faire comprendre à la femme qu'elle ne doit pas se serrer, peut-être ce jour-là, la femme se laissera-t-elle convaincre ; je dis peut-être, car qui oserait se vanter à l'avance qu'il convaincra une femme.

Elle sera plutôt alors touchée—car mieux vaut s'adresser à son cœur qu'a sa raison—par les arguments réunis et concordants de ceux auxquels elle devra d'être saine, d'être belle et d'être aimée.

[Fin.]

Translation

if her body was such molded as her corset. "So become artists and declare openly that wasp-waists are ugly, since nature has not made them that way."

So when between the doctor, the corset-maker, and the man, there is a perfect accord on the need to make the woman understand that she must not over-tighten, perhaps on this day, the woman will be convinced; I say perhaps, because who would dare to boast in advance that he will convince a woman of anything?

Rather, she will be touched—for it is better to address her heart than her reason—by the combined and concordant arguments of those to whom she will have to be healthy, beautiful, and loved.[68]

[End.]

68 And here ends O'Followell's purportedly objective treatise on the health, hygiene, and medicine of the corset—not with experimental results, not with facts and figures, not with more anatomical diagrams, but rather with an appeal to emotion. Throughout the book, we have seen O'Followell plagiarize, lie, falsify, and demonize women. Placed in a larger context of both fashion and medical history, his contributions to modern understandings of and discourses about women cannot be ignored, and I will finish this discussion of them in the afterword.

REFERENCES

Balch, E. (1904). "Savage and Civilized Dress," in the *Journal of the Franklin Instituteo of the State of Pennsylvania, for the Promotion of the Mechanic Arts*, Vol. 157 (5).

Barthes, R. (1967). *The Fashion System*, trans. Ward and Howard, Berkeley, CA: The University of California Press.

Bendall, S. (2022). *Shaping Femininity: Foundation Garments, the Body, and Women in Early Modern England*, London: Bloomsbury Visual Arts.

Berlanstein, L. (1984). *The Working People of Paris, 1871–1914*, Baltimore, MD: The Johns Hopkins Press.

Chandrasekhar, S. (1981). *"A Dirty, Filthy Book": The Writings of Charles Knowlton and Annie Besant on Reproductive Physiology and Birth Control and an Account of the Bradlaugh-Besant Trial*, Berkeley, CA: University of California Press.

Edwards, L. (2017/2018). *How to Read a Dress: A Guide to Changing Fashion from the 16th to the 20th Century*, London: Bloomsbury Academic.

Entwistle, J. (2000). *The Fashioned Body*, Malden, MA: Blackwell Publishers.

Gibson, R. (2020). *The Corseted Skeleton: A Bioarchaeology of Binding*, Switzerland: Palgrave Macmillan.

Gould, S. (1982). The Hottentot Venus, in *Natural History*, 91: 20–7.

Gross, R. (2022). *Vagina Obscura: An Anatomical Voyage*, New York, NY: W. W. Norton and Co.

Heine, H. (1850). *Le Cantique des Cantiques*.

Hooks, J. (1947). *Women's Occupations Through Seven Decades*, United States Department of Labor.

Kenealy, A. (1904). *The Curse of Corsets*, no other information given.

Klebs, A. (1909). *Tuberculosis: A Treatise by American Authors on its Etiology, Pathology, Frequency, Semeiology, Diagnosis, Prognosis, Prevention, and Treatment*, New York, NY: D. Appleton and Company.

Levin, J. (2018). "The Statutes Project: Women," https://statutes.org.uk/site/tag/women/

Lord, W. B. (1868/1870). *[Freaks of Fashion] The Corset And the Crinoline*. London: Ward, Lock, and Tyler.

Newton, M. (1974). *Health, Art, and Reason: Dress Reformers of the 19th Century*, London: John Murray.

Perrot, P. (1994). *Fashioning the Bourgeoisie: A History of Clothing in the 19th Century*, Princeton, NJ: Princeton University Press.

Pozzilli, P., et al. (2019). 'Venus by Botticelli and Her Pituitary Adenoma,' in *Endocrine Practice*, 25 (10): 1067–73.

Racinet, A. ([1888] 2022). *The Costume History*, Cologne, Germany: Taschen.

Ribeiro, A. ([1986] 2003). *Dress and Morality*, Oxford: Berg.

Senate of the United States. (2018). *Serial No. J–115–61: Confirmation Hearing on the Nomination of Hon. Brett M. Kavanaugh to Be An Associate Justice of the Supreme Court Of The United States.* https://www.govinfo.gov/content/pkg/CHRG-115shrg32765/pdf/CHRG-115shrg32765.pdf

Shrimpton, J. (2016). *Victorian Fashion*, Oxford: Shire Publications.

Styles, J. (2007). *The Dress of the People: Everyday Fashion in Eighteenth-Century England*. New Haven, CT: Yale University Press.

Veterans Affairs. (2018). *Study Finds Epigenetic Changes in Children of Holocaust Survivors, from the Office of Research and Development*.

Figure 5.16 Bath Fashion Museum, corset number I.27.86, exterior view. Heavily worn woven red silk brocade, with tabs and darts. Child's corset with very little deviation in size between waist and bust. Dimensions: bust 57cm; waist 55cm; hips 54cm; front 26cm; back 35cm; side 21cm. Ratio: 1:.96:.95. Photo © Rebecca Gibson, 2023.

Figure 5.17 Bath Fashion Museum, corset number I.27.86, interior view. Photo © Rebecca Gibson, 2023.

AFTERWORD:
O'Followell's Impact: Women and Medicine in the Twenty-First Century and Beyond

END MATTER

Medicine, like all research, draws on what came before it. While O'Followell never directly quoted J. Marion Sims, the so-called father of modern gynecology, and may not even have known about him, the disregard shown for his patients in an effort purported to be beneficial and helpful is incredibly reminiscent of Sims' experimental surgeries on enslaved Black women. These experiments, whence came the popular myth that the cervix has few to no nerve endings, are indicative of a disregard for the point of view of the patient, and despite this being common in both France and the US at this time, that disregard has had lasting and significant impact (Gross 2022; Jackson 2019; Owens 2018). This myth, reported as accurate at the time of this writing by no less than WebMD,[1] is used to justify such things as IUD insertion without anesthetic, and is used to (once again) dismiss, deny, and negate the pain of women, trans men, and intersex people with uteruses.

It is, however, just a myth—patently false. The nerve pathways of the clitoris, vagina, and cervix were mapped in a 2011 study (Komisaruk et al.)[2] which showed that not only were there many functioning nerves and nervous system pathways in the anatomy in question, but that the identity of the person doing the stimulation mattered. When men[3] stimulated the women in the study, whether the men were the scientists or the women's[4] partners, the fMRI showed less nerve activity than when women self-stimulated. To put it in non-medical terms, men could not find their way around women's anatomy, but the women themselves could, whether pleasurable or painful—and this lack of ability on the part of the men was not because the nerves did not exist, but because the men were not taking women's self-reporting at their word. People whom society genders female are systemically not listened to, and in addition to creating inequities as in all systemic discrimination, it unnecessarily multiplies pain and suffering.

---

1   WebMD, infamous for its symptom-checker that generally leads people to the worst possible conclusions about their health, has long been derided by the medical community for the fact that it employs sweeping generalizations. This article "What is Cervix Penetration?" was "Medically Reviewed by Dan Brennan, MD on June 27, 2021," (WebMD Editorial Contributors 2021).
2   All previous studies had been done on people with penises.
3   All previous experimenters were men or the stimulation was directed by the women's male partners (Komisaruk et al. 2011).
4   All research participants identified as women (ibid.)

307

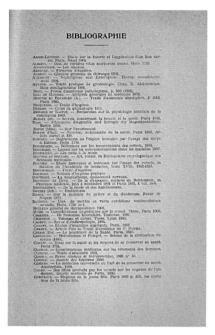

Figure 6.1 Bibliography of *Le Corset*, part 1.

The reasons I bring up this myth are twofold: 1) this dismissal of women's self-reported lived experiences has become the background radiation of our daily lives, present in medical situations, but also in work, home, sports, and legal proceedings, among other realms, most importantly in rape cases; and 2) the impetus to infantilize women by negating their own experiences, choices, and bodily sensations is one that has become buried deep within the patriarchal psyche of our time, and which is deeply linked to discussions around the corset. When women say something is severe (pain—cervical or otherwise, the results of rape, forced childbirth), doctors like O'Followell tell us it is not; we are overreacting. When women say something is inconsequential or even beneficial (the effects of the corset, the psychological results of abortion, the choice to not have children), doctors like O'Followell tell us it is not; we are brainwashed. When we get angry about the above gaslighting, doctors like O'Followell tell us that anger is not justified, and label us attention-seeking, pill-seeking, unreliable narrators, bad historians of our own medical past; we are hysterical.

Where, in all this telling, are we? It starts to look like there is no place for people to think what they think and feel what they feel and make choices that work for themselves. At the very least, having medical society proscribe one's thoughts and feelings, a direct result of O'Followell and doctors like him . . . well, that is not very feminist, is it? And yet, women have always been a part of French medical history—not always as doctors, but as midwives, informal caretakers, and as experts on their own bodies, from conception to quickening to childbirth (Broomhall 2004; McHugh 2007; Weston 2013; Wilson 1993). Women have provided official and unofficial care, sworn oaths, devoted their lives to understanding, caring for, and healing the female body, yet the first female doctor in France was not certified until 1875 (Pigeard-Micault and Debbasch 2007), a full seventy-one years after medical licensure was required to practice (Crosland 2004; Huard and Imbault-Huart 1975; Pinell 2011; Weisz 1978 and 2003).

At the beginning of this book I asked several questions. Let us investigate how *Le Corset* and my translation, *The Bad Corset,* have answered them:

308

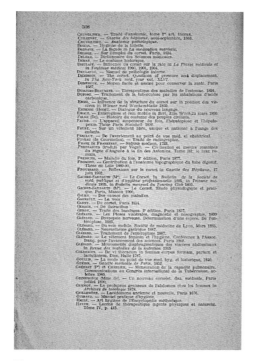

Figure 6.2 Bibliography of *Le Corset*, part 2.

What medical inaccuracies can be shown in O'Followell's work? I have brought in twenty-first century experts as well as late nineteenth- and early twentieth-century experts, his contemporaries, to demonstrate how his scientific method, medical understanding, and praxis were deeply flawed, and often times deliberately falsified or plagiarized. Time and time again in *Le Corset* O'Followell allows his agenda to lead his narrative, rather than using clear and unbiased data and allowing that data to speak for itself. The only things O'Followell got almost consistently correct were his discussions of basic anatomy, which I mostly left out in order to keep the translation uncluttered and on topic. For example, his assertion that "The ribs are twelve in number; they are divided into true ribs numbering seven, and false ribs numbering five,"[5] is in fact mostly correct (we currently count only the last two ribs as "false," but from his standpoint any not directly connected to the sternum were false), but adds nothing to this translation. And regardless, it should not be unexpected or surprising for a doctor to be able to correctly describe basic anatomy.

No, it is in the treatment of disease and disorder that he falters. While so much of medical knowledge was, at that point, still yet to be created, there was a fin de siècle rush to become known for isolating a disease, discovering a disorder, or creating a new treatment. Like his friend (and corset creator, let us not forget, see Chapter 1 of *The Bad Corset*) Dr. Glenard, of Glenard's Disease, it seems O'Followell badly wanted to gain renown as the man who fixed the corseting problem.[6] O'Followell's work in *Le Corset* aggregates the corset "knowledge," theorizing, pontificating, and opinions of the day. While many doctors, pundits, and lay-people published on the topic in various fashions—magazines, theses, medical and scientific journals, to name but a few—O'Followell collected many of their works into one place, and then used his book to, by turns, agree with (Glenard 1899; Murchison

1877), argue with (Corbin 1830), blatantly misrepresent (Fouveau de Courmelles 1897), and occasionally plagiarize what they said (Lord 1868; Platon and Sepet 1902).

5 "Les côtes sont au nombre de douze; on les divise en varies côtes au nombre du sept, et en fausses côtes au nombre de cinq," page 21.

6 Whether or not he did is a question I cannot answer: as I mentioned in the preface to this book, no data exists on who, and how many, read *Le Corset* when it was published.

309

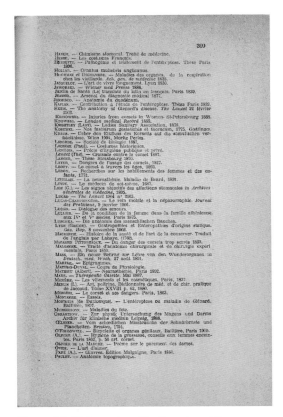

Figure 6.3 Bibliography of *Le Corset*, part 3.

O'Followell went so far as to co-opt the diagnosis of enteroptosis into a corset-use disorder. He defined it, somewhat against other doctors of the day, as a disorder with neurological and physiological effects, including both confusion and a lowering of the organs. And yet, despite the excessive number of pages in *Le Corset* spent on this disorder, the effects remain unproven in regard to the corset. This, unfortunately, is typical of the text of *Le Corset*. O'Followell's reach of medical knowledge and theory exceeds his grasp, and his grudge against corseted women overpowers his scientific method and logic. He allows the desire for control of this issue to swamp facts, twist interpretations, and destroy any veracity in his arguments.

Why did O'Followell hate and blame women so much? This is, perhaps, a question without a clear answer—we cannot go back in time and ask him to spell out the reasoning behind his misogyny. On the other hand, we can see very clearly in *Le Corset* that he did hate women, and he did blame them for their own illnesses and injuries. His loathing of them, disrespect for them and their choices, disregard for the whole person he was treating—even when he made mention of the habits of that person—fairly pours off the page. In this, he shares similarities with certain other people in various (though not all) other abolitionist movements, all of which had intersecting ideologies. The Dress Reformers/Bloomers, the Temperance/Teetotaler Movement, and the various Eugenicists movements all declared what they considered to be good intentions, but which were about control and containment of the choices of adult people.

310

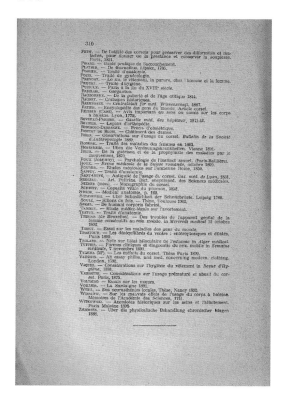

Figure 6.4 Bibliography of *Le Corset*, part 4.

Whether decrying the corset (Dress Reformers) or tipping over barrels of the demon gin (Temperance) or institutionalizing people who had the misfortune to not fit their ideas of people who should be allowed to reproduce (Eugenics), the root of these movements is control—to make people, to make fully adult citizens, conform to someone else's notion of proper behavior. Personally, I am not an anarchist; we live in a society, and that society needs to have (mostly) agreed-upon rules, enforceable laws, that work to make the social environment tolerable for (most)[7] people in it. But when those rules and laws are not applied equally, when they further disadvantage an already historically disadvantaged population, when they are created to regulate personal private decisions made by fully adult citizens, that crosses an ethical line.

And we know, from examination of the text of *Le Corset*, that O'Followell was in favor of crossing that aforementioned ethical line many times, not just in regard to forbidding women control of their own bodies. That he believed, more even than was standard during his time, in the so-called hierarchy of races and supported eugenics. That he resented and hated women who controlled their own fertility. That he placed so much emphasis on that fertility, that he was willing to consider, twice, laws that criminalized the act of corseting, particularly if the act could be shown to compromise a woman's fecundity. That his definition of woman reduced her to the products of her womb. He decried coquetry, fashionability, and that a corseted waist should appeal to a man. She was feminine only if she was fertile. He hails (or rails against—it was not clear) Dress Reformers as feminist, but . . . were they?

It is no accident that even though men corseted as well (though not to the extent that women did), O'Followell exclusively addressed women in *Le Corset*. Although he couches his final chapters in arguments about liberation and feminism, discussing the Dress Reform movement and the success of Amelia Bloomer, his text is considerably more focused on preserving fertility and berating women for any abortion (accidental miscarriage or purposeful abortion) that he believes might result from corseting. Though not writing on the topic until seventy-six years later, this is a theme developed in the work of Michel Foucault, where he deals with ways in which society exerts control (1984). O'Followell views the corset as having taken over the psyches of women, controlling them, and yet his own ways of "discipline and punish"—keeping the body under control by forbidding the "bad" corset, keeping the mind focused on concerns regarding societal wrongdoing by emphasizing motherhood and childbearing, and setting up systems to physically reprimand women who stepped outside that control and focus—was to support laws against wearing the corset.

7 There is functionally no way to please everyone, so we have compromised with an ideal of pleasing and/or serving the most possible. Note: this is an ideal—no country has achieved it, and most countries, including the US, often backslide into grift, parsimony toward the needy, and a notably jobsworth mentality toward moving beyond current laws toward actual assistance. Still, one can dream.

ToC1

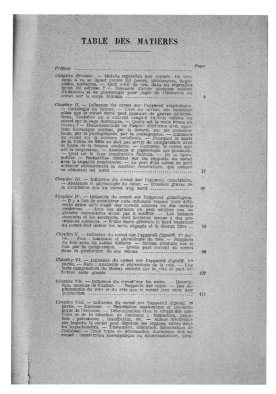

Figure 6.5 Table of Contents of *Le Corset*, part 1.

And can we reconcile these ideas—the feminine and the feminist—without being reductive and cliched? Absolutely. Let us define our terms, first, and see how very compatible the two are. The feminine is a rather nebulous concept, circularly defined, and tautological: the property of being feminine is to have qualities that we associate with womanliness. However, to be womanly is, by default, to be feminine. What those qualities are is another insoluble question; for if we go to the base ideas such as strength/lack of strength, aggression/passivity, preference for bright colors/preference for muted colors, well, those are all represented in varying amounts between all genders. If we go to the very specific (women are strong in childbirth, passive at home, prefer bright colors, etc.), then not only will these specificities fall apart very quickly—as there are very "feminine" women who espouse a variety of strengths/do not have children/are not passive/hate pink—but we will also be as reductive as O'Followell, restricting womanhood to a set of arbitrary and untrue reductions.

We can, however, circumvent this particular mess by leaning into the tautology: if to be feminine is to be womanly, then anything that makes us feel womanly is feminine, and we can all set our own definitions of what makes us feel womanly. In the year 1908, it was feminine to have long hair in a Gibson Girl-esque up-do with a few curls left loose. Fifteen years later, it would be feminine to sport a cheekbone-length bob with gentle undulating waves—no woman of class and style would be caught dead with long hair in 1923. As feminine styles came and went, women redefined themselves. This also makes being feminine feminist.

To be feminist is to live your life according to the principle that all genders should have equal access to spaces, opportunities, and autonomy. To be feminist is not about some flattening version of equality where we add women to various situations and stir, nor about some leveling effect where women cast off femininity to become more like men, but about the understanding that a fully adult human being is a thing of self-determination—each person must be allowed to choose what is right for themselves. Whom to love, whom to marry, whether to marry at all, whether to have children, whether to have an abortion or continue with a pregnancy, what to study in school, what profession to pursue, and yes, what to wear, are all issues where the choice is, or should be, private, personal, and self-determined. If a person feels feminine in jeans, a t-shirt, and sneakers, they are no less feminine than a person in a corset, a long skirt, and high heels, because society does not get to determine what feminine is—it is simply rubbish at it, and so we can self-determine.

ToC2

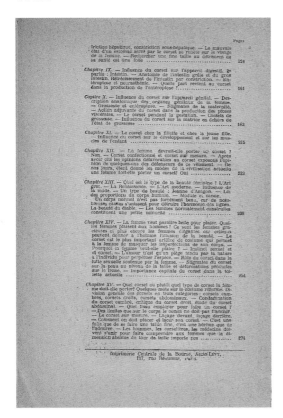

Figure 6.6 Table of Contents of *Le Corset*, part 2.

Can we rehabilitate the corset from its position as the scourge of women by women, allowing modern-day corset-wearers that nuance of the multiple aspects of fashion? Certainly. Primarily, I have demonstrated via *The Corseted Skeleton* (2020) and *The Bad Corset* that corseting itself is not a scourge, and there is not one extant historical piece of evidence for women dying with corseting as the direct cause of death. All evidence, from doctors' accounts, to the erstwhile "corseted livers," falls to failures of logic, modern medical understandings of the body, or, in the case of O'Followell, lies and fakery. As I showed in *The Corseted Skeleton,* not one woman among the 3,815 buried in the St. Bride's Parish graveyard over a span of seventy-nine years had corsets, corseting damage, bisected livers, chest deformity (not related to rickets), or anything at all that could be traced to corseting listed as their cause of death. Corsets did not kill, and based on a definition of "harm" that centers the lived experiences of the wearer, they did not cause quality of life issues. They could, of course, exacerbate existing issues—that is undeniable, and it is there in O'Followell if one reads the text with a critical eye—but *cause* them? No, there is no evidence of that; the corset was not a scourge.

Seeing that the practice was of women by women, but was not violent, traumatic, or necessarily harmful, what are better words to attach to the practice, then, that recognize the nuance and complexity? How about supportive, habitual, and affirming? Corsets supported not only a person's body, but their social standing, much the same way that wearing a bra today indicates that a person knows social rules and is following them. Corsets were habitual—both in that they formed part of a person's habit, or clothing, and in that putting one on in the morning became part of the daily routine. Habitual practices again form that social standing, and in O'Followell's time this habit could reinforce a person's personhood—they knew who they were partially based on what clothing they wore. In this way, corsets were affirming. They formed a part of people's identities for centuries. Whether whalebone or steel, homemade or off the rack, a corset served as the structure of the dress, dictating what type of clothing a person could wear, what looks they could pull off, and what role they had in society, and this role was extremely easy for people of O'Followell's time to read via the clothing choices. Just because we, today, have lost the ability to read that role as easily, does not negate the affirming qualities of the corset.

Ad1

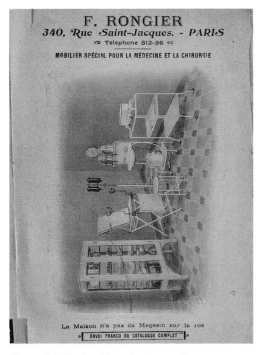

Figure 6.7 Backmatter advertisement.

And in this way, to answer the final question, corsets *can* be feminist. The essence of feminism is not to remove people from restrictive clothing, not to uncorset people who want to be corseted, but to give everyone, no matter their gender, the freedom to wear what pleases and affirms them most, even if or when that freedom extends to changing the shape, size, or appearance of one's body. O'Followell did not live and work in a culture oriented toward this type of freedom, and yet people were still using the corset to express their own identities, to create their bodies the way they wanted, and to do what pleased and affirmed them. In all clothing fads and trends, there will be people who follow such movements just to be trendy—we see that today just as much as we can look back in history and see women whose corsets followed *la mode*, however it would be a grave injustice to equate that to how the majority of people choose their clothing.

"Heroin chic" was trendy in the 1990s, but not attainable for the majority of people. In such a way, the extreme corseting and fashion following decried by O'Followell and others was not attainable for the majority of people. While magazines, the wealthy upper class, and the fashionistas of the day have always dictated what will be in vogue, the clothing of the rest of the public has always been a pastiche—old corsets with new dresses, old dresses "turned" and made new again with updated sewing patterns, old shoes with new buckles, borrowing from one era to another to make one's wardrobe into something that fit one's own image. Women during O'Followell's time who had never heard the word "feminist" were still choosing to make over their dresses to their own taste, and using their corsets in ways that were less restrictive, more supportive, and healthier than our modern misunderstandings have allowed for. In this way, it is not the corset that is a violent and oppressive tool of the patriarchy, it is the theorist who refuses to move beyond preconceived notions of what violence and oppression look like to see that the corset was, and still is, a legitimate feminist mode of expression. Far from being the bad corset, we must be open to reimagining it under the lens of choice, freedom, identity, expression, and yes, feminism.

REFERENCES

Broomhall, S. (2004). *Women's Medical Work in Early Modern France*, Manchester: Manchester University Press.

Crosland, M. (2004). "The *Officiers de Santé* of the French Revolution: A Case Study in the Changing Language of Medicine," in *Medical History*, 48: 229–44.

Corbin, (no first name given). (1830). "Des effets produits par lescorsets sur les organes de l'abdomen," *Gazette Médicale de Paris*.

Foucault, M. (1984). *The Foucault Reader*, ed. Paul Rabinow, New York, NY: Pantheon Books.

Fouveau de Courmelles, F. (1897). *Traité de Radiographie Médicale et Scientifique*, ed. Octave Doin.

Glenard, F. (1899). *Les Ptoses Viscérales, Diagnostic et Nosographie*.

Gross, R. (2022). *Vagina Obscura: An Anatomical Voyage*, New York, NY: W. W. Norton and Co.

Huard, P., and M. J. Imbault-Huart (1975). "La Clinique Parisienne Avant Et Apres 1802," in *Clio Medica*, 10 (3): 173–82.

Jackson, G. (2019). *Pain and Prejudice: A Call to Arms for Women and their Bodies*, London: Piatkus.

Komisaruk, B., et al. (2011). "Women's Clitoris, Vagina, and Cervix Mapped on the Sensory Cortex: fMRI Evidence," in the *Journal of Sexual Medicine*, 8 (10): 2822–30.

Lord, W B. (1868/1870). *[Freaks of Fashion] The Corset And the Crinoline*, London: Ward, Lock, and Tyler.

McHugh, T. (2007) *Hospital Politics in Seventeenth-Century France: The Crown, Urban Elites, and the Poor,* New York, NY: Ashgate Publishing.

Murchison, C. (1877). "Clinical Lectures on Diseases of the Liver, Jaundice, and Abdominal Dropsy: Including the Croonian Lectures on Functional Derangements of the Liver," Delivered at the Royal College of Physicians in 1874, New York, NY: W. Wood.

Owens, D. (2018). *Medical Bondage: Race, Gender, and the Origins of American Gynecology*, Athens, GA: University of Georgia Press.

Pigeard-Micault, N, and K. Debbasch. (2007). "A History of Women's Entrance Into Medicine," https://www.biusante. parisdescartes.fr/histoire/medica/presentations/entree-femmes-en-medecine-en.php#04

Pinell, P. (2011). "The Genesis of the Medical Field: France, 1795–1870," in *Revue Française de Sociologie*, 52 (5), 117–51.

Platon and Sepet, (no first names given). (1902). "Hygiene de La Femme: Enfant—Jeune Fille—Femme—Mère et Aïule."

WebMD Editorial Contributors. (2021). "What is Cervix Penetration?," https://www.webmd.com/sex/what-is-cervix-penetration

Weisz, G. (1978). "The Politics of Medical Professionalization in France 1845–1848," in *Journal of Social History*, 12 (1): 3–30.

Weisz, G. (2003). "The Emergence of Medical Specialization in the Nineteenth Century," in *Bulletin of the History of Medicine*, 77 (3): 536.

Weston, R. (2013). *Medical Consulting by Letter in France, 1665–1789,* Burlington, VT: Ashgate Publishing Company.

Wilson, L. (1993). *Women and Medicine in the French Enlightenment: The Debate over* Maladies des Femmes, Baltimore, MD: Johns Hopkins University Press.

INDEX